Praise for Stephen Bourne

'Stephen Bourne brings great natural scholarship and passion to largely hidden stories. He is highly accessible, accurate, and surprising. You always walk away from his work knowing something you didn't know, that you didn't even suspect.'

–Bonnie Greer on *Mother Country*

'A powerful, revelatory counterbalance to the whitewashing of British history'

–Bernardine Evaristo on *Black Poppies*

'A magnificent piece of work. I was gripped throughout, laughed out loud at times; became blazingly angry at the injustice, hypocrisy and expediency...and sheer waste. And, at times, delighted by the courage and refusal of many to bow down to prejudice or to dampen our full potential as human beings.'

–Keith Howes on *Fighting Proud*

'One of the soldiers, gatekeepers and champions of our community. I am in awe of his diligence and insight.'

–Russell T Davies on *Playing Gay in the Golden Age of British TV*

'Informs, delights and surprises'

–Cleo Sylvestre on *Trailblazers of Black British Theatre: From Ira Aldridge to Cleo Laine*

Thursday's Child

A Life Between the Lines

Stephen Bourne

JACARANDA

This edition first published in Great Britain 2026

Jacaranda Books Art Music Ltd
27 Old Gloucester Street,
London WC1N 3AX

www.jacarandabooksartmusic.co.uk

A CIP catalogue record for this book is available from the British Library

ISBN: 9781806750283
eISBN: 9781806750306

Cover Design: Rodney Dive
Typeset by Siliconchips Services Ltd, UK
Printed and bound by CPI Group (UK) Ltd, Croydon, CR0 4YY

Thursday's Child is dedicated to my parents:
Arthur and Kathleen Bourne

Table of Contents

Author's Note

In *Thursday's Child*, Black is used with a capital B. Black with a capital B refers to people of African descent. 'Black' is capitalised when I refer to people in a racial, ethnic or cultural context to signify a shared identity, history and community. I am aware that capitalising 'Black' is not universally accepted.

Though every care has been taken to trace or contact all copyright holders, I would be pleased to rectify at the earliest opportunity any errors or omissions brought to my attention.

Preface

There is a saying, '*Thursday's child has far to go.*' I was born on a Thursday in October of 1957, and I have come far. Much further than I could have imagined. Along the way, I have explored overlooked aspects and people of British history. I do not describe myself as an academic; my approach to history is personal. I take particular care to avoid using daunting words that end in 'ology'. If I had to give myself a title I would choose 'community historian'. But I normally wouldn't choose.

I was still at school in the 1970s when I began to look for history books about Black people in Britain. In those days, we didn't know about Mary Seacole, Walter Tull, or the Empire Windrush. Black history was not taught in schools, not even African-American history, although imports of African-American history books were available at this time. I am certain this had a lot to do with the rise in Black consciousness in Britain and the subsequent appetite for knowledge. I remember a history textbook at school which referred to the Transatlantic Slave Trade, but not in any depth and most crucially lacking a Black perspective. During the bulk of our history lessons we learned about Henry VIII and Elizabeth I, however, missing was mention of the Black Tudors in England, such as Henry VIII's trumpet player John Blanke. In those days, Black British history books were rare to find.

I remember getting my hands on a copy of James Walvin's *Black and*

White – The Negro and English Society 1555–1945 (1973) via an inter library loan. My local bookshop on Peckham High Street wasn't only diverse; it was radical in its offerings. If I wanted to find something of quality on Black British history, they were always a great help. I found the staff at the bookshop to be extremely friendly and helpful. They assisted me in my quest for information. I didn't have a lot of money, just my earnings from a Saturday job as a Sales Assistant. This is what I bought my books with. Self-taught, I soon learned how to make use of the British Library. It was here I discovered copies of Ita Ekpenyon's pamphlet *Some Experiences of an African Air Raid Warden* (1943) and the newsletters of the League of Coloured Peoples. This was an exciting experience for me. Until this visit, I had only used the local public libraries in Peckham and Camberwell. My first visit to the British Library made me realise that there was a whole world of discovery opening up to me.

My early findings also included Edward Scobie's *Black Britannia* (1972) and Folarin Shyllon's *Black People in Britain 1555–1833* (1977), both purchased from the bookshop on Peckham High Street. BBC television served as a great repository, too, despite their *Black and White Minstrel Show*, and gave us two superb documentary series: *The Black Man in Britain 1550–1950* (1974) and *The Fight Against Slavery* (1975). From reading these books and watching these programmes I realised that they were the tip of a huge iceberg, and that I wanted to see what was underneath the surface.

I knew that it would take more than my solitary lifetime to piece this story together. By becoming a historian, I joined a long corridor of individuals who understood the same basic principle as I – that our work was a stitch in an ever-growing tapestry of truths and untruths. I undertook this journey to be in the company of thinkers who didn't stop at the thinking part, who saw both *doing and undoing* as two sides of the same historical coin. Who pursued truth-seeking by way of revealing forgotten archives and clarifying misrepresented ones. I chose this path, but there are also happenings in my life and in this story that have chosen me, like my dear Aunt Esther, the inspiration for so much of what I do, a Black Briton of Guyanese heritage adopted by my family as an orphan during the Second World War. When I was a boy, she was my first primary source on Black British History and one whose stories would come to have a significant bearing on the historian I'd become.

At the age of 12, I rejected the notion that we lived in a fully integrated society where race didn't matter, all of us brothers and sisters under our skin. In 1969, as I was beginning to take an interest in Black British history, Madeleine Bell was the lead singer in the multi-cultural pop group Blue Mink. I loved her singing, I really did, but Blue Mink's hit single 'Melting Pot', which reached as high as number three on the charts, was a miss. The entire song is replete with crude solutions for racial harmony but none more reductive than the verse about racial mixing. This recording was released just one year after Enoch Powell made his racist 'Rivers of Blood' speech, which rang a different tune, predicting racial tumult if British people didn't oppose high immigration. The British public was receiving mixed messages about integration and none of them particularly helpful. No matter their intentions, naïve pop songs like 'Melting Pot', despite their good intentions, were not going to solve anything.

In 1970, the popularity of the far-right National Front was on the rise. I was a teenager at the time with a developing consciousness, and the Black struggle was increasingly playing a part in that development. I believed researching Black history would help to counteract the racist attitudes that were being expressed by the far-right. This seed was planted by my Aunt Esther, who may have been adopted into my white working-class family, but was fully aware of her identity as a Black woman. Her father had instilled in her a sense of Black pride, which manifested itself in Aunt Esther knowing from an early age that Black people had their own heroes. Her father taught her about the boxing champion Jack Johnson, the Edwardian composer Samuel Coleridge-Taylor and the 1920s musical star Florence Mills.

When I started this work, I didn't know anyone at that time who could help me, so it felt like I had to do this work, the work of being a community historian, all by myself. I now know the truth is more nuanced than this.

More than fifty years on at the Windrush 75 commemoration hosted by the Imperial War Museum, I realised that despite being largely ignored by mainstream media, my work *had* reached the very people I had wanted to reach, the people at the heart of my scholarship, the Black community. Not the intelligentsia but those who want to learn about their past in books that are accessible to them. On that day, I understood that Thursday's child had come very far indeed.

Thursday's Child developed because on several occasions I had been asked with genuine curiosity why I write about Black British history. I have never experienced any criticism for being a white 'interloper', or seen as a 'culture vulture'. My prerogative has always been honest. I'm not oblivious to how I'm perceived and the ways I occupy space, but I've largely been left alone to carry on with my job as an historian. I am passionate about what I do, and I always aim to be a diligent and conscientious researcher and writer.

At my Black history talks, I often explain to attendees that when I left school, through no fault of my own, university and the world of academia was beyond my reach. People, especially those from the working classes, relate to this and show respect when I explain that I am mostly self-taught. They connect with that. I explain that I taught myself to research by using reference libraries and archives. I also figured out how to write books on the fly. I've struggled to find a literary agent in my career, so I've had to navigate the world of publishing by myself, with little or no support. These setbacks aren't unique, however, they are mine, and they're the obstacles that have shaped me as a resilient writer. When progress was hindered, I persevered. The reward for my wilfulness has been a long and productive writing career.

Being a writer is a wonderful way to live. I love creating something out of nothing, working at the coalface, filling voids. I have achieved this by being rigorous, self-disciplined, and organised. I have avoided living in chaos. I have not tried to be all things to all people, and this alchemy has endeared people to my work.

When The History Press commissioned me to write *Deep Are the Roots* (2021), a book I wrote on Black British theatre, I discussed with my editor the possibility of writing it in a different style to my previous books. I explained to him that when I started out as a professional writer I was always told to write objectively, not in the first person. For years, I had never tried to personalise my books. I stuck to an academic, impersonal way of writing, but with *Deep Are the Roots*, I chose to take a different path. I wanted to avoid distancing myself from the subject by being objective. This is why readers found *Deep Are the Roots* to be a personal history and not an objective one. As a result, the book became semi-autobiographical, and I began to seriously consider the possibility of writing a full-length autobiography.

So, when I considered documenting my life through the lens of being an historian of all things Black and British, the most sensible option was to pursue the writing of an autobiography. My original intention was to focus solely on my Black British history work but when I discussed the proposal with my publisher, Valerie Brandes, and her Jacaranda publishing team, they strongly recommended that I also include my life as a gay man and my work as an historian in this field. At first, I was worried by the challenge, but the combination of the two strands worked much better than I expected. There were similarities, such as being made to feel like an outsider and being misrepresented in the mainstream media.

For those seeking guidance on writing, you must be single-minded and push ahead with what you believe in. With Black British history, the 'racism narrative' (as I call it) is very dominant in our culture, and it is part of our nation's history. It cannot be avoided. But if I have learned anything as an historian of Black Britain, it is to keep an open mind.

I have discovered over 50 years that there is a bigger picture. I am so thankful that I have dedicated my life to this work because I have found so many extraordinary, inspirational lives in what have been difficult, challenging times, and these lives have enriched and empowered me.

Chapter 1

Lucky Number 13

I am often asked why I became interested in stories about the London Blitz, and the reason is simple. I was influenced by the older women in my family, as so many youths are. As a teenager, I listened as they illustrated in vivid detail what life was like during the Blitz. Their stories of coping with the trauma of living with the threat of falling bombs were tales I was moved by. I was struck by their depictions of the air raid shelters, of trying to keep themselves and their children safe. They were undeniably strong, feisty women. My maternal grandmother Mary, affectionately known as 'May', came from Merthyr Tydfil and spoke with a Welsh lilt; the others spoke with Cockney accents. You'd have thought they came from the East End, but they, all of them, lived on Fulham's Dieppe Street, situated off North End Road in London.

The first raids of the London Blitz, otherwise known as Hitler's Blitzkrieg ('lightning war'), began on September 7, 1940. From mid-September to mid-November, raids took place day and night across London. Initially, the targets were the East End docks. However, by the end of the Blitz in May 1941, across London, more than 2,000,000 houses had been damaged or destroyed and at least 40,000 people were dead. But the bombs fell elsewhere, too – Coventry, Belfast, Cardiff, Liverpool, Sheffield, Hull, and numerous other cities – though London bore the brunt, battered by approximately two-thirds of the tonnage of bombs dropped during the Blitz and the target of 71 raids against the 79 aimed at other cities.

According to Aunt Esther and great-Aunt Mag, one of the worst attacks came on the evening of December 29 and went into the early hours of December 30, 1940. Watermains were broken and fires burned all night. Then like a map set alight at its edges, folding into great plumes of smoke snaking through the streets until it felt like there would be nothing more. Local firefighters stood no chance against the raid. This is how that night was described to me growing up. The City of London suffered damage over a larger area than it had during the 1666 Great Fire of London – and the night was referred to as the Second Great Fire. The physical damage was only second to the psychological.

May was a coal miner's daughter from Dowlais, a small village situated in Merthyr Tydfil. In describing her childhood surroundings she told me, 'The steelworks and collieries were surrounded by mountains, so there was a lot of countryside around us. We lived near a famous beauty spot called the Brecon Beacons.' It was a quaint existence for the most part, and my grandmother always spoke about it with fondness. It was clear to me that she looked upon Dowlais as her real home, even though she spent most of her adult life in London.

Her parents were Irish, from the city of Cork, with hardened spirits. When May's father, John Murray, struggled to find work, he relocated to Wales with his wife Mary and their young son Jack, my great uncle. By the time May was born in 1911, her father was working as a coal miner. She recalled that 'Later on, Dad was offered a job as a banksman. He worked the cage that took the miners underground, he was responsible for the safety of all the men. He had to inspect them before he took them underground because some of them used to smuggle cigarettes under the peaks of their caps. Dad also worked in the lamp room where he looked after the miner's lamps until he was about 60. He had to give up then because he got coal dust on the lungs which turned to heart trouble and very bad asthma. He was an invalid until he died in 1948.'

Throughout her life, May identified as Welsh but always acknowledged her Irish ancestry. She felt part of both communities. In Dowlais, there was a large Irish community. May was raised Catholic but told me there was no friction between the Irish and the Welsh: 'We lived side by side. We had a Welsh woman living next door to us on Harrison Street who spoke both English and Welsh. She walked into our house without knocking and sat and talked to my mother for hours.' The Irish community had their own Catholic church in Dowlais, St Illtyd's, which my grandmother and her family attended regularly. My grandmother and her siblings were educated at the Catholic school which was attached to the church. The Irish community celebrated St Patrick's and other saints' days. The Welsh had their celebrations too, like St David's Day. Every summer there was a fete in Cyfarthfa Park where everybody was welcome. The Irish and Welsh communities mixed together and showed respect for each other.

May had four younger brothers and five younger sisters. All of May's brothers worked as coal miners, some of them down in the same pits as their Dad. I remember my grandmother telling me about a terrible accident. 'Jack had overslept one morning and was late for work. He had to walk three miles underground to the site, but when he arrived on this particular morning, there had been a gas explosion.' Over 100 men were killed in the explosion. Jack escaped death by minutes, all because he had overslept. Horrified by what had happened to his fellow miners, some of whom were his mates, Jack frantically tried to dig away the rubble to find the men. In doing so he injured his hands very badly. They didn't find all of the men. The pit was sealed off and Jack stayed away from work for three months, suffering from shock. He then left the pits and took a job in a factory in Manchester. My grandmother continued, 'Some years later, my youngest brother, Danny, was also involved in a pit disaster. He was only 16 at the time. The pit collapsed and he was crushed. He refused to go down a pit after that. Then the war broke out and he joined the army. He served in the Royal Pioneer Corps all through the war and never worked down a pit again.' Stories like this remind me of the harsh hands my ancestors were dealt in their youth. My grandmother and her family lived in a small coal miner's house. There was no electricity, only a tin bath and a toilet in the yard. They lived in cramped conditions and suffered hardship, especially during the General Strike of 1926 when food and clothing were scarce for the families in their community. My grandmother told me that because they didn't have much space, and had to share beds, there was bickering between some of the sisters. She was particularly close to her sister Kitty, who never married and remained at home with their parents. So did brothers Mick and Jim. My grandmother was also fond of her sister Bridie, who also married a Londoner. I saw a lot of Aunt Bridie when I was growing up. She donned a Welsh accent, was tiny in stature and, unlike my grandmother, chain smoked. Because they lived in London, my grandmother and Bridie remained close for the rest of their lives. As for my grandmother's family, I often wonder about what parts of them are still alive in me.

May came to London aged 14 to work as a servant, though that didn't last long. She was outgoing and friendly, too much so for a job that expected her at most to be docile and compliant. It didn't take long for May to realise the job didn't suit her, so she soon took up a position as a barmaid in The Crown pub on North End Road. She was excited to be working in the bar because she felt she could be herself. All she ever knew was tight-knit spaces, and she found one again in Fulham at The Crown. At the pub she met a local coalman, Bob Joyce, whom she married in 1930 at the age of 19. My grandmother told me that they were attracted to each other straight away. He was tall and handsome, but rather shy. She was charming. She said they suited each other and it was a loving relationship. Together they had three children: my mother Kathy and her brothers, Mike and David. Bob worked as a coal delivery man in Fulham with his horse, Nobby, and cart. Despite Bob working as a coal delivery man, his path never crossed that of John Murray, who dug the coal in Dowlais. May raised her family at 13 Dieppe Street with Bob's mother Hannah, affectionately known as 'Gran'. My grandparents' neighbours included Gran's daughter Mag, and soon-beloved Esther Bruce, a Black seamstress born at 15 Dieppe Street.

In March 1941, Gran 'adopted' Esther Bruce into our family after her father Joseph was killed in an accident. He was knocked down by a taxi during one of the blackouts. Such accidents were common during the war, even though vehicles were expressly asked to drive slowly. Esther was 29 and suddenly had no family of her own. Gran, who had a big heart and was known in her community for helping anyone in need, offered her a home. She had known Esther since she was born on Dieppe Street in 1912 to mixed Guyanese-British parentage. Esther didn't remember her birth mother who died in 1918, a casualty of the flu epidemic. She was raised in the Dieppe Street community by her Guyanese father. Esther recalled her mature adoption during some of our many conversations and always made it sound like a natural thing. Gran had a reputation in their community for being a giver. She was an unofficial midwife at a time when expectant mothers could not afford to go into hospital and pay for their babies' delivery. The National Health Service did not come into existence until 1948. To earn a little extra money, Gran read tea leaves and told locals their fortunes. Esther recalled, 'We had been neighbours for years and went to the same air raid shelter. When Gran said, "Come and live with me, love", I thought it made sense. I moved into 13 Dieppe Street and shared a room at the top of the house with Gran. She was like a mother to me. She was an angel.' An angel and a fortune-teller.

I believe Gran and Esther formed a union because first and foremost, they were friends. Gran did not express any prejudice towards anyone and became the mother Esther never had. It all seemed natural to me, too, growing up. Gran was not politically motivated or trying to make a point by befriending Esther, but I also learned that Gran's decision had much to do with her class. I discovered that working-class families were more likely to embrace outsiders into their circle than the upper and middle classes. Refuge was offered to all walks of life by people like Gran during the war. I even found out in my research that persecuted gays in London's East End found safety and protection with families, which was a pleasant discovery.

When Esther came home from work and went to the shelter, she'd find Gran cooking their tea. They had fires in there, and stoves, and they'd stay the evening and all through the night. Gran would say, 'What do you want, love? Sausages and a baked potato?' Despite the bombing, they found ways to have a good time and take care of each other. It was warm. They sang songs like 'Run Rabbit Run', 'Don't Dilly Dally' and 'Roll Out the Barrel'. These were amongst the songs I heard my family sing at parties when I was a little lad in the 1960s. Everybody pulled together. When a neighbour came in, they were welcomed. If a stranger came in, they weren't turned away. Sometimes the bombs came too close and it became frightening, but nothing deterred these women from tending to each other. There wasn't a threat that could prevent them from their rituals.

Esther looked upon Gran as the mother she didn't get to grow up with. By all accounts, Gran was a hard-working woman and a great lady. It didn't matter who you were or what troubles you had; if you went to Gran, she would put you wise. Gran was good to everybody, that was just her nature. If you were ill she came and sat with you. She really was a marvellous woman, and a marvellous woman to my dear Aunt Esther. Sadly, I never knew Gran. She died in 1952, five years before I was born. However, Esther, my grandmother, and my mother always spoke to me about Gran. She clearly made an impact on everyone who knew her, especially her family. I learned a lot from their memories of Gran, and most important were the feelings of family love and unity, especially in difficult and challenging times, such as the war. Today

I understand how I became the person I am and how I developed my career as a historian of Black Britain. Esther was a big influence. However, I regret not being successful in promoting the working-class lives of the other women in my family. I have tried but there have been obstacles. I don't think historians have given enough attention to the lives of working-class women in Britain. Maybe this is something I can address in the future? Only time will tell.

In 1941, Esther, who had been working as a seamstress since leaving school, was conscripted for war work. She took a job as a cleaner in Fulham Hospital before moving to Brompton Hospital where she cleaned three wards, one of which was the forces' ward. This is where they put the servicemen who had been wounded. Despite what they'd suffered, Esther fondly remembered the men and their antics as colourful. She brought them fish and chips, she told me, which she had to smuggle in, otherwise she would have been in trouble with the matron. I imagine she saw some terrible injuries but she never spoke about this, not even when I asked her.

Esther also volunteered to do the quite dangerous job of being a firewatcher on the roof of the two hospitals. It was an extremely vital wartime job, especially during the air raids. As a fire watcher, Esther had to look out for incendiary bombs, or 'fire' bombs which would land on the roof and cause a great deal of damage while lighting the way for the more dangerous German bombers. It was her job to put out the fires using sand or a small water pump. The bombing largely ceased as the Blitz petered out in May 1941, but this didn't mean home front life became any easier. Food was rationed and when the situation worsened, Esther remembered whale meat being put on sale, 'I wouldn't eat it. I didn't like the look of it. We made a joke about it, singing Vera Lynn's song with new words: "Whale meat again!"'

Esther maintained contact with her family in Guyana [formerly British Guiana] throughout the war who were based in Georgetown.

Things were more stable there, and they had access to essential provisions. Gran and Esther, after discussing what they needed, would write letters to Esther's family stating their needs. A few weeks later, a great big box would arrive with tins of food. Those parcels made all the difference for Esther, Gran, and my family throughout the war.

I strongly believe that the key to understanding Gran's humanity – which included taking Aunt Esther under her wing – comes from a traumatic experience she had as a young woman. In 1895, when she was a teenager, Gran found herself expecting a child. At that time, unmarried mothers were frowned upon and ostracised. Most of them were forced to give up their newborn babies. There was no support for unmarried mothers. Her father was outraged and told Gran she had brought shame upon the family. He banished her to the local workhouse, known as the Fulham Infirmary. This was a grim and forbidding place. Workhouses were institutions launched in the 17th century but peaked in the Victorian era. They were seen as harsh, last-resort shelters for the poor and destitute. While she was there, Gran was forced to get down on her hands and knees to scrub steps. Members of staff constantly reminded her of her shame. Fortunately, shortly after the baby was born, the father of the baby was found and informed about what had happened. He immediately returned and married Gran. In the 1930s, still feeling ashamed and traumatised about her time in the workhouse, and the subsequent death of the baby at the age of five months, Gran broke down in tears and told my grandmother what had happened. However, this terrible experience did not break Gran. I believe it helped her to become a strong, loving, and compassionate woman. That is how my grandmother, Aunt Esther, and my mother described her to me.

The family home survived the air raids and soon became known as 'Lucky 13'. It remained standing until 1960 when the area was cleared for a new estate. At the end of the war, Kathy and her brother Mike left school and Wales (during the war they had been evacuated to their grandparents' home in Merthyr Tydfil) to return to Lucky 13, their beloved Gran, and Esther, who had become part of the family. Soon after, Esther took Kathy to St Paul's in the City. Like so many others, Esther found it hard to believe that the majestic cathedral had survived. For many, the structure symbolised the hope and strength of the British people. 'Look at St Paul's, there's not a mark on it', Esther told my mother as they stood hand-in-hand. 'We're lucky. Some poor souls have ended up with nothing – but we've got half a street.'

Chapter 2

Dunkirk to Doodlebug

I was 16 in 1974 when my paternal grandfather, Grandad Bourne, died at the age of 86. It was a sad occasion. Grandad had been a central figure in the Bourne family. I remember thinking that in the last six years of his life he seemed lost. He had been married to Nanny for over 50 years, and her passing in 1968 was felt very strongly by Grandad and the rest of the family. She was a lovely, caring person who never had a bad word to say about anyone. Following her death, Grandad lived with Dad's sister, my Aunt Hilda, and her family, in Ruislip, Middlesex. Soon after Grandad died, Hilda gave me his ditty box, a small wooden box he had made when he was a sailor. He kept his personal belongings in it when he served in the Royal Navy before and during the First World War. The box contained a number of items including his three war medals: the 1914–1915 Star, the British War Medal, and the Victory Medal. These were presented to him in 1919. The medals were given the nickname 'Pip', 'Squeak', and 'Wilfred' after characters in a *Daily Mirror* comic strip book by B.J. Lamb. There was also his 1939–1945 Defence Medal from the Second World War. I was thrilled to have been given the box but when I looked at the contents, I was disappointed that I hadn't taken the time to ask Grandad questions about his life. I discovered aspects of his life I would have liked to know more about, such as his childhood in the Essex countryside, his navy career, service in the First World War, and working as a fireman in the Second World War. Grandad was born in 1887 in the village of Tillingham in Essex. His father, George, a fisherman, had also been born there. His mother, Emma, had been born in Clare, Suffolk. They were country people and after marrying in 1885, had five children together. Tragically, George died in 1894 of exposure in the nearby Dengie Marshes when the children were young. Grandad's sister Lizzie once told me that Grandad, who was only six when he lost his father, was a troubled boy. When a teacher at the village school upset one of his sisters, Grandad picked up the blackboard and threw it at her. He needed some discipline so, aged 18, he joined the Royal Navy at Chatham.

His navy record (which I also found in his ditty box) showed that he served on a number of ships all through the First World War. When I was young, evidence of Grandad's navy career were the tattoos on his arms, which included the images of ships and the dancing lady. As children we would ask him to show her to us. He would roll up his sleeve, flex his muscles, and make the lady dance. He also had a large framed photograph of one of his ships, the HMS Illustrious, hanging above the fireplace in their kitchen. Smoke bellowed from it. Grandad used to tell me the ship was torpedoed and that he had to swim to shore. Dad said to take no notice, it wasn't true. That it was the smoke from the guns as they fired shells because the ship was on a training exercise.

Nanny Bourne was born Ada Allen in 1888 in Paddington, London. She remembered going to St Michael's Church of England School in Pimlico where one of her classmates was Edith Evans, soon to become one of Britain's most celebrated stage actresses. In *Ned's Girl*, his 1977 biography of Edith, Bryan Forbes said that the school 'maintained a reputation, if not for academic brilliance, then for solid Victorian qualities of decency and purpose'. Forbes's description of Edith's upbringing was one that was shared by Nanny: 'Without affluence yet without poverty – is that peculiar no-man's land of the lower middle class who have no pretensions.' When I was nine years old in 1967, I remember Nanny being fascinated by Edith's acclaimed performance in the film *The Whisperers* for which she was nominated for an Oscar. Nanny described the young Edith as a quiet, studious girl with long dark hair.

Nanny's life couldn't have been more different to Edith's. At the age of 20 in 1908, she gave birth to an illegitimate son, James. Unlike my great grandmother Hannah on my mother's side of the family, Ada was not banished to a workhouse, but remained with her parents who shared in the responsibilities of raising Uncle Jim until she married. In later years, Uncle Jim told me that he never felt stigmatised by his illegitimacy. In 1911, Ada married Henry Bourne and together they had nine children of whom five survived infancy: Harold (known as Terry), Henry (known as Harry), Hilda, Reginald and my father, Arthur, who was the youngest, born in 1931.

The Bourne family lived at 27 Reporton Road, Fulham. My Dad said that he had a happy childhood. He was the youngest of a large family and looked after by all of them. He adored his older brothers. They shared the same sense of humour, telling each other jokes and winding each other up. However, there was a tragedy in his young life. In 1935, when he was three years old, his 12-year-old brother George succumbed to diphtheria, a common child killer at the time. Aunt Hilda said that it was the only time she saw her father shed tears.

Grandad Bourne was tough and rarely out of work after leaving the Royal Navy in 1919. He could turn his hand to most things. On different occasions he was a railway porter and a bus conductor, but he lost that job when he had an argument with a fare-evading passenger. Grandad punched him in the face. Aunt Hilda told me that in the 1930s he sometimes worked at film studios. It was a boom period for British film production and there was a lot of work available. One time, Grandad's navy skills helped him to get a job making the huts for the African village in *Sanders of the River* (1935). This starred the great African-American singer Paul Robeson. Grandad also found work as a film extra. For the prison drama *King of the Damned* (1935) starring Conrad Veidt, he joined dozens of extras as a convict who joins a revolt.

Although this revolt was carried out for a fictional justice, Grandad maintained a strong sense of fairness throughout his life. This fairness was explained to me by my dad who recalled a memory from his childhood, walking along the road with his father when they heard a child crying out in pain. When they looked across the road, they saw a man beating a young boy. Grandad told Dad to stay where he was, walked across the road, thumped the man and said: 'See how you like it!'

I never saw this side of Grandad's personality. I only saw the humorous times. When I was young I asked my dad why Grandad walked along with his hands behind his back, looking at the ground. He said: 'Ask him.' So I did. Grandad's reply still makes me laugh. Pointing at the sky he said: 'Because you won't find pound notes up there, boy.'

When the Second World War began in 1939, Grandad joined the Auxiliary Fire Service (later known as the London Fire Brigade) and served at No. 7 Station, Fulham (685 Fulham Road). My uncles Terry and Harry joined the Army. Harry survived the 1940 evacuation of Dunkirk when more than 338,000 British and French soldiers were rescued from the French port as the Germans occupied France. However, more than 50,000 British troops were unable to escape and, of them, 11,000 were killed. The majority of the remainder were made prisoners of war. In 1986, Harry, a naturally chipper fellow, explained what had happened to him during a family gathering: 'I wasn't sober when I got out of Dunkirk. I was in a camp at the back of the line and we were ordered to move out, so we started walking, found a lorry, got on this lorry, came down to Dunkirk. We got sorted out there. The officer in charge told me I had to be a runner, so I'm running backwards and forwards taking messages from the beach to the headquarters which was at the back of the ditches. I noticed all these abandoned wagons and I found some chocolate and cigarettes in them, and rum. So I filled my water bottle with rum. One time I was on a run and I recognised my neighbour, little Billy. He said: "Hello, Harry" and I replied: "What the bleeding hell you doing here?" Poor Billy was miserable. "What's a matter?" I asked. "Got no fags?" Billy said no. I said: "Cop hold of these" and I gave him some fags. I also gave him some chocolate and a drop of rum. That helped to cheer him up. Then we were told to stay on the beach with our rifles and make sure no one comes off them. So we're stuck there all night like a couple of charlies, kipping on our guns.'

The next morning Harry and Billy heard the German bombers overhead. When the bombs started falling, they were ordered to go to the jetty and get on a boat: 'We got half way along this blimmin' jetty, but it was only a wooden thing with a great big hole in it. You should have seen the blokes jumping over it. Old Jerry [Germans] come over and done a bit of banging away [dropped bombs] but they got us on the coaster [boat] which took us out to the destroyer HMS Whitehall. We gets on this big ship and by all accounts it had been in dock for engine trouble and it still hadn't got a full engine going. Once it was filled up with men it starts off. The old naval blokes said, "Go down there and get yourselves a cup of tea or cocoa and a slice of bread", but Billy and I didn't fancy it. We found ourselves a place on the ship's upper deck and carried on drinking this rum. We both lay there and went right off to sleep until someone woke us up and said: "There's the white cliffs of Dover" and that was us come home. What a game it was. All kinds of boats came out to save us. We was lucky to get on a destroyer, cos they brought us back.'

Uncle Terry was not so lucky. A quiet introvert, he was sent overseas with the army, but in 1943, his wife Phyllis was informed that he was missing – 'believed killed. A deserter.' When it became known in their community that Terry had been branded a deserter, Phyllis and their two young children, Patricia and Michael, were abused by some of their neighbours. They had stones thrown at them and were spat at and called names, and yet they had done nothing. Their home was attacked and Phyllis faced destitution because, as the wife of a deserter, the army's regulations prevented her from receiving money from them. In desperation she went to the Salvation Army for help and they took care of her and the children.

Phyllis believed Terry was deceased until the army informed her that he had *not* deserted and was in fact still alive, though badly injured and traumatised. Serving in North Africa, he had gone missing after being blown up and losing his memory. He had spent three months in hospital. He had also witnessed the death of his best mate in the explosion.

Meanwhile, on Reporton Road, my dad and his brother Reg faced the London Blitz of 1940/41. They had been evacuated at the beginning of the war but along with thousands of other children, returned home when no immediate danger looked likely. However, it was a different story when the raids began in September 1940. Dad, aged just eight, and Reg, aged 14, got caught up in the excitement. He told me that one evening, Nanny left early to go to the shelter at the end of Reporton Road, situated in the crypt of St Peter's Church, to ensure she found a place to spend the night. Grandad had to attend his shift with the fire brigade and insisted that the boys join their mother at the church. After he left, Dad and Reg decided to stay in the house. During the raid, the bombing came closer to Reporton Road and Dad said that he and Reg started to panic: 'All of a sudden a stick of bombs fell nearby and the noise was deafening. The house shook and in terror we dived under the kitchen table. We never stayed in the house again during a raid and soon afterwards Mum and Dad arranged for us to be evacuated again.'

When me and my sister were children in the 1960s, anytime there was a thunderstorm in the middle of the night, Dad would wake us up and take us downstairs until the storm had passed. Storms reminded him of a terrible experience he had during the war, when on July 12, 1944 a doodlebug demolished his house, and he was caught in the blast with his parents and his maternal grandfather 'Pop' Allen. Dad never spoke about what happened until 1976 when he read a letter in a newspaper appealing for reminiscences about the doodlebugs. The request came from the historian Norman Longmate who was writing a book about them. *The Doodlebugs: The Story of the Flying Bombs* was eventually published in 1981.

Dad wrote down what he could remember and made copies using an old-fashioned stencil. I have kept this treasure. 'I had come home from school. It was late afternoon and I was playing in the street when I heard the flying bomb approaching. It was one of many that day so I didn't pay too much attention to it, but as it got louder I looked up and saw it coming over the row of houses opposite. When it started to dive towards me I ran into our house shouting to my mother and father. We managed to reach our passageway which had been reinforced with corrugated sheets and scaffold poles. We didn't have a garden, and so an Anderson shelter was out of the question. My grandfather also joined us from his room off the passage. I remember quite clearly that the engine of the flying bomb had not cut out as they normally did. It just got louder and louder until the explosion. I was terrified.'

The flying bomb landed on the opposite side of the road and demolished two houses. Most of 27 Reporton Road and the neighbouring houses were badly damaged in the blast. According to the air raid warden's report, this was Fulham's 70th flying bomb incident. Two people were killed and 26 seriously injured. Dad continues his note, 'The next thing I can remember was someone picking me up and saying, "This is Sandy. You will be alright now". He lived at the end of our road and was on leave from the navy. I was placed on a stretcher to await the arrival of the ambulance. It was then I realised my face was wet with blood and my eyes would not open. A little while later I heard a familiar voice. It was my brother Terry talking to me. He was on leave having been in hospital after being wounded in the army. He said not to worry, he was going to see if the others were ok.' Dad was taken to Fulham Hospital and given anaesthetic while his face was stitched. When he recovered, he was very sick and his face was bandaged. He could not tell if he could see. 'The next day I was taken with my mother to a hospital in Windsor which was being used for wounded servicemen and other war casualties. Mum told me that Dad was still in Fulham Hospital with a broken hip and cuts. Grandad was in a rest home with minor cuts. Mother had a broken arm and cuts. My recollection of this hospital was having the bandages removed, and each day a nurse would bathe my eyes to try and remove the dirt and dust. After a while I was able to see, thank God.'

Dad and Nanny were then taken to Hinchingbrooke House, a stately home in Huntingdon, Cambridgeshire, part of which was being used as a convalescent home for casualties of the bombing. By the time he recovered, the Germans had started to send over the V-2 rockets. Dad found them very frightening because, unlike the doodlebugs, there was no warning. So he was evacuated to Stourport-on-Severn, a town in Worcestershire. He remained there, with a kind, middle-aged couple, Mr and Mrs Colvin, until the end of the war.

27 Reporton Road was no longer habitable and was eventually demolished. Dad later found out that scavengers had stolen what little furniture and belongings survived the blast, except an antique clock that belonged to his grandad. It remained damaged until 2014 when Paul, one of Aunt Hilda's grandsons, restored it to its former glory, and for the first time in 60 years, it told the time again.

My parents were warm, loving, and caring people unafraid to show their feelings. They were very young children when the war started, and both of them experienced traumas. Mum was just eight years old when she lost her father in 1940, and not long after that, she faced the London Blitz, then the upheaval of leaving home – and her beloved Gran – to relocate to the safety of Merthyr Tydfil in Wales.

In a diary entry for March 30, 1952 my mother confirmed that 'K met A today.' A few months later, Dad completed his national service in the Royal Air Force. He told me that following their first date, Mum took him home to 13 Dieppe Street to meet Gran and Esther. When he entered the house Esther's dog Paddy ran to him, but when he put out his hand to stroke him, Paddy bit him. Things were off to a good start. When my grandmother, May, remarried in August 1952, she relocated to Peckham to live with her new husband, however, Mum refused to leave Gran, whose health had begun to fade. After Gran died in November 1952, Mum joined her mother in Peckham and continued her relationship with Dad until they were married in St Luke's Church, Peckham on March 27, 1954. Leaving Fulham behind, Peckham became their new home.

I think Mum and Dad were searching for security after the disruption and trauma of the Second World War. They found it with each other and remained very much in love until the end. I have one older sister, Linda, and we were fortunate to be raised by two devoted parents, who worked hard to provide us with a home and security. Dad was a pipe fitter by trade, and when I started school in 1962 Mum took a part-time job as a sales assistant in a shoe shop. We didn't have much money coming in, but we had a home that made us feel happy and secure. My sister and I didn't want for anything.

When I am asked why I write books about Black British history, I usually respond by explaining that it was the influence of having had Aunt Esther adopted into our family during the war. However, now that I am older and can look back over time, I realise that I have pursued my interests because of the loving, caring family I come from, in which Aunt Esther plays a large role.

I have many happy memories of my parents, though none as fond as the moments when they recollected their own youth in front of Linda and me.

Mum would say to Dad: 'Do you remember this one, Arf?' and she would start singing an old, forgotten song. The one I remember most is 'When I Grow Too Old to Dream' with music by Sigmund Romberg and lyrics by Oscar Hammerstein II. As much as my family history takes a page out of war history, it is nothing without love.

Chapter 3

Raised by Peckham and Camberwell

When I was born on October 31, 1957 Mum wanted to name me Frankie, after Frankie Vaughan, her favourite pop singer at the time. He was famous for kicking his leg up in the air while singing songs like 'Give Me the Moonlight, Give Me the Girl.' Thankfully, I escaped being called Frankie Bourne after Dad put his foot down. However, naturally, Mum objected to Dad's first suggestion, too, which was to name me Arthur Bourne Jr, so they compromised and the name Stephen John was entered onto my birth certificate. I have always liked my name, I think it suits me. Mum told me that I wasn't named after anyone, but Stephen was a popular name at the time.

Mum gave birth to me in St Giles' Hospital on Havil Street, Camberwell. Once upon a time, the hospital had been the Camberwell Workhouse for the poor and destitute. Inmates were forced to undertake hard labour, namely breaking stones and unpicking oakum. In 1930, it became the hospital where I started life. When I was born, we lived in rented accommodation, a Victorian council house – 151 Cronin Road – off Commercial Way in Peckham. Nan and Grandad lived downstairs and Mum, Dad, Linda and I occupied the upstairs rooms. Grandad – whose name was Horace Dulieu – was actually my Mum's step-father. Though he had inherited a French surname, he had lived in Peckham all his life. He had been born in neighbouring East Surrey Grove in 1896. He was still living there in 1916 when at nineteen, he joined the 10th Royal Sussex Regiment.

Horace was sent to France, to the Battle of the Somme, but only lasted four months. He was shot in the face by a German sniper. Mum told us that the bullet went through the bridge of his nose, causing severe eye damage. He lost the sight of his left eye, which had to be sewn up on the battlefield. My sister said that the injury saved his life because he missed the atrocities that were to follow. His brother Augustus Reuben was killed in action on August 22, 1918.

Horace returned to East Surrey Grove and worked until he was in his sixties. I remember him working as a night watchman at the Jones and Higgins department store at the bottom of Rye Lane, Peckham. He was a kind man and cared very deeply for all of his grandchildren, step- or blood-related. We adored him and made friends with our 'step' cousins, especially Sharon, Gloria, Derek and Richard. Nan's marriage to Grandad meant that she was Welsh of Irish ancestry and with a French surname. Complicated, eh? After making Peckham her new home, she worked as a cleaner at nearby King's College Hospital and then the head office of Kodak in Kingsway.

At 151 we had a beautiful garden that Grandad lovingly tended to. It was his pride and joy. We had an inside loo but no bathroom. Instead we took our baths in a large enamel sink in Nan's scullery in the basement. It was fun if you were a child, but not if you were a grown-up. Dad told me he had to take a bath sitting upright with his knees to his chest because there was no room for him to stretch his legs.

In his spare time, Dad enjoyed betting on the horses (which he called 'gee-gees') and playing darts at the Duke of Wellington pub just down the road, opposite the Rosemary Road bakery where everybody bought their bread. Dad also loved football and he sometimes played in a team on Saturday with my uncles. He never pressured me to take an interest in the game. I preferred to play with my sister's dolls anyways, or read a book. Dad also went fishing with his brother-in-law, Uncle George, so he had lots of male relatives to share his interests with. Every Friday evening Mum went to the pictures at Peckham Odeon with our next-door neighbour, Edna. I loved films and couldn't wait for Mum to tell me what she had seen.

I remember Cronin Road as a wonderful place to live. All around us there was a strong feeling of community, quite like Dieppe Street. Mr Macklin lived alone in a house covered with ivy. Grandad told us he'd once been a gentleman but had since fallen on hard times. His electricity and water had been cut off; soft-hearted Nan felt sorry for him. If she saw him walk past our house on his way to the Grand Surrey Canal (situated at the end of Cronin Road) to fetch water in his kettle, she ran out to him. 'Give me your kettle. I'll fill it up', she said. Mr Macklin was grateful, and when he could afford it, gave Linda and I sixpence when he saw us playing in the street.

Grandad's sister, Aunt Lil, had a grocer's shop on nearby Blakes Road. Now and again, Grandad took us to her shop to say hello to Aunt Lil. I looked forward to these visits because she always gave us a bag of broken biscuits. One day, in 1966, Aunt Lil was knocked down by a car on a zebra crossing on Peckham Road. Nan and Grandad took us to see her in St Giles' Hospital, but she looked very tired and hardly said a word. For a little lad of nine, I found the hospital a forbidding place with a strong smell of disinfectant. A few days later she died, and Grandad cried. This would have been my first experience of a family death but all I can remember is the deep sadness Grandad felt. Lil was his only sister and he thought the world of her.

One day, Grandad came home with a puppy. It was a beautiful brown cocker spaniel with large, floppy ears. Grandad called him Spikey even though he was as soft as a pillow. I adored him. Grandad took me, Linda, and Spikey for walks to the top of Cronin Road, and along Grand Surrey Canal. Some of the walks were punctuated by strange stories, like the time he told us about the police finding a dead body in the canal. In a different way to Grandad, Nan spoiled Linda and me. She bought us sweets and comics. She told us that she couldn't afford to do that for our Mum when she was young because our 'real' Grandad had died at the beginning of the war and she didn't have much money. I couldn't imagine life without my Dad.

My grandparents in Fulham also figured in my childhood. After losing their home in the war, they were rehoused in a basement flat in a large Victorian house on Fairholme Road, a short walk from West Kensington station. The road was run down and most of the houses had rooms rented out to tenants. One of the houses was a brothel, as I later discovered when I read Michael O'Mahony's *My Fairholme Road Days*, published in 1998. The basement flat was small and didn't have much daylight. It would have been the servant's quarters in earlier times. They never used the front room, which had bars at the window, installed in Victorian times to protect the house against thieves. While Grandad was at work, Nanny spent her days in the kitchen area at the back where a coal fire kept her warm. They didn't have a fridge. Their food and milk was stored in a pantry which had a mesh window at the back to keep the food fresh and flies out. They didn't have a television either. Nanny refused. She preferred the wireless and her weekly copy of the *Radio Times*. She was fond of digestive biscuits and listening to military band music on the radio. She could play the piano. They didn't have one, but Aunt Hilda and Uncle George did and when she visited them, Nanny would entertain us with her piano playing.

After Grandad left the fire brigade in 1945, he was employed as a security guard at St James' Palace where he occasionally met and chatted to Queen Elizabeth, later the Queen Mother. He then became a park keeper at Bishops Park in Fulham. That was his job in the 1960s when I was growing up. During the school holidays Mum took Linda and me to see them. Nanny was a sweet, kind lady. Dad later told me that Grandad would turn up for work at Bishops Park and then disappear into a pub for a few pints. When he came home he was always pleased to see us, and when he rubbed his stubbly chin on our faces, he smelt of beer. He would then put his arm around Nanny and try to kiss her but she would push him away with the words: 'Lay orf, 'arry.' After Nanny died in 1968, Grandad went to live with his daughter and her family. And I, continuing her legacy, started to buy the *Radio Times* with my pocket money. And still do.

On Sundays, when Dad was having a darts match at the pub and Mum was preparing dinner, she would tell Linda and me funny stories about her childhood in Fulham. We were fascinated by her descriptions of life with Gran and Aunt Esther, and we were amused by the antics she shared with her cousin Rosie who lived next door on Dieppe Street. One time Rosie took my Mum to the top of 13 Dieppe Street and threw a lighted firework out of the upstairs window. It landed amongst their Uncle Charlie's chickens which he kept in the backyard. Suffice to say, the fireworks scared the life out of them. Chickens are not known to fly, but apparently these ones could. On most occasions when the girls were up to trouble, Charlie would run out of the house and shake his fist at them to a chorus of their laughter: 'You effing little bleeders! You wait till I get my hands on you!' Linda and I would fall about laughing at this anecdote. Mum always referred to her Uncle Charlie (her Dad's brother) as 'Oatsie'. When I asked her why, she'd explain it was Cockney rhyming slang for his name: 'Charlie rhymes with oats and barley so we called him Oatsie.' I loved hearing these stories and, better still, writing them down. To this day, I can still feel the stitches from all the laughter brought on by Mum and Auntie Rosie's stories and jokes.

Mum and Dad worked hard to provide Linda and me with experiences we'd remember. They didn't have much time to take us anywhere throughout the year, but in the summer Linda and I looked forward to getting away from the city and experiencing the joys of the seaside. We usually went away with Aunt Hilda, Uncle George and their three children, our cousins, Kay, Dennis, and Alan. Sometimes we went to

Hayling Island just east of Portsmouth, and in 1963, we had a brilliant time in Ventnor on the Isle of Wight. We also went to holiday camps in South Devon including Torquay and Ladram Bay as well as Portreath in Cornwall and Cilgerran in Wales. They were memorable holidays. Linda and I still reminisce about them, and the ease our parents seemed to fall into. They were relaxed and enjoyed being away from the stresses of London and their working lives, especially when the sun came out. Dad went fishing with Uncle George, while Mum sat and talked to Aunt Hilda. Linda and I often went on adventures with our cousins Dennis and Alan. I remember when we were staying in Cilgerran the four of us discovered a disused, overgrown railway line and explored it. That was exciting. Although Mum and Dad took Linda and me on holiday every year, we never travelled overseas. They just couldn't afford it. I didn't visit another country until 1976 when I went on a day trip to Calais in France, organised by my school.

When I was very little my favourite television programme was *Watch With Mother*, a daily BBC television programme aimed at pre-school children. Mum told me I sat glued to the set when the puppet Andy Pandy and his friends Teddy and Looby Loo came on. She added that if there had been an earthquake in Peckham I wouldn't have taken any notice. I could hardly contain my joy when Mum made me an Andy Pandy rag doll from a pattern she found in her *Woman's Own* magazine. It was one of my favourite possessions, I kept it for years.

In 1962 our local council announced their plans to install bathrooms (which we didn't have) and convert our houses into self-contained flats. Council tenants were informed they could continue living in them while construction took place. Mum and Nan were thrilled because it would mean that they would have separate flats with bathrooms. Six months later the council informed Mum and Nan they had changed their minds and were going to move us out. We were going to be rehoused because the houses on Cronin Road and the local area were going to be demolished. The council had decided to build a brand new council estate in the area, one of the largest in Europe. So we said goodbye to Cronin Road in March of 1963 and moved into a ground floor council flat in a small block called Voltaire on a nearby housing estate called Sceaux Gardens. Linda and I had bedrooms overlooking Peckham Road, and in general we were pleased with the new flat. It had a bathroom, with a proper bath, and central heating. We were in a lively area right across from the fire station, which was a bit of a shock after the peace and quiet of Cronin Road. But we came to appreciate the noise of traffic, police car sirens and the clanging sounds of the fire engines at all hours of the night. Eventually, these things became white noise to us, and Linda and I learned to live with it. There was a bus stop outside which came in handy, too. It took me a bit of time to appreciate the move. I loved our home on Cronin Road, and it was great to have Nan and Grandad living downstairs.

It wasn't before long that Nan and Grandad moved into a flat in a block of flats called Woodene on the Acorn estate in Peckham not far from us. We didn't have a garden in Voltaire, just a stone porch which the council deemed insufficient space for us to keep our dog, Spikey, who we sent to live with relatives outside London. Spikey settled into his new home and we visited him a couple of times, but he died soon after our move which was devastating to me.

A few years later, Cronin Road was demolished to make way for the North Peckham Estate as part of the council's postwar regeneration of the area. Then, in the late-1990s, Southwark Council demolished that. What Hitler's bombs failed to do in the London Blitz, my local authority did twice in my lifetime. However, it didn't take long to get used to living on a big council estate. Children adapt. One of the benefits was that our primary school was next door. It took Linda and me exactly two minutes to walk from our front door to our school, Oliver Goldsmith, situated on the corner of Peckham Road and Southampton Way. It was a Victorian building which had opened in 1899. I quickly appreciated that the council estate was a big, exciting adventure playground, and

I soon made friends with other kids. It was a large estate and in those days a child could walk alone to the shops to buy his or her mum a loaf of bread.

Marie Curie and Lakanal were the names of the two high rise blocks of flats on the estate. They had long corridors, with about fourteen units, seven on each side. On the estate, we innocently played games like 'Tin Can Tommy' but 'Knock Down Ginger' was the one we enjoyed most of all. It was hilarious. Each member of the 'gang' would stand at a front door, while another held the lift open. On the word 'go' we would all bang as hard as we could on the letter boxes and then run as fast as we could to the lift, bundle in, and pray that the lift door would close before the tenants opened their doors. All the while giggling at the thought of people opening their front doors to no one, but if you were the last child in the corridor, and didn't run fast enough, you could find yourself trapped outside the lift and at risk of being caught by one or more of the irritated tenants. When that happened, plan B was to run for the fire exit and escape down the back stairs. I was never a leader of the pack. I was a quiet kid on the sidelines, but I always joined in because I enjoyed the camaraderie and fun.

In the summer of 1968, word spread around that a film was being made close to the Grand Surrey Canal in Wells Way, so groups of us children found our way to the location. We were impressed by the film equipment and huge searchlights. We learned that the derelict houses behind St George's Church were going to be set ablaze and demolished that evening for a sequence about the London Blitz in a film called *Battle of Britain.* When we saw the film at Peckham Odeon we discovered that it was the sequence featuring Ian McShane as the RAF pilot who returns home on leave to discover his wife and children have been killed in an air raid.

I enjoyed school. I started in September 1962, just before my fifth birthday. Most of the other children came from similar backgrounds as myself. From working-class families. I felt safe and secure at Oliver Goldsmith. I enjoyed the company of the other children. Some of them enjoyed my company too. I do not recall having any special friends at this time, but I got on with most of my classmates.

Most of my teachers did well to nurture a family feeling amongst the pupils. I remember feeling like I didn't have to fight to belong in our classroom. They didn't see us as cogs but as children who would one day become adults; future historians, doctors, dreamers, and the like. I also never felt unsafe at school, although I know, even then as a boy I knew, that there were kids who did. Every once in a while, our inclusive bubble would get popped by ignorant questions from certain members of staff. There was a very old teacher at the school and as the stereotype goes, he was also strict and grumpy. I remember him always asking the Black children, 'Where do you come from?' We were young so I doubt their replies were anything more than earnest, but I could see a fuse burst in his brain when they'd politely say, 'I'm from Peckham.' Felt like a kind of small justice against prejudice, his defeat.

In the 1960s, Oliver Goldsmith welcomed a new generation of children from African and Caribbean backgrounds, their parents having come to Britain as part of the 'Windrush Generation'. What we were failed to be made aware of, not in schools, history books, or general popular media, was that there had been a Black presence in Britain since at least the mid-16th century. Black historical figures from the past were invisible, and there was a wall of silence around Britain's Black history. However, I was lucky for two reasons. I was a curious boy, and to pair with my curiosity, I had an adopted aunt who had been born Black and British long before the Empire Windrush docked at Tilbury in 1948. Unlike my contemporaries, my relationship to Aunt Esther gave me, from an early age, an awareness of the pre-1948 Black presence in Britain. Consequently, I did not share in the wildly popular view that the postwar immigrants from Africa and the Caribbean were a threat or agree with those who, in the late 1960s, began suggesting that immigrants be repatriated.

Every year Oliver Goldsmith organised a May festival which was an ambitious but thoroughly enjoyable event that drew lots of proud mums and dads into the school playground to watch the May Queen crowned. This was followed by some entertainment from us children, including my personal favourite: dancing together around the maypole. In the 1963 iteration of the festival, I danced the sailor's hornpipe with my classmate Eric, both dressed in sailor costumes. My mum told me that I looked very nervous trying to remember the steps as Miss Ash pounded on the piano. It didn't help having older boys from nearby Peckham Manor (they had climbed over a wall behind the school) standing in the background and jeering, but Eric and I got through it.

During the autumn, Oliver Goldsmith also had a harvest festival and encouraged every child to bring a tin of soup or a packet of tea to school. These would be included in a small parcel and distributed free of charge to senior citizens in Peckham and Camberwell. It seems extraordinary now, but young children like myself were trusted to leave the school unaccompanied, in groups of three or four, and take the food parcels to the homes of mostly appreciative senior citizens. I say mostly because I shall never forget walking all the way to a house in Kimpton Road, off Camberwell Church Street, and having an elderly lady look disgustedly inside the parcel I handed to her. She said, 'Oh, no, not bloody tomato soup again. You gave me that last year and I hate it!' But she kept the parcel.

The most enjoyable time I spent at Oliver Goldsmith was in the fourth and final year (1968–69) before I left to go to secondary school. We had a young teacher who would sometimes get bored and play us his favourite records instead of teaching the day's lessons. Maybe it was his dream to be on stage instead of in the classroom. Whatever the reason for his distraction, I loved these interludes; he'd play the biggest hits on the pop charts which I adored. I remember him playing us 'Michelle' by The Beatles and 'Lily the Pink' by the Scaffold, which felt to me then like a spiritual experience. However, my love for music predates this teacher. 1967 was the year I purchased my first seven inch record, 'Hello Goodbye' by The Beatles.

There was only one issue that I had with school. It was sums, or what people today call 'maths'. I hated the subject and couldn't multiply to save my life. When I was about ten years old, Mum and Dad went to Oliver Goldsmith for a parents' evening. Upon their return, they informed me that my teacher was generally pleased with me but that I needed to work harder at maths. As soon as they said that, my bottom lip began to tremble in the way children's lips can when they're upset, and I burst into tears. Dad being Dad, put his arm around me and gently said: 'Don't worry about it, son. Just remember that when you're grown up, the only maths you need to worry about is how to add up your wage packet at the end of the week.' I never worried about sums again.

I was just four years old when Mum introduced me to the magical world of cinema. She took Linda and me to see Hayley Mills play twins in a Walt Disney comedy called *The Parent Trap*. In 1968, I wrote my first fan letter to Hayley. I cannot remember what I said or how I found out where to send it, but Hayley did receive it and she kindly sent me a signed photograph, which I still treasure. I keep it safe in an album of signed photos of my favourite film and television stars. I appreciate that film stars of yesteryear would respond to their fan letters, or at least employ someone to do it for them. I often wonder if this still happens. Thanks to Hayley and my mum, I became a toddling film buff, and Peckham Odeon on Peckham High Street became my second home. It provided a source of never-ending escapism – joy, thrills, and magic – except the time Mum and Dad took me and Linda to see *Lawrence of Arabia*. I couldn't have been more than five, and I suffered. Afterwards, all I remembered about the film was sand and more sand and some bloke in a white frock, and that it went on forever.

Lawrence notwithstanding, I spent many happy hours in the Odeon, especially during the school holidays. Every Saturday morning Linda and I took off to the Odeon with an army of other local children for

'Saturday Morning Pictures'. This was a programme designed to entertain kids and usually consisted of worn-out scratched black and white serials from the 1930s called *Flash Gordon* (in the 1960s he was well past his sell-by-date), and cartoons, such as Donald Duck and Tom and Jerry, which we'd already seen on the television. There were also Children's Film Foundation serials which were fun, even if most of the child actors spoke with middle-class accents and had trained at acting schools for children.

In addition to our Saturday morning ritual, Linda and I had great fun going to see Walt Disney features, usually during the Easter and Summer holidays. In those days you could sit through the main feature twice if you hid from the manager on the floor when the lights came up. We watched Disney animation classics going back as far as the 1930s (*Snow White and the Seven Dwarfs*), the 1940s (*Bambi, Dumbo*) and 1950s (*Cinderella, Lady and the Tramp*), which had yet to be seen on television. My favourite was *Peter Pan.* Sometimes we'd act out the film with kids from the estate and I'd always elect to play Wendy. I remember when Nan took us to see *Mary Poppins.* Films like that were training grounds for my perception of the adults in my life. Masking emotions and putting on a happy face. It's interesting how even as young people we can intuit these things. Mary Poppins is a nanny who looks after other people's children, but doesn't have any of her own. In Peckham we had a nan, our grandmother, but not nannies, so Mary's profession was something of a mystery to me. Mary Poppins doesn't have a romance in the film, not even with Bert, the chimney sweep she befriends. At the end of the film she leaves the children with their mum and dad, and flies away, never to be seen again. For me, at the age of seven, *Mary Poppins* was a film about loneliness, and I identified with that. Although I was a happy child, I sometimes found emptiness inside, not knowing why it was there. I know that when I played Wendy from *Peter Pan* I sensed that other children thought it was a strange thing for a boy to want to do. They didn't say anything. We were very young and we were friends. To me, playing Wendy instead of Peter or Captain Hook or one of the lost boys was the most natural thing in the world, but I felt that it wasn't really acceptable behaviour. Yet, when Dad came home and gave me a funny look when he found me parading around the living room with a curtain wrapped around me, still pretending to be Wendy, he didn't chastise me. He didn't tell me that boys do not play Wendy because Wendy is a girl. I bless him for that. Sometimes women said to my Mum: 'Look at his beautiful eyelashes. He should be a little girl.' I didn't mind and I didn't take any notice of some of the boys at school who called me horrible names like sissy or poofy because I spoke softly and didn't want to play football. I wasn't like other boys but I was never put under any pressure to behave like them. As far as I was concerned, no grown-up in my family or at school appeared to be bothered that I was 'different'. I was an innocent, gentle child who enjoyed escaping into worlds of make-believe (especially cinema), my Hayley Mills scrapbook, and Enid Blyton's Famous Five.

Enid Blyton created a world so far removed from the one I knew in Peckham, and, thanks to her, I spent many blissful Sunday mornings in bed with Julian, Dick, George, Anne, and Timmy the dog. In Enid Blyton's books, children inhabited worlds in which they discovered tunnels under the sea, travelled the countryside in caravans, made friends with travellers and chimpanzees, explored castles and stumbled into the most exciting adventures. The children in Enid Blyton's books came from privileged backgrounds. I read Enid Blyton's books to escape into worlds where there were islands, castles, mountains, seas, ships, and rivers of adventure. In the Famous Five books, George was easily Enid Blyton's most interesting character. Her real name was Georgina and she hated being a girl. She refused to answer to her real name, and she was always being mistaken for a boy with her very short hair. Only Julian, Dick, Anne and Timmy, her faithful dog, knew the truth about George. She was, like me, an outsider. I had the sense that should we have had the chance to see George grow up, we would've been delighted to see her fully embrace her identity in Blyton's world. George was brave, defiant and tough, forever in conflict with sexist Julian. She always stood up to him and struggled jolly hard to assert herself and to be what she wanted to be.

When I was eight years old, encouraged by Linda, I started visiting our two local libraries in Peckham Hill Street and Camberwell Church Street (some 30 years later I worked there as a library assistant). I was overjoyed to find dozens of Enid Blyton's books available to read, not just the Famous Five stories. Though we enjoyed reading them, we also enjoyed defacing them. Linda and I drew speech bubbles filled with obscenities coming out of Julian, Dick, George, and Anne's mouth. This was usually followed by squealing laughter. As children, Linda and I were very close, and in addition to sharing a love of reading, we also shared a sense of humour. We would visit places of local interest such as the Cuming Museum on Walworth Road and the art gallery on Peckham Road. We would also travel on the bus to Greenwich where they had a ship called the Cutty Sark and wonderful green space. Sometimes our neighbour Carol would come with us. She was about the same age as Linda. When Linda reached her teenage years, she found other interests and friends her own age to share them with. But we have remained close. Friends forever.

I was often criticised at Oliver Goldsmith by some teachers for reading Enid Blyton's books. I didn't understand why, and I was hurt by their comments. As far as I was concerned, Enid Blyton was the greatest writer ever. Other books were offered to me, mostly adventure stories aimed at boys, like Robert Louis Stevenson's *Treasure Island* and Daniel Defoe's *Robinson Crusoe*, but I didn't want to read them. Linda recommended Mary Norton's *The Borrowers*, but the illustrations frightened me, especially the one which had the tiny Pod family running away in terror when someone discovered them living under the floor boards. I did read, however, another book recommended by my sister: Mary Norton's *Bedknobs and Broomsticks.* I enjoyed it tremendously because it was like reading a Famous Five book, with a magic bed that transported the children to all sorts of exciting places. It is still one of my favourite fiction books.

Since that time I have read plays by William Shakespeare, Oscar Wilde, Bertolt Brecht and Harold Pinter, poems by John Keats, Wilfred Owen and Sylvia Plath, novels by Jane Austen, Charlotte Bronte, Emily Bronte, Charles Dickens, Thomas Hardy, Alice Walker and Samuel Selvon, and short stories by James Joyce, but my favourite work of fiction will always be Enid Blyton's *The Valley of Adventure*, first published in 1947. For Christmas 2007 I treated myself to an original hardback copy – with the dust jacket intact – from the internet for £35. Once again I relived the adventures of Jack, Lucy Ann, Philip, Dinah, and Kiki the parrot. I first discovered and read the book at the age of ten in 1968 and even after 40 years it captivated me still. I live in the hope that one day BBC Radio 4 will invite me to be a guest on *Desert Island Discs* so that I can choose *The Valley of Adventure* as my book to take to the island.

Linda and I loved watching television. This was one of the joys of growing up in a working-class household. Most of the time we were allowed to watch what we wanted. In the 1960s, we witnessed the spectacle of Valerie Singleton doing extraordinary things with sticky back plastic and squeezy bottles in *Blue Peter* and were moved to tears by Ken Loach's *Cathy Come Home*, a gut-wrenching drama documentary about homelessness. Our early evening's entertainment always began straight after school at 4:30 with *Crossroads*, a daily soap opera. In *Crossroads* a kind, well-spoken lady called Meg Richardson ran a motel near Birmingham which was always full of interesting characters. For instance, the motel's cleaner was a busy-body gossip called Amy Turtle who was always poking her nose into other people's business. After *Crossroads* we had a range of children's programmes to choose from on two channels: ITV and BBC1. We watched practically *everything: Squiddly Diddly, Marine Boy, Atom Ant, The Munsters, Flipper, Daktari, The Flying Nun, The Singing*

Ringing Tree, Batman, Gentle Ben, Lost in Space, Junior Showtime, Robinson Crusoe (which had that lovely theme tune and French-speaking actors who were dubbed into English so their lip movements were out of sync) and, of course, BBC1's *Blue Peter* (I never took to its ITV rival *Magpie*). I was so proud when the programme's editor Biddy Baxter awarded me blue and silver badges, but my proudest possession was my signed photograph of the presenters, Val, John, and Pete.

Every Saturday afternoon I waited patiently for Dad's racing to finish so that I could leap into his warm armchair and watch *Doctor Who.* I can still recall seeing the very first episode on November 23, 1963. I was just six years old. It was so eerie and frightening. The series quickly captured the imaginations of the nation's children. At playtime in school on Monday mornings, groups of children huddled together and discussed what terrors we had seen on Saturday afternoon: Daleks, Cybermen, the Yeti.

From time to time Linda and I, if we nagged our parents hard enough, were allowed to stay up late to watch serious, adult programmes. One I shall never forget is the 1968 screening of Alfred Hitchcock's film *Psycho* when it was shown for the first time on British television on BBC1. Mum had seen it at the cinema when it was first released and she told us how scary it was, so naturally Linda and I wanted to see it for ourselves. We begged Mum and Dad to let us, which they eventually did, but warned that we would be very sorry. Were we sorry... nothing, not even *Doctor Who*, had prepared us for *Psycho*, perhaps the scariest film ever made, especially when Marion Crane is stabbed to death in the shower. I became a quaking ten year old who sat huddled on his dad's lap throughout the film, and then insisted on sleeping in his sister's bedroom that night. I shall never forget Mum saying afterwards: 'Well, I warned you.'

It wasn't just entertainment that TV offered, but I witnessed so many of the life-changing events of the 1960s through our household television. I recall the passing, in 1965, of Winston Churchill. Someone in my family commented, 'He was a Tory bastard but he got us through the war.' After his funeral, which we watched live, I was presented with a jigsaw puzzle showing his coffin going into St Paul's Cathedral. In 1966, I was upset about the terrible Aberfan disaster near Merthyr Tydfil when 116 children were killed during the catastrophic collapse of a colliery spoil tip. My nan, who came from Merthyr, cried her eyes out. In America in 1968, there was the assassination of Dr Martin Luther King Jr and, in 1969, in London, the death of Judy Garland. For me, the 1960s were a decade of extremes. I could be watching *Blue Peter* at 5pm and then at 6pm on the news, children being napalmed in Vietnam. At the end of the decade I remember being furious when a favourite children's television programme called *Banana Splits* was cancelled for a live news report on the landing of the first men on the moon.

In 1968, there was only one present that I wanted for Christmas: a Petite Typewriter (the junior version). It had been advertised on television for weeks. A little girl happily tapped away. When I asked Mum and Dad if I could have one, they agreed. I wasn't troubled when my Petite Typewriter turned out to be pink. However, this prize acquisition soon caused me some embarrassment when we visited Aunt Hilda and Uncle George over the Christmas holiday period. When Aunt Hilda asked me what I had received for Christmas I proudly replied 'A Petite Typewriter'. Uncle George looked surprised and my teenage boy cousins, Dennis and Alan, burst out laughing. Aunt Hilda told them to stop and Dad, defensive and as protective as ever, explained: 'Well, it's what he asked for. He's going to be a writer one day.' I quickly learned to type with one finger.

It was around this time that my true nature began to reveal itself. I was looking at a mail order catalogue with Mum and Auntie Rosie. When they flicked through the pages showing men modelling suits, I blurted out that I wanted to be a male model when I grew up. Auntie Rosie was unimpressed and said quite firmly, 'You don't want to do *that* for a living, boy.' I asked her why and she replied: 'They're all a bunch of queenies!' She didn't mean any harm, but I realised that being gay (though I didn't know that word at the time), was going to be an issue as I grew older.

Chapter 4

Secondary Modern, Second Class

I was a gay little boy who made it through the 60s relatively unscathed. Unbeknownst to me, the other shoe had to drop. And drop it did the day I started secondary school in September 1969. When I was just 12 years old, I was slapped across the face by the PE teacher for refusing to take part. I suspect that I was slapped for what my teacher suspected of my sexual orientation *and* because I refused to take part. I had never been hit before. My parents had never laid a hand on me. Traumatised, I absconded and returned home in tears. This was my life at St Michael and All Angels, a secondary modern on Wyndham Road in Camberwell. Most of the kids were from working-class families in the area – Brixton, Camberwell, Walworth and Peckham, nothing too far out the way, and we were a lively lot. It was a Church of England school that promoted Christian values but practiced a philosophy much less forgiving. Corporal punishment and bullying were the norm.

In some ways, I was lucky to have been offered an education. Both my parents were part of the working-class generation that left school at 14 and went to work. It was during the Second World War that the 1944 Butler Education Act made secondary education free for all pupils. The resulting offering was a three-tier system of grammar, secondary modern, and technical schools. The 11-plus examination was administered to measure academic ability, ultimately determining which school children would go to. Grammar schools emphasized academic excellence and were reserved for the highest achievers, where secondary moderns mainly focused on practical subjects. In addition to English and Maths, girls were taught needlework, housewifery, and cookery while boys did woodwork and metalwork. I didn't think it was fair. I loathed woodwork and metalwork. They were a complete waste of time for me. I would have preferred to learn how to cook. St Michael and All Angels was a relatively new building when I arrived. It had been opened in 1955 by HRH Princess Marie Louise, the 83-year-old granddaughter of Queen Victoria. She planted a tree to commemorate the occasion. The school had been built on the site of a Victorian primary school that had been destroyed in 1943 during an air raid, recalled Reverend Shaw, the Vicar of St Michael's parish from 1947 to 1954. The Reverend campaigned for the site to be cleared and for a new school to be built there.

I was a quiet, soft-spoken boy and hence, an easy target for verbal abuse. Name calling was common. I was often called poof, queer, bendy boy, bum boy and shirt lifter. I didn't have to tell anyone I was gay. There were occasions when some of the teachers at the school could be insensitive. I remember sitting at the back of a classroom when our maths teacher introduced a new teacher training student to us. 'She's interested in giving sewing classes during the lunch hour', the teacher said. He then persuaded some of the girls to join in. Then he spotted me and I cringed, knowing what was going to be said next. 'What about you, Stephen? Boys can learn to sew too.' The other kids roared with laughter. I felt humiliated and I resented the teacher for embarrassing me.

Another time, a teacher tried to explain to us what isolates are. 'They're people who don't fit in', he said. He drew a diagram on the blackboard to show us what he meant. First, he drew a large circle to represent 'society'. Then he drew a line from the large circle and joined it to another, much smaller circle. This, he said, represented the 'isolate'. Then he looked at me, and I was horrified when he described me to my classmates as an example of the isolate, someone who 'didn't fit in'.

What made me return to school every day and walk through those gates? There were days I couldn't face going to school, and this meant that I either persuaded Mum I was ill or spent time in the public library in Camberwell or walked the streets of nearby Walworth, until home time, but mostly I did as I was told. I think it was a mixture of fear of getting into trouble and guilt about embarrassing my family, that made me go to school. I came from a close-knit family. Mum and Dad worked. They paid their rent every week and never fell into arrears. There was always food on the table, and a roof over our heads. Mum and Dad provided a safe, comfortable, loving home environment, and the last thing I wanted to do was upset them. I remember Mum telling Auntie Rosie about the times I tried to avoid going to school. Auntie Rosie, who never had any children, responded: 'If it was up to me, Kath, I'd march him to the gates and leave him there!' But Mum and Dad were not like that. They were concerned, and it upset me to see them worried or upset, so most of the time I kept my fears to myself, while trying to cope with a difficult situation. What helped me through these unhappy adolescent years was television. I watched a great deal of television, and the continuity of long-running drama series like *Coronation Street*, *A Family at War* and *Upstairs, Downstairs* kept me going. They provided me with something to look forward to.

These series were my constant in a decade of dynamism and change. My teenage life was soundtracked by the best of pop. Every Sunday I would take the radio from the kitchen to my bedroom and listen to the run-down of that week's pop charts. I also looked forward to BBC television's *Top of the Pops*. I did not go to pop concerts and at that time music was a solitary pastime. Other sounds made it in too, glam rock, disco, punk, reggae, but none of them did the trick quite like pop did. In one of our lessons the teacher asked us who our favourite pop or rock stars were. Answers included Marc Bolan, David Bowie, David Cassidy and Jimmy Cliff but when my turn came I blurted out 'Judy Garland' and everyone fell about laughing, including the teacher. It just hadn't occurred to me that, in the early 1970s, Judy was not considered cool.

Nor was talking about sex. At least in the classroom. My sex education was pretty much non-existent, although I do recall a short looped film that my biology teacher showed us of a woman giving birth. Of course we all, especially the girls, groaned in horror as the baby came out, covered in blood. But that was it. No birds and bees, nothing, just a woman on a screen in agony. As far as the school was concerned, sex didn't exist. My own sex life was non-existent. I knew nothing about gay sex and learnt very little about straight sex, just what I overheard in the school playground from other boys. There was one awkward experience when I took a girl to a school disco. It was my only attempt to pass for straight, but it felt alien and uncomfortable. I led a solitary life as a gay working-class teenager. I didn't know of any other gays at school or in my community. There was no information either. Sexuality was never discussed at school or in the home.

By the age of 14 I had learned how to truant without being caught. In fact, I became quite skilled at it. I would get my name in the afternoon register and then bunk off for the rest of the day. Now and again I would catch a bus to Tower Bridge and explore the nearby docklands area. I was a film buff. I loved old movies. Sometimes I would visit the Cinema Bookshop in Great Russell Street off Tottenham Court Road which has since sadly closed. This is where I purchased books about the movies. The first was David Shipman's *The Great Movie Stars – The Golden Years*, first published in 1970. It replaced Enid Blyton's *The Valley of Adventure* as my favourite book and I read over and over again profiles of Humphrey Bogart, Joan Crawford, Bette Davis, Robert Donat, Clark Gable, Jessie Matthews and many others. I avidly watched their old movies on television. Other times I would attend a matinee of a new film in the West End. I remember seeing films like *Cabaret* with Liza Minnelli and *Lady*

Sings the Blues with Diana Ross even though I was underage. I must have looked older. I also loved the 'disaster' movies that were popular at that time: *The Poseidon Adventure, Earthquake* and *The Towering Inferno.* However, I avoided films like *The Exorcist,* having witnessed a lad in my school having a nervous breakdown after seeing it and being kept off school for several weeks to recover.

The Duke of Edinburgh's Award was a new teenage rite of passage at the time. One morning, we were herded like cattle into the school hall to be given a presentation about this scheme, which was aimed at teenagers. I got very excited and dreamed of being awarded a Gold (in my head, an Oscar), though I would have been just as happy with a Silver or Bronze. This was how they classified achievement but also how they measured the difficulty and extensiveness of one's wilderness tasks, with Gold being the most arduous, most taxing expedition. My heart sank when it was explained that, for the scheme, the Duke of Edinburgh expected us to climb a mountain in Scotland, swim the Channel, build a raft on a lake with oil drums, and sing 'Ging Gang Goolie' around a camp fire in the middle of nowhere in the winter. I searched through the leaflet we were given, hoping to find activities I enjoyed such as 'keep a Diana Ross scrapbook', 'read your mother's *Woman's Weekly* magazine', or 'bunk off school after lunch to go to the West End with your pocket money to see *The Towering Inferno*', but I was disappointed to find that these activities were not included. I am sure the Duke of Edinburgh meant well, but clearly his award scheme wasn't intended for gay lads like me.

When I reached the age of 16, I joined the National Film Theatre (NFT) on London's South Bank. I remember the first film I saw there was a 1944 Hollywood melodrama called *Since You Went Away* starring Claudette Colbert, Jennifer Jones and Shirley Temple as an American family during the Second World War. I also went because I wanted to see the great African-American actress Hattie McDaniel who I had seen in *Gone with the Wind,* the 1939 classic. When I joined the NFT, I believed that a whole new world, far away from Peckham Road, would open up to me, and it did, in part. Due to costs, I did not go to the NFT very often, but I quickly discovered that the NFT anyway was part of a world to which I did not completely belong. Apart from one or two teachers at school, I did not know of anyone else who belonged to the NFT. I realised that it belonged to the world of the white middle-class. It was not part of my world. I felt as if I was a stranger but once I sat down to watch a film at the NFT, I felt at home, just as I did at the Peckham Odeon or the two cinemas at the Elephant and Castle. Being introverted didn't help. Perhaps if I had been more confident in myself, I could have overcome my self-consciousness in these middle-class spaces. It took time to find my way.

Meanwhile, I visited the library of the British Film Institute, then situated on Dean Street, off Oxford Street, but I had to get a letter from my school to confirm I was honest and reliable and could be trusted not to half-inch any of their books or movie star files. I wanted to research what they had on Black stars of the screen and I was thrilled with the files they gave me, especially those which had material relating to Hattie McDaniel and the 1940s MGM star, Lena Horne.

My movie star book-buying was partly paid for by a Saturday job I started at the age of 15. My mum worked for True Form, a shoe shop on Rye Lane, and they were always on the lookout for Saturday staff. Mum had to get permission from the Inner London Education Authority (ILEA) for this to happen, and I was only allowed to work for four hours. One year later this increased to seven hours but it was so long ago I cannot remember what I was paid. I know that it was enough to pay for the occasional book or record. So I never wanted for anything. I continued working on Saturdays at True Form until I decided I needed a change of shoe shop and joined the staff of Stead and Simpson next door. We were supervised by an elderly disgruntled woman called Miss Tuite. She had worked for the company for decades. I didn't like her old-fashioned ways and was shocked when she announced to me that if there was another vacancy, staff were not allowed to encourage a 'coloured boy or girl' to apply if they made enquiries. 'Tell them we have no vacancies', she said. At True Form they always employed Black staff. When I told my Mum what Miss Tuite had said, she explained that True Form was part of the British Shoe Corporation (BSC) and did not discriminate, but Stead of Simpson was independent of the BSC and could do what they liked. I didn't remain at Stead and Simpson for long. As soon as a vacancy arose at Freeman, Hardy & Willis which was further along Rye Lane, I successfully applied and went to work for them. I then reported Stead and Simpson to the newly formed – in 1976 – Commission for Racial Equality but for years, when I walked past Stead and Simpson, I never saw a Black sales assistant.

In 1973, we were informed that St Michael was 'twinned' with Lancing College, a public school for boys on the West Sussex coast. None of us knew what this meant, or cared, until pupils from the college arrived at our school to stage a production of Terence Rattigan's one-act play *Harlequinade*, a witty farce, first staged in 1948. All the pupils of St Michael were herded into the school hall one afternoon to watch this production, and it wasn't long before we started to giggle at their posh accents and overtop, less-than-flattering acting. When the play continued past home time, some of the older kids started to leave the hall. Teachers stood by trying to stop them, but the more determined kids pushed past them saying: 'I'm going home. I have to make tea for my little brother and sister' or 'This is boring. I don't want to watch it anymore' or 'My Mum will kill me if I'm late home.'

Worse was to come. Soon after this visit, a teacher decided to return the favour by staging a production of Harold Brighouse's comedy *Hobson's Choice* at Lancing College following several performances at our school. To our dismay, he chose my school year to enact it. The main problem was that the play was set in Salford in Greater Manchester in 1880. We were South London kids from housing estates, and couldn't have been further from the characters we were expected to play. Some of the kids tried hard, but we couldn't manage Northern accents and the boys in the cast, including me, refused to cut their long hair. The teacher did hire the right costumes for the period the play was set, but that would soon be undone when a visit to the Young Vic to see a professional matinee production just made us feel more inadequate. I quite enjoyed the Young Vic version, recognising Peter Bayliss, who played the horrible father of Dennis Dunstable in the television sit-com *The Fenn Street Gang* as Henry Hobson, and Anne Stallybrass, from the popular BBC drama series *The Onedin Line*, as his daughter Maggie. In our school version, I was cast as Freddy Beenstock. It was my first and only acting role.

Our three school performances went down well with pupils and parents, and we enjoyed the trip to Lancing on a hired coach, but our performance of *Hobson's Choice* was disappointing. First, to avoid over running (like *Harlequinade*), the teacher cut acts two and three, so the Lancing chaps only saw acts one and four. All my lines disappeared, not that I minded, and the two acts we performed didn't make much sense. The highlight of the trip for me was the guided tour we were given by some of the boys, who were very friendly. We were shown their tennis courts, the beautiful grounds around the school building and their very own chapel. It was another revelation of class differences. This was how the 'other half' lived, and it made an interesting day out of an otherwise boring school routine.

I wondered what sort of schooling the boys at Lancing College received. A secondary modern education meant a second class education. The schooling we received wasn't great, no wonder many of us kids played truant. Some of my classmates left to go to work as soon as they were old enough. We didn't know what O- or A-Levels were. We did the Certificate of Secondary Education (CSE). I later found out that these courses had been devised for less-than-bright kids. They were graded from one to six, and anyone who achieved a grade one result reached the equivalent of Grade C, which was the lowest pass at O-Level. CSE's took two years to complete. By the end of our third year at the secondary modern, we had to choose two options in addition to four compulsory subjects which were English, Maths, Religious Knowledge, and Social Studies. I chose Art and Biology, but I was informed that I could only take Biology with Chemistry, but I didn't know one end of a test tube from the other. My knowledge of biology was also limited. My recent biology project had consisted of making a scrapbook of pictures of cats. The teacher was unimpressed and gave me a very poor grade on that year's school report. Reluctantly, I agreed to take Art with Typing. My typing capabilities at the time were encapsulated by a solitary but rather fast-pecking index finger. Sadly, History was not offered, which I would've embraced.

There was another reason we had been encouraged to take part in a school production of *Hobson's Choice.* It was one of the books we were going to study for CSE English. It was one of the first plays I had read, and it was hardly inspiring. Another book we were given to read was Valerie Avery's *London Morning,* first published in 1964. It was a book about working-class life around the Old Kent Road as seen through the eyes of a child, something I could relate to. It was a refreshing contrast to some of the other books we were given to read for the CSE which I found difficult to comprehend. The other books included Shakespeare's *Macbeth* and George Orwell's *Animal Farm,* but I struggled with the language they used. Indifferent teachers didn't help either. In 1974, working-class kids were not expected or encouraged to think. With few exceptions, our teachers decided that most of us were destined for shop work or jobs in factories, so what was the point of educating us? *London Morning* was a wake-up call for me. It was the first book I read that made me realise that it was possible to write about subjects I was familiar with, composed in my own language.

In those days Peckham Odeon would organise matinee screenings of films relating to school exam texts. Crowds of local secondary school kids were herded into the Odeon to see the 1954 animation film of *Animal Farm* and Roman Polanski's brutal and bloodthirsty 1971 film of *Macbeth.* Some kids found this version of the Scotland-set play too gruesome and waited outside until it ended. I'm not sure how much these screenings helped us understand the texts. Meanwhile, in the real world, 1973 and 1974 were the years we faced power cuts and IRA bomb scares. The power cuts were fun because we were sent home early from school to spend the evenings in darkness, with candles and no telly. Our school had occasional IRA bomb scares which meant that we all had to leave the building and congregate on the playground while teachers searched the school for bombs. It was common knowledge that it was a small group of boys in the school who would contact the office from a local phone box and make the false call, but the teaching staff had to take the threat seriously.

In the months leading up to the CSE examinations and leaving school, we were encouraged to think about possible career options. One day, the Deputy Head called me into his office in great excitement and informed me that he had found me a job as a messenger for the law courts in the City of London. Every year he recommended one or two boys to a friend who worked in the City. Much to his annoyance I told him I didn't want the job, after all, this was the same teacher who had embarrassed me in front of my classmates when he said I could join a sewing class. I simply didn't trust him. 'But it is a great opportunity for you, Stephen', he said. I shook my head. I had other ambitions and they didn't include being a 'messenger'. I have no idea how my working life would have panned out if I had taken the job, but I am glad I didn't take up the offer.

Sometime after this, I had an interview with our careers officer. He asked me what sort of job I would like to have when I left school. I told him I loved cinema and wanted to work for the British Film Institute. He advised me to write to them and ask if they had any jobs. So I did. Seemed simple enough. I remember putting at the end of the letter that I wanted to work for them so much, I would even accept a job as a tea-boy. To my dismay, I received a short reply from them which said that only university graduates were considered for employment at the British Film Institute. They advised me to go away and study for O- and A-Levels. I couldn't heed this advice because they weren't offered at St Michael. Clearly, a job at the British Film Institute was out of my league. For now.

In 1974, I sat for my CSE exams. During the CSE typing exam the teacher whispered in my ear, 'You'll never pass using one finger', to which I replied, 'I will if you don't tell the examiner!' I was a fast one-finger typist and generally unorthodox as a teenager. I also wasn't the most attentive listener when it came to negativity. I passed the exam. I spent the next few months dreaming about achieving outstanding results, going to university, and then working for the British Film Institute but when the results came, I was crushed. I didn't achieve a single Grade One, the equivalent to an O-Level pass. I felt terrible. I thought I had worked hard at the subjects I liked and believed I was going to be awarded at least three Grade One results in my three favourite subjects: English, Art and Social Studies, which would've enabled me to study at a further education college, and then hopefully progress to university. Instead, I was awarded Grade Two results in each of those subjects, and everything else from Grade Three to Six in other subjects. My disappointing CSE grades left me feeling defeated and a failure. Any thoughts of going to university and working for the British Film Institute flew out of the window. So, at the age of 16, I left school in the summer of 1974 and continued to work for True Form, the shoe shop, where I had been a Saturday assistant for a year. Mum had been employed there as an assistant for about ten years. I was proud of my mother and what she did for a living. I felt no shame in working with her in a shoe shop, we got on and worked well together, but I wanted to do something else with my life.

I never saw a future for myself. I left school with nothing. No useful qualifications. No confidence. I believed I had intelligence and potential, but I found myself stuck in a dead-end job in the shoe shop. Tail between my legs, I remembered the school's careers officer telling me that his door was always open for advice. I made an appointment to see him and he advised me to return to school in September and join the sixth form of Archbishop Temples, a comprehensive school on Lambeth Road. We didn't have a sixth form in the secondary modern and so the careers officer explained that, with my parents' support, I could study for GCE O- and A-Levels at Temples and hopefully go to university. Mum and Dad encouraged me, so I enrolled in time for the autumn intake at Temples.

Behind the scenes, a much more informal, although no less valuable, education was taking place. My favourite history class was family history, taught by my Nan Dulieu in Peckham.

Nan was an eloquent storyteller with a clear memory. She also lived through the war, and her descriptions of life on the home front during the war inspired me to read widely about the subject. It was easy to find books about the Second World War in the adult sections of the public libraries in Peckham and Camberwell. One that I borrowed was Angus Calder's *The People's War – Britain 1939–45*, first published in 1969, which drew on first-hand testimony and a mass of neglected social documents to tell the story of Britain during the conflict. Reading this was a turning point in my education because Calder gave me the bigger picture of ordinary people's lives in the war.

Enthused by Nan's memories of the war, I was keen to visit and talk to more of the older women in my family in Fulham about that period. School often took a backseat to this more informal education and so I'd skip class to spend mornings, afternoons, even whole days with these matriarchs. Once there I would visit my Great Aunt Mag (my late grandfather's sister) in Barclay Close and then catch a bus to Wandsworth Bridge Road where Aunt Esther lived.

History began to interest me because the women in my family made it feel intimate and lived. They made me feel like a participant and not a pawn. Theirs were working-class women's voices, largely missing from history books. Aunt Esther's experiences gave me insights into the life of a working-class Black woman in Britain. It was through her I learned that Black people occupied all segments of British life and society prior to Windrush.

My favourite lessons took place outside the classroom. For example, in Angus Calder's *The People's War*, I learned about Ita Ekpenyon, a Nigerian air raid warden in London during the Blitz who in 1943 published a short pamphlet entitled *Some Experiences of an African Air Raid Warden*. When I asked a teacher at school if the pamphlet could be found, she advised me to try the British Library, which was then housed at the British Museum.

An appointment was made for me to visit the British Library's Reading Room and, on entering that vast, intimidating building, I made my way to the counter and asked for Ekpenyon's pamphlet. I was trembling because I had never been inside such a place before. I felt as if I was an imposter. The only libraries I knew were those in Peckham and Camberwell. Even my visit to the British Film Institute library hadn't prepared me for this. There were rows and rows of grey coloured seats and desks. Everything looked formal and uninviting. There were book shelves with balconies that went up and up to the roof which was high above. I had never seen anything like it. At the main desk I was instructed to take the pamphlet to a desk and there I read Ekpenyon's informative descriptions of life as an air raid warden during the London Blitz. The Library made a photocopy of the pamphlet for me, which I still have, and on that afternoon I found myself aware of another Black Londoner in the Second World War. Common sense dictated that there were probably many others waiting to be discovered.

My first contribution to a book was in 1974 when I was still a teenager. I had acquired a copy of Leslie Halliwell's 1970 edition of his popular film encyclopaedia *The Filmgoer's Companion*, but I was disappointed that several pioneer Black stars of British movies, such as Robert Adams, Earl Cameron, Orlando Martins, Nina Mae McKinney, and Elisabeth Welch were missing. I had read all about them in an early book on the subject called *The Negro in Films*, by Peter Noble, a British publication from 1948. So, on the second-hand typewriter that my dad had purchased for me (to replace the Petite Typewriter that I had worn out), I typed out short biographies of these actors. I carefully adopted Halliwell's style and sent them to him through his publisher. I waited patiently for a reply to no avail. However, when his revised edition of *The Filmgoer's Companion* was published in 1974, I was over the moon to discover that he had included all of my entries. My joy was short-lived when I checked Halliwell's acknowledgements and there was no mention of me.

I was ten years old in 1968 when the Conservative MP Enoch Powell made his inflammatory 'Rivers of Blood' speech on immigration from the Commonwealth. 'In this country in 15 or 20 years' time the Black man will have the whip hand over the white man', Powell warned. 'As I look ahead I am filled with foreboding. Like the Roman, I seem to see the River Tiber foaming with much blood.' At the same time, in homes up and down the country, Powell's fictional disciple, Alf Garnett, shouted racist abuse in BBC television's *Till Death Us Do Part.* This was a popular situation comedy series that was shown between 1965 and 1975 and its lead character, Alf Garnett, was depicted as a racist, working-class Tory. I was disgusted, however, it didn't surprise me that the 1970s witnessed a rise in the popularity of the right-wing and racist National Front. I haven't yet forgotten the horror of watching – from my bedroom window – members of the National Front marching along Peckham Road with a police escort, which some of us interpreted as police protection. It didn't surprise me when a decade later, in 1981 and 1985, young, mostly Black youths vented their anger and frustration with the police on the streets of Brixton and Peckham. In 1972, ITV launched *Love Thy Neighbour*, the situation comedy series which ran successfully until 1976. My copy of the *TVTimes* described the premise of the show as being about racial prejudice 'with a difference' that would 'make us laugh a lot'. But when I watched the first episode the day it came out on April 13, my heart sunk. The 'comedy' dealt with the conflict between a white bigot and his Black neighbour. The white bigot used racist slurs against his neighbour, which made me feel uncomfortable. With 14–17 million viewers, *Love Thy Neighbour* was just as popular as BBC1's *Dad's Army* (1968–1977), but none of its viewers learned anything about Britain's Black community from this nonsense. An antidote was needed and it came two years later, though it probably didn't attract millions of viewers.

In 1974, I was drawn to a fascinating five-part television series on BBC2 called *The Black Man in Britain 1550–1950*. It was hosted by the Black actor and singer Derek Griffiths. The show highlighted aspects of Britain's Black history over 400 years. It really captured my imagination because it was well written, engagingly presented by Griffiths, and introduced me to new Black British stories from the past. In Part One, *The Heart of Darkness*, I learned about Elizabeth I's proclamation to repatriate Black people back to Africa in Tudor England and the evils of the slave trade. For Part One, James Walvin was recruited as the 'academic adviser'. I was also introduced to some of the Black historical figures from the 18th century such as Francis Barber, the Jamaican manservant to Samuel Johnson in London from 1752 until Johnson's death in 1784. And Ignatius Sancho, who was sold into slavery but secured his freedom and became a British abolitionist. Part Four, *Soldiers of the Crown*, focused on men from the Caribbean who supported the British and joined the armed services during the Second World War. One of the interviewees was Sam King who, in 1983, became the first Black Mayor of Southwark, my London borough. I got to know him quite well. Part Five, *Revolution and Manchester*, included an illuminating interview with C. L. R. James, the Trinidadian historian, Trotskyist activist, and Marxist writer who spoke eloquently about the Pan-Africanist, George

Padmore ('He was one of the greatest politicians of the time'); and the 1945 Manchester Pan-African Congress. Some names I later learned about were missing, such as Ira Aldridge, the celebrated Shakespearean actor of the Victorian era, Jamaican 'doctress' Mary Seacole, and Dr Harold Moody, a British civil rights leader and a founder of the League of Coloured Peoples. Also, women's voices were mostly hidden. None of the Caribbean women, such as Nadia Cattouse and Connie Mark, who were recruited into the Auxiliary Territorial Service (ATS) in wartime, were interviewed in *Soldiers of the Crown.* Despite these omissions, this was a groundbreaking series that touched upon subjects seldom written about in books or covered in British broadcasting.

One of the few books which did an excellent job at the time at addressing this absence was James Walvin's *Black and White – The Negro in English Society 1555–1945*, first published in 1973. What is important to acknowledge about this series is that its producer Tony Laryea was Black and British and the series adviser was the Guyanese writer Mike Phillips.

Hungry for more information, I was disappointed to find that, apart from the slave trade (mostly written from white historians' perspectives), there was no mention of Black people in our school history books or, with the exception of James Walvin's *Black and White*, the history books I searched for and found in our local libraries. As a youngster I realised that my quest for knowledge would have to come from first-hand accounts, so I began to question Aunt Esther about her life.

It came naturally to me. I found my way into history, but I did not call myself a historian because I thought only people from Oxford and Cambridge universities could be historians. I found a different way of learning history, by talking to older relatives and people in the community, and realising that their life stories are part of British history.

Chapter 5

Just Comprehensive Enough

In September 1974, I entered Archbishop Temples School in Lambeth. The building was a shock. Unlike the sleekness of St Michael, Temples was a dilapidated Victorian dwelling. It had a roof that let the rain in and flooded some of the classrooms. The building wasn't fit for purpose. Cabins had been installed on the playground to serve as extra classrooms for some of the pupils, but these were also damp and in disrepair. There was an annex on a nearby street which was in terrible condition. It was no wonder some kids at Temples staged a protest shortly after I arrived, demanding better facilities. The protests made the teatime television news and some of the local and national newspapers.

The first thing I noticed in the room that accommodated the sixth form was the informality and friendliness of the students. They were from similar working-class backgrounds, but appeared to be more advanced academically than the pupils I had known at St Michael. This likely had to do with the better standard of education they had received throughout their time at the comprehensive. I felt at ease. The year I arrived, only a handful of students from St Michael joined the sixth form. Within a few weeks, most had left, either to find work or a place in a college of further education. They just didn't fit into Temples' somewhat unconventional mould of education, which was more informal and friendly than what we had been used to. All who remained from the secondary modern was myself and Terry Geater. It wouldn't be long before we'd make friends with the sixth formers at Temples.

I also liked the teaching staff. When they introduced themselves they were as laid back as the sixth formers. Some of them even encouraged us to call them by their first names. They treated us as adults. A group of them were lefties, wore jeans and lived in grand apartments in houses around Clapham Common (to which we were occasionally invited). They were keen to do the right thing by their underprivileged working-class pupils and they never came across as patronising. They were so different from the dull teachers at St Michael. At Temples I discovered that teachers could be fun. However, I wasn't prepared for the rigours of the academic work that awaited me. My CSE courses hadn't prepared me for O- and A-Levels. In my first year (1974–75) I signed up for four O-Levels in English Literature, English Language, Art, and Sociology. The English teacher was excellent. She got me to enjoy texts like William Shakespeare's *Romeo and Juliet* and Emily Bronte's *Wuthering Heights.* No small feat. I loved and still love a bit of romance, so when the teacher hired Franco Zeffirelli's acclaimed 1968 film of *Romeo and Juliet* for a screening at the school, I was all-in. The film, entertaining as it was, also helped me break down the language Shakespeare used, which had previously been a challenge to me.

Another book we studied was Laurens van der Post's *The Lost World of the Kalahari*, but I struggled with it. How on earth did the people who chose this book for an O-Level expect working-class kids from South London housing estates to understand life in a desert in southern Africa? There was no film for van der Post's classic. Despite my incomprehension, I managed to achieve a Grade A in my English Literature exam, which was a lovely surprise and boosted my confidence. I have often wondered if this had something to do with the answer I gave about *Wuthering Heights* in the exam. I stated a case for the novel's hero, Heathcliff, a foundling orphan from Liverpool, to be of mixed heritage. I suggested that his father had come to Liverpool from Africa or the Caribbean, and his mother was white, thus giving a whole new dimension to his relationship with the white Cathy Earnshaw. I also passed my English Language and Art exams, but failed Sociology, which I attribute mostly to a boring teacher.

I liked Nancy Spender, my art teacher. It couldn't have been easy for her to teach art in one of the horrid cabins on the playground, but she persevered. We all did. When she passed away in 2001 an obituary in *The Telegraph* described her as a painter who had been 'much underrated'. True to them but not to me. At Temples, she was known as the sister-in-law of the poet Stephen Spender which meant very little if not nothing to me at the time. In my school report for 1975 she said: 'Stephen is very gifted. He has worked hard throughout the year developing his own ideas. He deserves to do well.' Those few words meant a lot to me.

I soon made friends with Gill from Temples. It began when I heard her talking to someone about Judy Garland. My ears perked up and I joined in. Gill and I discovered that we were both huge fans of Judy. We both considered her the greatest singer of all time and we attended screenings of her films when they were shown at the National Film Theatre on London's South Bank. These included an all-nighter on January 4, 1975 (I still have the programme note), beginning at 11pm and ending at 7am. I managed to stay awake for *Everybody Sing*, but slept through *Girl Crazy* and *Meet Me in St Louis*; woke up in time for *I Could Go On Singing*. Sadly, my favourite Judy Garland musical, *Easter Parade*, was not included.

Gill told me about her membership to the Judy Garland Club. Naturally, I joined and we attended meetings together at the Russell Hotel in Bloomsbury. My favourite memories of the club meetings include the time Dora Bryan attended and entertained us with a chorus of the song 'Hello, Dolly' which she changed to 'Hello, Judy, well, hello

Judy, it's so nice to have you back where you belong.' Dora raised the roof and brought the house down. Another time, the camp television star Larry Grayson appeared and entertained us with his affectionate memories of Judy on screen and his attendance at many of her British concerts.

The club happily acquired bootleg copies of Judy's 1963–64 American television series, but the funniest memory I have is the screening of her final MGM film, *Summer Stock*. It had been made in Technicolor but the print was in black and white and kept breaking down. We were a devoted bunch and remained patient until the big pay-off came when she sang 'Get Happy,' only for our excitement to be short-lived. You can imagine our shock – our horror – when we realised she was dubbed. The mysterious British ghost-singer didn't sound anything like Judy.

It was at the club meetings that I befriended Ken Sephton, the editor of the club's quarterly journal, the *Rainbow Review*. He was one of the most outgoing and kind-hearted people I have had the joy of knowing. He had been a club member since the 1950s and was a walking encyclopaedia on anything to do with Judy and the movies. He was slim, polite and kind; but most of all, keen to engage Gill and me in conversation. My first encounter with Ken was during a tea break when he approached us with a tray of biscuits and asked if we'd 'like a custard cream?' Ken and I remained friends until he was lost to dementia, following the death of Brian, his partner for 50 years. He never recovered from the shock and died in 2017.

Beyond Judy, Gill and I also shared our admiration for the singer-songwriters Stevie Wonder, Labi Siffre and Joan Armatrading (who we saw in concert at the Hammersmith Odeon in 1977). All three created memorable, soulful songs, sung to perfection. We also enjoyed the antics of the comedy legend Dame Edna Everage. To my joy, I discovered that Gill and most of the sixth formers had worked in the Easter holidays of 1970 as extras on a film called *Melody*. As the film buff I was, I was fascinated by their tales of filming with Jack Wild and Mark Lester, the young stars of the Oscar-winning musical *Oliver!* In *Melody* they co-starred as schoolboys from different social backgrounds. I was told that the wardrobe lady on the film insisted that the extras carry satchels, which they laughed at because no self-respecting Lambeth kid from a working-class background would be seen dead with such a thing. They remembered Jack Wild with affection and told me how he would play football with the extras when they were not filming. However, they said that Mark Lester was kept away from them, hidden from view in a caravan with his private tutor. The pupils were paid £1 a day. None of the staff appeared in the film. Archbishop Temples was going to be used as the location for the fictitious school attended by Wild and Lester, but the production company was unable to agree to the 10-day window which the school's governors wanted so another school on Hammersmith Road was used instead.

When *Melody* was released in 1971, I went to see it at Peckham Odeon. I loved it. When I heard that Jack Wild was making a personal appearance at a department store on Oxford Street to promote the film I knew I wanted to see him so I went with Linda. We took the number 12 bus from Peckham. When we arrived we discovered many people who had the same idea, filled with, I'm sure, nervousness and excitement. I didn't have any memorabilia for Jack to sign like the people ahead of me, just my bus ticket. So I handed him that. Sensing my shame, I didn't want him to think I was a halfway-fan, he gave me his trademark grin and without saying much, autographed the back of the ticket. In 2003, I told the story of Jack autographing my number 12 bus ticket in a letter to *The Stage* newspaper. I added that I had long since lost the ticket. Someone must have brought it to Jack's attention because several weeks later, he sent me a letter of thanks and a signed photo via *The Stage*. Just three years later this gifted and popular actor died at the age of 53. His rapid rise to success at an early age led him to alcoholism. He will never be forgotten as long as films like *Oliver!* and *Melody* are revived.

Throughout 1974 and 1975 the slum dwellings existing behind St Michael and All Angels were demolished to make way for new school buildings. The plan was to expand St Michael, vacate Temples, and relocate the pupils and staff to the new school which was going to be called Archbishop Michael Ramsey, named for the 100th Archbishop of Canterbury. They even built a small church at the front of the building. For the school year that began in September 1975, I found myself back in Camberwell in a brand new sixth form suite. On returning I discovered that many of the teachers from my former secondary modern had either been demoted or made redundant.

We were somewhat cocooned in the sixth form, away from the younger pupils in the school. One of them was Michael Collins who in 2004 gave the following insight of what he experienced in his Orwell prize-winning book *The Likes of Us – A Biography of the White Working Class*. 'Teachers drifted into the abyss of a dark and deep humiliation each week, finding themselves at the mercy of unruly teenagers who would shower them with paper pellets, elastic bands, matches, spit.' I was glad to be confined to the sixth form suite where we had a small kitchen with a tea urn. We also had our own toilets. Collins was also one of the pupils who took part in a television documentary about the school called *Our School and Hard Times*, first shown on ITV in May 1977. Sixth formers like myself did not participate, but I recall seeing the television crew around the building with their cameras and sound equipment. A review by Ken Burgess in the *Coventry Evening Herald* in May of 1977 summarised the documentary saying it 'lingered over blue-hazed shots of high-rise flats and concrete tower blocks, giving them the appearance of water colours, and photographed children making their leisurely but happy way to school. Inside the school we saw English, music, and drama…It seemed a happy school but we were not shown the truants, the misfits, the pupils and the teachers who couldn't cope.'

Against this veneer, I still enjoyed being a sixth former at Archbishop

Michael Ramsey. However, school wouldn't be the place where I could pursue my interest in Black British history. Despite being a multi-cultural school, with many pupils from African and Caribbean families, Black history was never discussed. So I taught myself. A teacher advised me to visit a radical bookshop in The Cut, opposite the Young Vic, where I acquired some other pioneering books on the subject, including Dilip Hiro's *Black British, White British* (1971). It wasn't long before we had our own radical community bookshop in Peckham called The Bookplace, opposite the Odeon on Peckham High Street. When it opened in 1977, I was over the moon: a bookshop on my doorstep. It catered to the local culturally diverse community and though it had a radical, politically left-leaning focus, it stocked a wide range of books and journals, and prioritised accessibility.

It was at The Bookplace that I purchased another groundbreaking book, Edward Scobie's *Black Britannia – A History of Black People in Britain* (1972). I was also introduced to the concept of community publishing, an innovative venture for Peckham. For the next decade they published and distributed a number of books by local writers, mostly African and Caribbean Britons who felt alienated from 'serious' institutions like schools. The Bookplace offered a safe haven and encouraged young people to write short stories, poems, and plays. They even published some of them in inexpensive pamphlets. I still have copies. The writing produced by these young people was largely drawn from personal experiences and from observations of the inner city environment in which they lived. They provided a valuable insight into the world of local Black youths, expressed in their own words and dialects. This greatly influenced my own approach to writing history books.

When I was growing up, there was next to nothing available about the history of Black British film, television, theatre, and radio. I found plenty of material about African-American entertainers and jazz musicians. By the age of 16, I had read books about Dorothy Dandridge, Louis Armstrong, Sammy Davis Jr, Duke Ellington, Eartha Kitt, Lena

Horne, Sidney Poitier, Paul Robeson and, my favourite, Ethel Waters. As a teenager I read every book I could find about Black cinema, but they were all written by Americans, like Ed Mapp (who would later become a friend), Thomas Cripps, Gary Null, Donald Bogle, Daniel J Leab, and Eileen Landay. Bogle's work in particular opened up a whole new way of thinking about Black actors in the movies that made them feel more *real* by countering reductive tropes. Despite the great work of writers like Bogle, and with the exception of Thomas Cripps, none of them truly gave Black British cinema the recognition it deserved. The only *British* book I had found on the subject was Peter Noble's *The Negro in Films*, but as groundbreaking as it was, it had been published in 1948. In Britain we had Jim Pines and *Blacks in Films* (1975), but Pines's work was theoretical. Pines was an African-American who had made Britain his home.

In the 1970s, there was a shop on the corner of Rye Lane and Peckham High Street close to where I worked that sold soul music and reggae records. It also sold copies of the glossy African-American magazine *Ebony* which I often purchased. My tastes were eclectic to say the least and on a given day I could be found browsing through the *Ebony* magazines on Rye Lane, then perusing the bookshelves of The Bookplace. There were times when I wanted to read discourse on Black British life in journalistic form because I found it more digestible, but the options back then were limited. The Bookplace did stock the radical Black journal *Race Today* (I still have some copies I bought during this period).

In my second year in the sixth form I opted to study for an O-Level in General Studies with an excellent teacher called David Pink. He informed me that I had to put together a project of my choosing. He was impressed when I told him I was going to write about Black British history and how Black people were portrayed on television. He suggested that I interview a Black actor or actress I had seen on television, and I chose Cleo Sylvestre, who had been a familiar face in the soap opera *Crossroads*. In 1976, Cleo was acting at the Young Vic and so I wrote to her. She invited me to join her for a coffee at the theatre and we engaged in a lively discussion about her career as a Black British actress. At home, I typed up my notes and at the end of the year the teacher praised the project in my school report. I passed the O-Level. Since that time, Cleo remained a close, supportive friend until her passing in 2024.

David Pink was one of the sixth form teachers who encouraged us to take an interest in subjects beyond the O-Level. I remember him giving us copies of Richard Adams's *Watership Down* to read and taking us one afternoon to the West End to see the film *All the President's Men* starring Dustin Hoffman and Robert Redford. He also hired a print of Gillo Pontecorvo's brilliant film *Queimada* (1970) (also known as *Burn!*) about a slave uprising in the Caribbean. It starred Marlon Brando and featured a splendid score by Ennio Morricone.

My success in the two English O-Levels led to being signed up for a two-year A-Level course in the subject. There were only a few of us in the class, including Gill. One of our teachers, Jenny Boshell, had a wonderful, charismatic personality. She would sit cross-legged on the classroom desk and bring alive John Webster's Jacobean tragedy *The Duchess of Malfi*. When she found out we had never seen an opera, she booked tickets for a school trip to the Royal Opera House to see *Rigoletto*. Then there was Felicity Powell, who came from a privileged background but felt the need to train as a teacher once her children had grown and left home. Felicity wanted to work with educationally disadvantaged students. We adored her and she helped us to understand Iris Murdoch's complex novel *The Sandcastle*. When we were challenged by some of the themes and characters in the book, Felicity encouraged us to write to Ms Murdoch through her literary agent. To our delight Ms Murdoch replied and answered our questions. I kept the letter for several years until I stupidly loaned it to someone who never gave it back to me.

Last but not least was Farrukh Dhondy, who taught us Shakespeare's

Coriolanus. He was an Indian-born left-wing activist who had been educated at Pembroke College, Cambridge and who had been involved with the British Black Panthers. He was also part of the radical *Race Today* collective, a friend of Darcus Howe, and wrote widely on the experiences of Black working-class pupils in the British school system.

I liked Farrukh. He was an intellectual but cared deeply for his pupils, even if some of them of the younger ones in the school were disruptive. He wasn't the most disciplined teacher, and in some of our *Coriolanus* classes he would talk about anything but Shakespeare's text. We didn't mind because we often had illuminating discussions. He took us to the theatre to see George Bernard Shaw's *The Devil's Disciple* and Peter Shaffer's *Equus.*

However, there was an occasion when Farrukh tried to out me by informing the class that I was a 'homosexual' long before I had the courage to come out as gay. Same-sex relationships between men had only recently been partially decriminalised with the 1967 Sexual Offences Act and it was illegal for two men to engage in a sexual relationship before the age of 21. The Gay Liberation movement was also a recent phenomenon, although it hadn't reached Archbishop Michael Ramsey. The bi-weekly newspaper *Gay News* was on sale, but I never saw a copy. My sexuality was *my* secret. Though I was comfortable in my own skin, I wasn't ready to tell anyone. Farrukh was out of line.

When I arrived home that afternoon I was overcome with emotion. My secret was out and I wasn't ready. I burst into tears in front of Linda and our parents. I told them what had happened, but I denied that I was a homosexual. My parents made an appointment to see the headmaster, Mr Aggett, and he asked Farrukh to apologise to me. He never did. A few years later, in my own time and on my terms, I found the confidence to come out as gay. I first came out in 1979 at the age of 21 when I made several anonymous calls to Gay Switchboard, a helpline. The gentlemen who took my calls were kind and supportive. Then, in 1980, I told my sister. That was my first attempt at coming out face to face. Linda reacted well, but

I asked her to keep it to herself. I wasn't ready to share my secret with the world. Several years passed before I told my parents. In 1983, when I bumped into Farrukh Dhondy at a recording of a television series, I informed him he had been right, but was wrong to try and out a young, impressionable, and frightened lad at an inner London comprehensive school in 1976.

Before I left the school, Farrukh had *East End at Your Feet* published, his first collection of short stories. I still have my 1977 copy, dedicated to the pupils of Archbishop Michael Ramsey. He has had a successful career as a writer and for a number of years, was the Commissioning Editor for Multicultural Programmes at Channel 4, the fourth television channel, launched in 1982. I have no idea if he regretted trying to out me, he probably forgot all about it, but in the 1980s when I approached him for testimonials to support job applications or a place at college, he always obliged.

I spent three relatively happy years at Archbishop Michael Ramsey and was sorry to leave in the summer of 1977. Gill did well enough to go to university as did Terry, my friend from St Michael. However, I did not achieve the necessary qualifications to go to university. One A-Level was not good enough. I needed two. In a way I found myself back at square one, but my passionate interest in Black British history had become an important focus in my life and I had enough sense to understand that one never knows what is waiting around the corner.

Chapter 6

All About Love and Rage

My first job after leaving school was in the Peckham dole office in Blenheim Grove, across the road from Peckham Rye overground station. My work involved taking benefit claims from the unemployed and processing them. In Margaret Thatcher's Britain many people were unemployed. Too many. Every day I was faced with dozens of claimants and benefit claims to process. It was depressing, laborious work. One day as part of my training I was taken to the North Peckham Estate by the visiting officer whose job it was to call upon claimants and make sure they were not fiddling the dole. I hated going into people's homes and having to listen to the officer pry into their business. On one occasion he returned to the dole office covered in blood. Someone on the North Peckham Estate had wounded him with an air gun. It was deliberate, and from then, I swore against ever becoming a visiting officer. These types of incidents weren't exceptional. There were also times that we, the staff, had to call the police and request officers to come to Blenheim Grove and escort us to the nearest bus stop at the end of our working day. This a result of threats made to us on the front counter by angry claimants, another part of the job I loathed.

My time at the dole office was marked by Margaret Thatcher and the Tory government's tenure in office. My grandmother disliked her intensely. Nan told me that Thatcher wanted to get the working-class as low as she possibly could. 'The Prime Minister? She comes from a grocery shop in Grantham. Well, she must have seen some hard times when she was a child with people coming into the shop. You'd think she'd have a little bit of feeling for the working-class, but she hasn't. She can't have much of a memory. I've never been a Tory because I was a kid under the Stanley Baldwin leadership and look what he did to South Wales! I haven't forgotten the General Strike. He crucified us and she's doing the same. The mines have gone. The steelworks have gone. I'd like to meet Mrs Thatcher and tell her a few home truths'. Aunt Esther wasn't a fan either. 'She is no damn good for this country, she's dragged this country down, which is why I've always voted Labour.'

My days at the dole office were brightened by Sonia Pascal. She was a co-worker who was also my best friend and soulmate. In her spare time, Sonia loved to perform her poetry in public. To get away from the daily grind of the dole office, we spent our lunch breaks in a pub on Peckham High Street, putting the world to rights and sharing common interests in Black culture. It was Sonia who put the idea in my head that Black British history is all around us. 'We just have to look for it', she said. She told me not to listen to those who complained that whites had 'erased' the history of Black people. 'It isn't true', she said. 'You can walk into any organisation, like the Imperial War Museum or the BBC, and if you dig hard enough, you will find Black history.' It made sense to me, and, over time, especially when I undertook research in the archives of places like the Imperial War Museum and BBC, I discovered that Sonia was right. She seemed to have an instinct that I was going to go far with my interest in Black British history. Sonia was a wise and inspiring friend and she encouraged me to keep an open mind.

Sonia and I were aware that the dole office gossips had convinced themselves that we were an 'item' but this was not the case because I was gay. Our colleagues did not know this. I had to keep it a secret because when I joined the civil service I signed the Official Secrets Act which included a paragraph that stated I was not a 'homosexual'. By signing my name to this, I reassured the powers that be that I was not a 'security risk' to Margaret Thatcher and the United Kingdom.

Working at the dole office didn't interrupt my cinema going. In addition to trips to the National Film Theatre, I still enjoyed going to our local Peckham Odeon. By the end of the 1970s Peckham Odeon had been split into three different screening rooms, one large, two small. I didn't enjoy going into the two smaller screening rooms. Small spaces make people act up. In 1979, I took Mum to see *Kramer vs. Kramer* which happened to be showing on one of the smaller screens, but we were forced to leave before the end because a group of alcoholics kept disrupting the film. When one of them bounced an empty beer can off of Meryl Streep's face, we'd had enough.

I was thrilled when I saw that there was going to be a double-bill of Diana Ross in *Lady Sings the Blues* and *Mahogany* at the Biograph Cinema near Victoria Station. *Lady Sings the Blues* had barely started when I became distracted by men bobbing up and down, constantly moving from seat to seat. It was the most bizarre thing, to go to the cinema and do everything but watch the film on screen. But I soon realised these people, mostly men, weren't *just* restless when one of them sat what felt like on my lap. When I refused what he was serving and got up from my seat to leave, he shouted out after me, 'Not your cup of tea, dear?' When I told my sister she looked shocked. 'That's a queer's cinema!' she exclaimed. 'Why did you go there?' I replied that I wanted to see Diana Ross in her first two movies. I had no idea about gay life and where the 'scene' was. There was no one to tell me. I didn't know that by the 1960s the Biograph had become a popular meeting place for gay men and that the Sunday tabloid *News of the World* had demanded that this 'scandalous cinema of vice' be closed down.

Meanwhile, the Peckham Odeon, in decline, became the Ace Cinema and partly survived by screening films of interest to the local

Black community. These included *Black Joy* starring Norman Beaton, *Babylon* starring Brinsley Forde and a double-bill of two popular Jamaican films: *The Harder They Come* starring the reggae singer Jimmy Cliff, and a hilarious comedy called *Smile Orange*. Black youths packed into the Odeon to see Jimmy Cliff as a reggae singer forced into a life of crime, and then they stayed for the laughter that came with watching *Smile Orange*. Unlike me, they understood the Jamaican patois and didn't need to read the subtitles. All of these films extended my own knowledge and appreciation of Black cinema. The Odeon finally called it a day and closed in 1983 and with it a chapter of my youth. It was quickly demolished to make way for a job centre, yet another reminder of high unemployment in Thatcher's Britain.

My love of cinema extended to buying movie magazines every month. My favourite was *Films Illustrated*, launched in 1971 and edited by David Castell. I would describe this as one of the 1970s pre-eminent magazines for film fans. There were others, including *Photoplay*, *Films and Filming*, and *Film Review*. I bought all of them. They were stored in my bedroom, alongside my weekly editions of *Radio Times*. My parents were convinced my bedroom floor was going to collapse under the weight. David Castell and his team also published a series of small books on different movie stars, such as Sean Connery, Robert Redford, Liza Minnelli, and Barbra Streisand, which were all fun to read. However, I took issue with Castell's *Superstars of the '70s*, published in 1974. It was a comprehensive celebration of Hollywood stars with a sprinkling of British screen personalities. I thoroughly enjoyed the book but was saddened that Castell omitted Black stars of the period. So I wrote to him at the editorial office address given in *Films Illustrated* and drew his attention to the absence of Richard Roundtree – the star of *Shaft*, *Man Friday*, *Earthquake* – and Diana Ross, the Oscar-nominated star of *Lady Sings the Blues*. Castell wrote back and apologised for these absences. Seven years later, when he published a revised edition under a new title, *Screen Stars of the '70s*, he included Diana Ross and wrote to me to say that he had featured her as a direct result of my letter. Meanwhile, he published several of my letters in *Films Illustrated*, and when I wrote to him for advice about how to get a magazine feature published, he invited me to meet him for a coffee at the National Film Theatre. That was in 1981. It wasn't long before he became an important part of my life.

In 1982, while I was on holiday in Ventnor on the Isle of Wight, I accepted an invitation from David to visit him at his home in the lovely seaside town of Bembridge. He was a warm gentleman. Tall, blonde, romantic. I quickly ended my stay at my hotel and spent the rest of my holiday with him. I developed feelings for him quickly. I was a late starter, losing my cherry at the age of 24. I didn't want to waste any more time. There was an age gap. He was 14 years older, but I trusted him. He brought me breakfast in bed on a tray and added a rose in a small vase. We shared a love of the movies, and he was friends with most of the broadsheet film critics of the day, such as Dilys Powell, as well as the filmmakers David Puttnam and Richard Attenborough. He was a gay man, though not an activist and, as far as I'm aware, didn't contribute his efforts to publications like *Gay News*. In 2004, my friend Keith Howes, the features editor for *Gay News* in the 1970s and early 1980s, reflected: 'In my few dealings with David C I found him always courteous and sweet, but not really knowable. When I joined *Gay News* I think he viewed me as a bit of a threat to his protected image. He was *very* much in the mode of many gay men who were in their late 20s, early 30s in the mid-1970s: They did not want to risk their hard-won security and position.'

As a lover, he was sensitive and protective. In his company I felt content and secure. This was not a holiday romance. We continued to see each other. He had a collection of videotapes (I think they were called Betamax cassettes then) which included some of his favourite musicals. We watched a few of them together, while cuddling on his settee. My favourite was the remake of *Goodbye Mr Chips* starring Peter

O'Toole and Petula Clark. This was the perfect musical to fall in love to. To this day, the soundtrack still reminds me of these happy times. I also recall him showing me *Bells Are Ringing*, an MGM musical starring Judy Holliday. David owned a fabulous collection of LPs, and he played me some of them, including the cast recording of the London stage version of *Gypsy* starring Angela Lansbury. I never thought about a long-term future with David because this was something new to me. I had nothing to compare it with. I just enjoyed what we had. It was the best relationship I ever had.

In addition to *Films Illustrated*, David kept himself busy as the film critic for *The Sunday Telegraph* and he had his own series on London's Capital Radio. He had a dreamy, reassuring speaking voice, suited to the radio. He told me that his attempt to present BBC-2's *Film Night* in 1975 didn't work out. Television wasn't his medium. He also had a home in Mornington Crescent, not far from Capital Radio's base at Euston Tower. Despite his busy schedule, he made time for me. I enjoyed my occasional weekend trips to Bembridge and visits to his apartment in London. These were happy, romantic times that I have never forgotten. Same-sex relationships between men under the age of 21 were against the law, and it had taken me a long time to come out. When I met David I was ready, at 24, to experience a same-sex relationship. It made me feel complete and blissfully happy. The relationship lasted for several years. By the mid-1980s, though, we drifted apart as I began a new chapter in my life as a film student, but we kept in touch until the early 1990s.

Away from the dole office, and in my spare time, I volunteered and trained as an adult literacy tutor at Cambridge House on Camberwell Road. This was in 1981. Cambridge House had been set up in the Victorian era in 1889 to provide social services to the inner city poor and to campaign for social justice. In 1963, they began to provide adult literacy services. When I volunteered, there was a national campaign to encourage adults who hadn't learned to read and write when they were at school. What motivated me was my father. Dad's schooling had been interrupted by the war. When he left school at the age of 14 he could read but his spelling was poor. He was self-conscious and embarrassed by this, more acutely when my sister and I went to school and excelled in reading and writing. He eventually asked us to help him when he became the secretary of the tenant's association on the housing estate where we lived. After he had taken notes at meetings, he would ask one of us to check his spelling, and I would type them for him.

Following some training, I was assigned two students, a young Rastafarian who wanted to be able to read his Bible, and an Irish labourer, who was a recovering alcoholic and had been disowned by his family. He was living in a local hostel. It was interesting work, and I hope I did some good. One event that's stayed with me is the time that Kenneth Williams, the famous *Carry On* star, visited Cambridge House as part of his support for the adult literacy campaign. The tabloids portrayed him as an embittered, sad figure in his private life, but there was more to him than that. Tutors and their students gathered to meet Williams, who seemed to have a sweet spot for adults who couldn't read or write. He listened to the students, engaged with their stories and showed a completely different side to his public persona. The rapport he had with them revealed a generous, caring side to his personality which we rarely, if ever, saw on television or read about in the newspapers.

Up until this point in my life I was still living at home with my parents. I moved out of our home in 1982 and into a council flat on the top of a tower, also in Southeast London. I had spectacular views of the whole of London. From my bedroom window I had a panoramic view of the metropolis that took in Battersea Power Station, St Paul's Cathedral, and Canary Wharf. Thanks to Mary, a neighbour and soon a friend, I became involved in the tenant's association on the estate, like my father. Mary had lived in the tower block since she was a child. She loved her community and was a force of nature. I later became godfather to her daughter Becky. I happily made more new friends on the estate who were my kind of people. Working-class. People who kept me grounded. There were other changes, too. It was Sonia who made it possible for me to have my first article published in a magazine. In 1982, she introduced me to the editor of *Root*, a glossy lifestyle magazine for Black British women. The editor commissioned me to write several articles. The following year Sonia took me to see the playwright and director Don Kinch. After arriving in London from Barbados, Don established the performing company Staunch Poets and Players in 1979. When Don planned to launch and edit a new Black monthly magazine called *Staunch*, Sonia encouraged me to offer him my services as a feature writer. I found these experiences to be extremely formative.

I was working in the dole office when the Brixton uprising began. I have never described them as riots. A few years later the historian Peter Fryer put into words my internal rationale in his *Staying Power – The History of Black People in Britain* (1984): 'Riot', being a four-letter word, is excellent for headlines; but its use to describe what were in fact uprisings by entire inner city populations, black and white together, served to obscure the true nature and causes of these events. Even Lord Scarman in *The Scarman Report*, published in 1982, avoided using the word 'riot' and described what happened in Brixton as 'disorders'. From April 10–12, 1981 the tension which had existed for years between police officers and Brixton's Black youth erupted into violence. One of the triggers was the aftermath of the tragic New Cross Fire (January 18, 1981 where thirteen African-Caribbean youths, all aged between 15 and 20, lost their lives). People were incensed that the police weren't taking the investigation of the cause of the fire seriously. It was generally believed to be racially motivated. Consequently, the Black People's Day of Action was organised by the activist John La Rose and others for March 2, 1981. With over 20,000 attendees, it was Britain's largest demonstration for a Black cause to date. People of every colour came out in droves. Sonia and I attended the march starting in New Cross, going via the Elephant and Castle and continuing along Blackfriars Bridge. It was here that the police attempted to stop marchers going to Fleet Street. It was feared there would be trouble in the heart of the area where right-wing journalists were based. They had done much to fuel racism and negative media images of Britain's Black community. In spite of this interruption, and a confrontation with the police, the marchers eventually reached Hyde Park.

In 1981, our Black youths felt alienated in our inner cities. They were, as a condition of their being, harassed and victimised by the police all the time. Margaret Thatcher and her right-wing views didn't help either. Her appalling language about immigrants 'swamping' the country inflamed the situation. The police blatantly used the repressive 'sus' law to stop and search and bully and harass young Black men. In South London we had three police stations with bad reputations: Peckham, Brixton, and Carter Street, situated off Walworth Road. It was common knowledge that people who were arrested begged their arresting officers to take them anywhere except the cells at these three stations. As a kid growing up in the area, if we saw a policeman, we ran for it. In 1980, my own fear and mistrust of the police deepened when I was frisked by two officers for no reason opposite my parents' flat on Peckham Road. It was one of the most frightening experiences I have had. It was embarrassing, too, because people on buses were staring at us. I trembled because all I could think about was a lad I had grown up with on our housing estate who had been picked up by the police, taken to Brixton Police Station, and beaten up in a cell. My negative experience with those police officers on Peckham Road fostered a sense of empathy for people of colour who were likely stopped on a more frequent and more violent basis.

I wasn't in the least surprised when, a year later, following 'Operation Swamp 81', Brixton was swamped by police officers who stopped and searched everyone Black. Black youths took to the streets and fought back. The uprisings spread to other parts of the country such as St Pauls

(Bristol), Toxteth (Liverpool), and Handsworth (Birmingham). Brixton became a no-go area. Many shops and buildings were burnt out. The Brixton uprising spilled over into Peckham, and we were suddenly in the thick of it. On Rye Lane, shop owners were advised to close early and board up their windows. The dole office was told to do the same. For just one afternoon and evening, Peckham was a ghost town. The silence was eerie. Fortunately, the violence that Brixton had witnessed over several days and nights was not repeated in Peckham. However, from our living room window, we witnessed a number of police officers chasing Black youths along Peckham Road or up Talfourd Road directly opposite us. Thatcher and the police made sure that the uprising was suppressed, and eventually tensions subsided. Meanwhile, the unemployed continued to flood into our office to make claims, keeping Sonia and I extremely busy, and stressed, but we still found time to share our interests.

When Sonia eventually left the Peckham dole office she joined a radio journalism course at the London College of Printing. From there she worked for BBC Radio London on the weekly magazine series *Black Londoners*, launched and presented by Alex Pascall in 1974. We never lost touch. In 2004, we spoke on the phone and she told me how excited she was with a gardening landscape course she had taken on. A few months later she suffered a heart attack and passed away at the age of 45. Her passing was a shock to everyone who knew and loved her. It was an emotional experience that I found difficult to comprehend. Apart from losing older family members, such as Nan Dulieu and Aunt Esther, I hadn't lost a friend in this way. She was always full of life and never had a bad word to say about anyone. Sonia had gently given me the confidence to begin my professional career as a writer. I miss her and I will never forget her.

Chapter 7

Brief Encounters

In February 1982, Sonia and I went to the Festival of Black Independent Filmmakers at the Commonwealth Institute on Kensington High Street. One of the highlights was Menelik Shabazz's acclaimed film *Burning an Illusion.* Its leading actor, Cassie McFarlane, gave a stunning performance portraying a young Black woman who becomes politicised by the events she witnesses in then-contemporary Britain. For her performance Cassie deservedly received the *Evening Standard*'s British Film Award for Most Promising Newcomer. In Isabel Appio's review of that evening's screening of the film she commented in the *Caribbean Times* (February 26, 1982): 'The most overwhelming audience turnout was for *Burning an Illusion* which had eager viewers spilling into the aisles. Females reacted openly: cheering Pat (Cassie McFarlane) through her journey as she confronts her troublesome boyfriend and discovers a more rewarding political identity. It was proved that night that there is a vast and receptive audience who at the moment is starved of films dealing with subjects with which they can identify.'

Sonia and I were part of that starving audience. Later in the month, curiosity took me to the National Film Theatre (NFT) to see Paul Robeson in *Sanders of the River* (1935). It was being shown in an Edgar Wallace retrospective. Wallace had written the novel on which the film was based.

The NFT's programme booklet described the film as a 'Cornerstone of the Cinema of Empire…an adventure epic that now stands as a monument to everything that was 'the White Man's Burden', adding that 'Paul Robeson steals the picture as the loveable rogue with the magnificent bass voice.' I had only seen Robeson in two of his films: *Show Boat* (1936) and *The Proud Valley* (1940). They were worthy of him, but *Sanders* was a controversial film that the great singer and actor has since disowned. This happened after its producer, Alexander Korda, added scenes that transformed it into a glorification of the British Empire and colonial endeavours. Apart from Robeson's magnificent singing voice, there was nothing about the film that I liked. For me, it was nothing more than racist propaganda and an insult to Robeson. The screening prompted me to write the following letter of complaint, published in *Time Out*, a popular weekly London listings magazine. It appeared in their issue of March 5–11, 1982:

> 'I recently saw Menelik Shabazz's film *Burning an Illusion* at the Commonwealth Institute, which made me realise how misunderstood and unexplored the Black filmmaker/actor is in this country and how rarely Black Britons are given opportunities to see themselves portrayed with any degree of realism on the screen. Conversely, I saw the 1935 British film *Sanders of the River* at the NFT. The enthusiastic "nostalgic" reaction of the white, middle-class audience to this crude and racist film was quite disturbing. This film should be withdrawn by the National Film Archive until such time when this country has given an opportunity to its Black filmmakers, actors, and writers to realise their potential in the medium.'

I also wrote something similar to Ken Wlaschin, the Programme Director of the National Film Theatre. In a reply dated March 3, 1982, he disagreed that *Sanders of the River* should be withdrawn: 'It is my feeling that films presenting older stereotypes are valuable reminders of changing attitudes and should perhaps be shown more widely in educational contexts than at present.' I seized this opportunity to write to Wlaschin again and proposed that *Sanders* be shown again at the NFT in an educational context, in a retrospective of Black British films from the 1930s to the 1980s. The NFT had never done this before. As far as I was aware, there had been only a handful of Black film retrospectives since they had opened in 1957. These included Jim Pines's *Blacks in Films – The Changing Image* in June/July 1971 which included 23 screenings, but only two of them featured British titles (*Sapphire* and *Death May Be Your Santa Claus/Reggae*). Pines mainly focused on American movies. On March 16 Wlaschin responded positively. 'I think this is an intriguing idea indeed' he wrote, and invited me to meet him at the NFT to discuss the proposal further. I was thrilled. I had been a member of the NFT since 1974 but it had never occurred to me that I would curate a season of films on my own. I wasn't used to collaborating with organisations at this level. On meeting Wlaschin I felt intimidated, but I must have said the right things. When Wlaschin asked me what I did for a living, I told him that I worked at the Peckham dole office. He seemed amused, but I quickly added that I had been a member of the NFT for almost ten years, and had attended many screenings. Consequently, the retrospective, entitled *Burning an Illusion – Black Actors in British Cinema*, was scheduled for June 1983 and my suggestion to curate a small exhibition in the NFT foyer of film stills, posters, and memorabilia relating to the films was also accepted.

It was an ambitious season: 28 feature films, including *The Thief of Bagdad* (1940) starring Rex Ingram as the impressive Djinni; *Men of Two Worlds* (1946) starring Robert Adams as a 'westernised' African concert pianist who returns to his village in Tanganyika to face hostility and suspicion from his people; *Pool of London* (1951) starring Earl Cameron, who later became a friend; *Cry, the Beloved Country* (1952); *Sapphire* (1959); *Flame in the Streets* (1961); *A Taste of Honey* (1961); *To Sir, With Love* (1967) starring Sidney Poitier; John Boorman's *Leo the Last*

(1969); Horace Ove's *Pressure* (1975); *Black Joy* (1977) starring the great Norman Beaton who attended the screening and shook my hand; *The Sailor's Return* (1978) starring Tom Bell and Shope Shodeinde; *Babylon* (1980) and, last but not least, *Burning an Illusion* (1981). These films were given prominence in the NFT's programme booklet, for which I wrote the introduction and the notes for all the films. I also offered to assist the programme booklet's editor in selecting film stills to illustrate the season.

At the British Film Institute's Stills Department, I was confronted by John Gillett, a highly respected film critic and researcher whose career at the BFI spanned 44 years until his death in 1995. Gillett asked me why I had included Paul Robeson's six British films, made between 1935 and 1940. I replied that most of them hadn't been seen since the 1930s, such as *Song of Freedom, Big Fella*, and *Jericho*, and that it was important to revive them and give audiences an opportunity to see them. Gillett informed that they were terrible films and none of them were worthy of Robeson and should not be shown. I informed him that I would prefer to see them for myself and make my own assessment. After choosing the stills, Rita, the booklet editor who accompanied me, turned to me and said: 'I'm so glad you came, otherwise I'd have picked all the jungle ones.' She was referring to her lack of awareness of Black British cinema, except those films from the past that had promoted a racist version of Africa and its people, such as *Sanders of the River*. I was impressed that I had made a breakthrough with a NFT season that had never been considered before.

Then came the bombshell. Two months before the season was to start, I received a letter dated April 8, 1983 from David Meeker, the BFI's Print and Copyright Researcher. He informed me that he had spent three very painful months negotiating for the three most rarely seen Robeson films and only very reluctantly did he have to accept that the negotiations had failed: 'In short, the reason why we can't show *Song of Freedom, Big Fella*, and *Jericho* is that their owner, Raymond Rohauer, has invested thousands of dollars in gathering together as many Paul Robeson films as possible in order to promote special tributes to Robeson around the world.' I was deeply disappointed and was only told the truth because of a friend who worked at the BFI. Apparently Rohauer despised the BFI and refused the NFT permission to screen the films for this reason. As far as I am aware, the BFI never publicly challenged him, preferring to avoid a lawsuit. Rohauer died four years later in 1987.

I immediately warned Wlaschin that the loss of those three films would give *Sanders of the River* more prominence and this would cause trouble. I asked him if he would agree to take *Sanders* out of the season, but he refused, reminding me what he had said in his letter about screening it in an educational/historical context. In an attempt to defuse any potential complaints, Richard Dyer from Warwick University was invited to give a lecture on Robeson's films during the season. Wlaschin tried to reassure me that this would help to offset any negative publicity, but surely enough complaints arrived. *New Society* (June 16, 1983) felt that the film should have been left out and asked '*Who put the NF in NFT?*' Two weeks later they published Ken Wlaschin's justification:

> 'The decision to show *Sanders of the River* in the context of a series demonstrating how Black actors in British cinema progressed…over a period of 45 years is, in our opinion, an extremely worthwhile presentation, but one which would have no value if it did not include the earlier films to show how things have changed. In the past, the NFT has shown, in context, German films of the 1930s, in which the portrayal of Jewish people was far more vile than in any of the films with Black actors made in Britain at that time. In our belief, the only way to be able to understand the present is through study of the past, warts and all. We have no intention now, or in the future, of repressing films from the past, and would be derelict in our duty to demonstrate both film and social history if we did so.'

While I understood Wlaschin's argument, I did not agree with it in relation to the season. I accepted that problematic films like *Sanders of the River* should be seen and debated, I just didn't want it in my retrospective without the other three Robeson films. 15 years later I did curate a Robeson film and television retrospective for the NFT, but I omitted *Sanders*. And I would do the same today.

Richard Dyer expressed his enthusiasm for the season in a letter he wrote on February 15, 1983 following the invitation to give a lecture about Robeson:

> 'I'm delighted to learn of your work and your season, both of which are much needed. I'd thought of proposing a Robeson season, but it seems much better that he should be seen in context and indeed that people should be made aware that there is a context. Hope you get *Big Fella* – I'd love to see it. It looks like a *huge* season – are you really going to show all those films? On the more substantial point you raise about Robeson, politics, art and Black performers, it is a difficult one and I do see your point – to certain people, to talk of Black actors as Black and as political, avoids their capacities as actors. One can imagine an unsympathetic voice saying – oh, well he was interesting as a Black actor, or she was just using acting for political reasons – and really demeaning their artistic skills. A season like yours which will, presumably, insist on skills and abilities to counteract that.'

On television, two popular Black magazine series, the BBC's *Ebony* and Channel 4's *Black on Black*, highlighted the season. *Black on Black* made an excellent short pre-recorded overview of the films which was superbly narrated by the actor Anton Phillips. This was followed by a studio discussion between the presenter Beverly Anderson, actress Eva Mottley (from the drama series *Widows*), and the singer Elisabeth Welch (who had co-starred with Paul Robeson in two of his films). Afterwards, the programme's producer, Trevor Phillips, sent me a letter: 'I am writing to thank you for all the help you gave us in compiling the story on Black actors in British cinema, which we undertook in *Black on Black.* Without your assistance, I suspect that we might not have got it on the air. As it turned out, the whole item was extremely well received; and perhaps more importantly, we were very pleased with it ourselves.'

One of the happy outcomes of the NFT season was my friendship with the actress Shope Shodeinde, who had starred in the film *The Sailor's Return* (1978). She portrays an African princess who marries an English sailor, played by Tom Bell, and settles with him in a hostile West Country village in the 1850s. I first saw the film when it premiered at the London Film Festival and again on its first television showing in 1980. It is one of my favourites, and a rare occasion that a British film acknowledged the Black presence in this country in the 19th century. In 1983, Shope was a member of the Black Theatre Co-op, and together they starred in *No Problem!* a Channel 4 sitcom. Shope invited me to the recording of an episode. The warm-up act was a young Gary Wilmot, who was met with enthusiasm from the young, predominantly Black audience. The actors of *No Problem!* also elicited a roar from the crowd when they came on. After the recording I bumped into one of the show's creators, my former school teacher, Farrukh Dhondy, who had left Archbishop Michael Ramsey to become a television writer. He was excited by the recording and asked me what I thought of it. I told him I enjoyed it and, judging by the enthusiastic reaction of the audience, thought it'd be a success.

Shope was a close friend who often gave me advice. 'Write everything down,' she'd say. 'You must write down everything that happens to you or you will forget it.' I took her advice and, since that time, I have made notes of just about everything that has happened to me. Which is why I can relay these anecdotes with any amount of detail.

My experience of working with the NFT on the Black British film season was positive. The NFT staff, including Ken Wlaschin, was helpful and supportive; however, what struck me most of all was that everyone who worked there was white and middle-class. As someone from a working-class background, I felt it strongly. They accepted me, though I expected only just. I never felt completely at ease but I recognised that I had made an important intervention and one that was making waves in the culture. Our work warranted a two-page spread in *The Voice* newspaper and had drawn a full-house to the largest cinema, NFT1, to watch *Burning an Illusion.* I had broken down a barrier. After Wlaschin left the organisation in 1984, my hopes of curating further Black film seasons were prevented by his successor, Sheila Whitaker. She was a self-proclaimed feminist who championed women in film, especially filmmakers, but that's where her inclusivity stopped. The NFT had never included a retrospective of a Black or Asian woman screen star, but this lack of precedent wasn't enough for Whitaker to consider my proposals for Josephine Baker, Ethel Waters, Elisabeth Welch, and Anna May Wong. I was heartbroken. Denied but not deterred. After Whitaker left the NFT in 1990, her successor, Mark Adams, looked at my proposals and willingly gave me the opportunities to honour Ethel Waters (1993), Elisabeth Welch (1994) and Anna May Wong (1995).

I first heard about Elisabeth Welch from my mother. I couldn't have been more than 7 or 8 years old. It was sometime in the mid-1960s, and she was singing on the radio. My mother said, 'That's Elisabeth Welch', and explained to me that she was a famous singer for whom Aunt Esther made dresses before the war. When Cole Porter and Ivor Novello were writing songs for Elisabeth, Aunt Esther, employed by Mary Coy Taylor, a dressmaker in Chelsea, delivered the dresses to her home in Cottage Walk, off Sloane Street. Aunt Esther adored her. 'She was elegant. I often listened to her singing on the wireless. Now and again Miss Taylor said, "Go on, Esther, take this dress to her house for me". She was a lovely person and always treated me with kindness.'

On May 28, 1982 I met Elisabeth for the first time. The occasion was the closing night of her triumphant series of one-woman shows at the Riverside Studios in Hammersmith. I attended the concert which, as promised in the programme, included songs by some of the great composers and lyricists of the 20th century. The conclusion of each song was met by a rousing ovation from the audience. Elisabeth was still in top form, and I was thrilled to be there.

After the concert I visited her crowded dressing room. Feeling shy, I stood in a corner. One by one, excited friends and fans greeted Elisabeth and expressed their joy at seeing her perform. Some years later when her friend Kenneth Partridge gave me access to Elisabeth's diaries, I found out that in her entry for that evening she listed some of the famous names who were in attendance: the lyricist Alan Jay Lerner (of *My Fair Lady* and *Camelot* fame); Anton Dolin, the dancer and former member of Diaghilev's Russian Ballet; the legendary actress and singer Evelyn 'Boo' Laye, who had attended the opening night of Elisabeth's first West End success *Nymph Errant* in 1933; and the architect Sir Hugh Casson, then-President of the Royal Academy, but at that time I didn't know who any of them were. The only person I recognised was the openly gay artist and filmmaker Derek Jarman who, in 1979, had directed Elisabeth in an unusual but magical screen version of William Shakespeare's *The Tempest*, in which she sang the famous torch song 'Stormy Weather'.

Once her friends and fans left, I remained hovering in the corner, too shy to approach her. Once she spotted me I was beckoned. I introduced myself and handed her a letter. She took my hand and I immediately felt at ease. 'Cold hand, warm heart', she said, 'I bet you're a Scorpio!' She was right. Some months later she responded to my letter and invited me to her home. In great excitement I told Sonia, who was thrilled for me. I couldn't wait to meet her again. Until then, I had never spoken to anyone famous at length, much less in their home. In the 1950s, Elisabeth had moved from Cottage Walk to nearby Capener's Close, off Kinnerton Street in Knightsbridge. This is where I visited her in 1982. I travelled across London on the underground and took with me a list of questions I wanted to ask her. I had never been to that part of London before and it was very different to what I was used to. Walking from the station to Kinnerton Street I discovered that I was entering an exclusive and rather grandiose environment. The houses were tall and elegant. The pavements were spotless. I later discovered that her Kinnerton Street neighbours included, at one time or another, Lord Louis Mountbatten, opera singer Leontyne Price, actress Hermione Gingold and the film director Brian Desmond Hurst. In her home, which she described to me as a 'mews cottage', I was impressed that Elisabeth had kept most of her elegant art deco furniture of the 1930s. There was also a baby grand piano and stacks of books and music sheets. The walls of her living room were pink.

Elisabeth was full of joy and happiness and it showed through her laugh, straight from the belly. That day, I learned that Elisabeth was more interested in the person she was talking to than she was in laying out the details of her own successful life. As I prepared to say goodbye, I told her that we had a family connection. Elisabeth looked puzzled, but I explained that it was through my Aunt Esther who had made dresses for her before the war. To help jog her memory, I showed her a photograph of my aunt, taken just after the war, and Elisabeth exclaimed, 'Yes, I remember her, the friendly coloured lady with the cockney accent!'

I did not expect to see Elisabeth again, but the following February I received a call from Andrew Youdell who worked in the British Film Institute's Regional Film Theatre department. Andrew explained that he had befriended Elisabeth at a party and had organised a private screening for her of the National Film Archive's print of *Song of Freedom*, the first film she had made with Robeson (the other was *Big Fella*). He asked if I'd like to join them.

On March 4, just a few months after visiting her in Capener's Close, I found myself sitting next to Elisabeth in one of the British Film Institute's quaint but cosy viewing theatres in Royalty Mews, off Dean Street. The screening of *Song of Freedom* brought back many happy memories for her. Over the next few years Elisabeth and I were occasional guests of Andrew's for lunch at Kettner's Restaurant in Soho. The lunches were habitually followed by afternoon screenings of films from the National Film Archive. While we lunched at Kettner's, it became a ritual for Alfredo Ivaldi, the tall, distinguished-looking 80-year-old-singing maître d' (who had worked at Kettner's for over 40 years) to approach Elisabeth. After reminding her that he had seen her in a cabaret in Paris in 1930, he serenaded her, much to her delight and the amusement of the customers. These were memorable, joyous occasions.

Shortly after meeting Elisabeth, I met Derek Jarman. He had heard that I had included a tribute to Elisabeth in my NFT film season. This was during the summer of 1983 when he was in the middle of a 7-year break from feature films. It wasn't his choice. No one in the British film industry would finance his work, and he hadn't directed any feature films since *The Tempest.* Derek described himself as a painter who made films. He was also an eloquent, outspoken campaigner for the rights of gay men. He wanted to hear more about my interest in Elisabeth and invited me to his minuscule studio flat in Phoenix House, just off Charing Cross Road, to discuss a project he had in mind. I had never ventured into the world of a painter before. I was quite unprepared for what I encountered.

Derek's flat consisted of a galley kitchen, a tiny bathroom and a single front room overlooking noisy Charing Cross Road and facing St Martin's School of Art. Fascinated, I studied the contents which included a mini-gallery of Jarman's own paintings, some books and lots of interesting 'arty' things. Then something moved under a large duvet on a double mattress on the floor. A tousled-haired, naked man, aged about 19, stood up and Derek, in his quaint, middle-class way, politely asked the lad if he would 'Go downstairs and have some breakfast.' Derek then handed him money for coffee and a croissant. The young man dressed and left.

We talked enthusiastically about Elisabeth, at which point Derek elaborated further on his invitation. He wanted to make one of his Super-8 home movies about her and if we could raise the money, possibly transfer it to 16mm and release it as a featurette. He wanted me to put together a proposal and work as a consultant on the project. I thought it was a great idea and was happy to get involved, but my enthusiasm faded as he explained it more: 'We could film Lis at home in Capener's Close, vacuuming the floor or dusting the piano, while singing "Stormy Weather".' I smiled and nodded but secretly found his ideas very silly and too eccentric for someone as wonderful as Elisabeth. It didn't take long for me to realise that Derek was a bit crazy, but it was exciting to meet him all the same.

A few weeks later Derek arranged for me to meet his producer, a handsome, well-spoken gentleman called Tim Bevan. He was tasked with raising money for Derek's projects. I liked Tim. He appreciated my ideas for a documentary film about Elisabeth. Unfortunately, nothing came of the project, but Tim would soon make his mark with the critically-acclaimed and award-winning *My Beautiful Laundrette.* Tim would go on to become one of the most influential figures in British cinema, and Derek found himself back on track with his film career with *Caravaggio* (1986).

I never saw Tim again, but I did correspond on-and-off with Derek for several years. When I was the film critic for *Gay Times* magazine in the early 1990s, I bumped into him at various press screenings. He was always warm and friendly, even after I wrote a negative review of his 1990 film *The Garden!* A few years after our discussions, David Robinson and Stephen Garrett co-directed a more conventional documentary about Elisabeth called *Keeping Love Alive* (1987). It magically captured Elisabeth in concert at the Almeida Theatre in Islington, interspersed with an interview of her conducted in her home. When I asked Elisabeth about the film she smiled and said that they had done a good job.

She was a private person. I expect she may have been wary of the project at first, but I'm sure her fears were quickly allayed because Robinson and Garrett treated her with respect.

In the 1980s, I began writing for most of the Black newspapers and journals that were available in this country. They included *Caribbean Times*, *Black Arts*, and *Artrage*. The latter two publications were published by the Minority Arts Advisory Service (MAAS). I was commissioned on a freelance basis and I was rarely paid. An exception was *The Voice*, a newspaper aimed at the Black community. *The Voice* launched in 1982 by the Grenadian broadcaster Alex Pascall and Val McCalla, a Jamaican accountant and entrepreneur. Freelancers didn't get paid much but I appreciated the exposure. I got to attend press screenings of new films, events like the London Film Festival, and all I had to do was write reviews and the occasional feature. It was valuable experience for a young writer. I also approached McCalla about writing a book about the history of Black movie stars, but the meeting was embarrassing. 'How many white women did Sammy Davis Jr have affairs with?' he asked. I shook my head, 'I have no idea.' He soon realised I wasn't interested in writing *that* sort of book, which would've made it more commercial. I was only interested in their professional careers. He showed me the door and I never saw him again. This encounter didn't change the respect I had for what he'd achieved with his newspaper and the opportunities it gave me. I continued to write for *The Voice* until the end of the decade when it descended into a tabloid and started publishing the most hateful, homophobic content, mostly on the 'Letters to the Editor' page. As a gay man I couldn't justify contributing to *The Voice* any longer so I withdrew my services until the homophobic content vanished. By then there were plenty of other Black newspapers and magazines on the market providing me with work, like *The Weekly Journal* and *Black Britain*. I also contributed to *Chic*, a popular glossy lifestyle magazine for Black women. One of the highlights was my interview with Gail Lumet Buckley about her famous mother, the legendary singer Lena Horne.

Meanwhile, more Black British history books began to surface. In 1984, there were two groundbreaking titles: a reissue of Mary Seacole's 1857 autobiography, *Wonderful Adventures of Mrs Seacole in Many Lands*, edited by Ziggi Alexander and Audrey Dewjee; and the Marxist journalist Peter Fryer's comprehensive *Staying Power: The History of Black People in Britain.*

Mary Seacole (1805–1881) was an extraordinary Jamaican-Scottish doctress written out of popular accounts of Victorian British history. During the Crimean War of the 1850s, she tended to wounded soldiers on the battlefields. Thanks to Ziggi and Audrey, the reprint of her book generated renewed interest in her story. Seacole received the recognition she was due. In 2004, she was voted first in the 100 Great Black Britons poll. In 2007, English Heritage honoured her with a Blue Plaque at her former home at 14 Soho Square in Westminster, and in 2016, an impressive memorial statue was unveiled opposite the House of Commons in the grounds of St Thomas' Hospital in Lambeth. It is believed to be Britain's first statue in honour of a named Black woman.

Peter Fryer's *Staying Power* has come to be regarded as one of the main sources of information about Black Britons from history. It is a chunk of a book. The paperback version that I purchased in 1984 has over 600 pages. In 2016, David Olusoga acknowledged in *Black and British – A Forgotten History* that it is 'a uniquely important book' for anyone 'who has ever written about Black history'. However, over time, I have come to the conclusion that Fryer's book has some limitations. I agree with Anne Rush who in her 2007 article in *History Compass* drew attention to Fryer's focus on people who had been politically active in Britain. She said they wrote more and so had more written about them, which created an imbalance in information. *Staying Power* also reflected Fryer's socialist outlook. There was nothing wrong with any of this, but it alerted me to the fact that there needed to be a much broader and inclusive exploration of Black British history.

In 1984, I befriended Junior Douglas, also known as J. D. He had curated an exhibition about Paul Robeson for Battersea Library and after learning about my film tribute at the NFT, invited me to come and see it. On a separate occasion, he invited me to a private viewing where I met Dame Peggy Ashcroft, who had played Desdemona to Robeson's Othello at the Savoy Theatre in 1930. She was theatre royalty to me. Dame Peggy told us that she had the utmost respect for Robeson as an actor and political activist and talked to J. D. and myself about her working relationship with him. On that occasion, J. D. also introduced me to C. L. R. James, the Trinidadian historian, journalist, and socialist. Though he looked frail in his wheelchair at the age of 84, he was a sharp thinker and talker. In 1936 James's play *Toussaint L'Ouverture* was staged at the Westminster Theatre in London with Robeson in the lead. In our brief conversation he expressed his appreciation for this long-overdue recognition of Robeson.

When J. D. successfully applied to the Greater London Council (GLC) for funding to expand the exhibition and present it at the Royal Festival Hall in London's South Bank, he asked me to join the project as a consultant. My primary interest was in Robeson's acting career, and so I focused on that section. At the GLC, Parminder Vir was the Head of the Race Equality Unit for Arts and Recreation. She was responsible for overseeing the exhibition and making sure that everything was in place for the opening on April 24, 1985. Robeson's son, Paul Robeson Jr, had accepted an invitation to travel from his home in the United States to open the exhibition, so everything had to be perfect. Parminder was a force to be reckoned with and not an easy person to work for. She lacked tact and could be dictatorial. On the morning of the day of the opening, J. D. was nowhere to be seen, so I had to listen to yet another of Parminder's rants, this time about the windows which hadn't been cleaned, the tables and chairs that hadn't been removed from the exhibition area, the carpet that needed cleaning, and so on. She had a right to be angry, but I felt like telling her I wasn't responsible for housekeeping at the Royal Festival Hall. Regrettably, I lacked the confidence to stand up to her.

Later that day, before the opening, J. D. came to me in great embarrassment to explain that I was not going to attend the reception for Paul Robeson Jr because 'Parminder only wants Black and Asian people there.' J. D. was upset, but it wasn't his fault. I understood that this was the world of radical Black politics, and I was not a part of it.

The opening of the Paul Robeson exhibition attracted a huge crowd of honorary guests and attendees from all walks of political and creative life. In addition to Robeson Jr, who was a gracious and charming gentleman, these included the Labour leader Neil Kinnock; C. L. R. James; actor Sam Wanamaker; a number of well-known Labour Party politicians who had known Robeson or just admired him including Jennie Lee, Illtyd Harrington, who at that time was Deputy Leader of the GLC, Bernie Grant, Tony Benn, Andrew Faulds and Lord David Pitt; the folk singer and actress Nadia Cattouse, who I befriended a few years later; Elisabeth Welch, Robeson's leading lady in two films; and Rachel Thomas, the Welsh actress who had co-starred with Robeson in the 1940 film *The Proud Valley*.

When I look back, I realise these brief encounters, even the difficult ones, helped to give me insights into Paul Robeson and the world of radical Black politics. In some ways, my work on the Robeson exhibition and dealing with the challenge of working for Parminder, was a significant 'coming of age' time for me. In fact, it helped to lead me to another exciting turning point in my life.

Chapter 8

Are We Being Served?

When I left school in 1977, I lacked confidence. I was plagued by self-conscious thoughts because I didn't have a degree. From time to time, I would enrol in adult education courses to help boost my confidence and broaden my knowledge, even signing up for an O-Level in sociology in 1981. I had failed it several times at school but this time round I felt sure I could pass the exam, and I did. During a period of unemployment in 1984–85, I was permitted to continue claiming the dole while attending a media studies course three days a week at the London College of Printing (LCP) in Elephant and Castle. This coincided with a summer school course I attended in 1985 about British cinema at the Watershed Arts Centre in Bristol. We compared British films of the 1940s with British films of the 1980s. One of the visiting guest speakers was the film producer David Puttnam who took to the stage following a screening of his 1981 Oscar-winning *Chariots of Fire.* Puttnam came across as a well-meaning smooth operator. He was a slick packager, ambitious but kindly, rather like an uncle who would give you pocket money. Derek Jarman despised everything Puttnam and his 'safe' films stood for, such as middle-class values and jingoism. Though in fairness, *Chariots of Fire* does tackle anti-Semitism. The general consensus was that the British films we saw from the 1940s were more interesting than those we saw from the 1980s. We were unprepared for the screenings of two of Michael Powell and Emeric Pressburger's films: *A Matter of Life and Death* and *Black Narcissus*, both made in the 1940s. These films captured our imaginations, as did Puttnam's *Local Hero.*

The same year I took part in the summer school in Bristol, I applied for and was accepted into a Bachelor of Arts degree in Film and Video at the London College of Printing. I had been encouraged to apply by a tutor on the media studies course. When I informed her that I didn't have the requisite A-Levels to apply for a degree, she laughed and explained that I could apply as a mature student even without the grades. I was astounded. It had never occurred to me that it was possible to apply for a degree without a couple of A-Levels. No one had told me that. Had I known, I might have applied sooner. I also applied for and was awarded a three-year grant from the Inner London Education Authority.

I was aware that the LCP's degree had an enviable reputation in film-study circles for being left of centre and accepting people from an array of backgrounds. Even though I wasn't out to everyone publicly, knowing this definitely made me more comfortable to apply. The school had a radical, left-wing and Marxist outlook on Thatcher's Britain which manifested itself in the experimental ethos it encouraged the students to adopt. The content of the course was inclusive. We studied the work of women filmmakers and Black and Third World cinema, none of which were curricular norms at the time. Most students I met from other film schools expressed envy toward our programme because we had tutors like the highly-respected feminist filmmaker and theorist Laura Mulvey, and the leftist director Ken Loach was one of our visiting lecturers.

The course officially began on September 23, 1985. I was 27 and immediately found myself amongst a diverse group of students. Although we came from different social, cultural, and political backgrounds, as well as age groups, we all had a desire to learn and experiment. I was not the only gay man. In that first week, Steve Whitson, an American with a larger- than-life personality and a background in lighting design, came over to me and said, 'I hear you're a sissy too.' We got along but we never became close friends, I suspect, because our interests diverged. Steve came from a background of avant-garde, experimental theatre, not film or television. After graduating we lost touch, but one day in 1992 he called me out of the blue. 'I'm decluttering and I have something for you. I know how much you love Hollywood movies. It's a signed photograph of Lauren Bacall and I want you to have it.' It is a striking black and white print of the Hollywood star walking along a street in New York. Lauren's smiling as she looks over her shoulder at the camera. He sent it to me in the post. A few months later, someone told me that Steve had died at the age of 46 from an AIDS-related illness.

In 1985, the AIDS pandemic was beginning to take hold. It was frightening. If it hadn't been for gay magazines and newspapers I wouldn't have learned about the risks of having unsafe sex. The pandemic did make me wary of having sexual encounters. I was careful. Understandably my parents were worried about me because they read the tabloids which were hostile. Thatcher's government deliberately turned a blind eye to much suffering. As a young gay man I had always shied away from the gay scene. I didn't go to gay pubs and clubs. I didn't know where Heaven was. I didn't step foot in the Vauxhall Tavern. It wasn't that I disapproved. I was reserved. I have always described myself as a sociable person who shies away from socialising. An introverted extrovert. In 1985, I took out a subscription to the monthly magazine *Gay Times*, partly to keep myself informed about what was happening in the gay community and the AIDS pandemic.

I had a small circle of close friends, some gay, some straight. They included Sonia from the dole office days, my cousin Karen, and the actress Shope Shodeinde. One of my closest friends, though, was Terry Bolas, who was a headteacher of a comprehensive school in North London. We befriended each other at one of the evening classes that I attended. It was called 'Gay Writing Today' and took place at Morley College in Lambeth. Terry was deeply interested in cinema, and he helped me to navigate my way through film school. He was a kind gentleman. Older and supportive of younger gay men. Easy to talk to. But at his school he had to keep his sexuality a secret. As far as I was aware, there were no openly gay headteachers in Britain in the 1980s. We occasionally met up for visits to the cinema. It was Terry who introduced me to Alfred Hitchcock's brilliant *Vertigo* when it was reissued.

My life at that time was mainly focused on my film studies, but as a young gay man I knew next to nothing about the lives of gay men in history. When I saw a copy of Heinz Heger's *The Men With the Pink Triangle*, published by the Gay Men's Press in 1980 in my local library, I was intrigued. On reading it, however, nothing could have prepared me for the terrible shock of discovering that gay men had been incarcerated, brutalised, and murdered in the Nazi death camps of the 1930s and 1940s. A few years earlier, in 1979, Martin Sherman's play *Bent* dealt with the same theme, although I had yet to see it. On reading *The Men With the Pink Triangle*, I realised that we, gay men, had a history – albeit a troubled and sometimes painful one – and that it had been suppressed.

Five days after starting the film degree, the second Brixton uprising took place in nearby Lambeth. It was sparked by the police shooting of mother Cherry Groce. From my living room window on the top of the high rise, I could see the flames and smoke. Brixton was burning again. It seemed that nothing had been learned since the 1981 disturbances. Certainly the police hadn't changed their ways. At the LCP, some students wanted to borrow video cameras from the film department and record what was happening on the streets. I cannot recall if they did, but I do remember the caution offered by the Head of the Film Department: 'If you take our video equipment to Brixton, make sure you take care of it. If you leave it unattended and it gets stolen by a young Black guy, then you cannot blame him for his actions because he is underprivileged and in a desperate situation. But you will have to find the money to replace the stolen equipment.' I couldn't make up my mind if I agreed with him. What if the 'young Black guy' was not part of the uprising but a thief? I was confused by the politics we were being presented with.

Before the end of the year, I had begun to extend my knowledge of gay culture. I went to see Derek Jarman in conversation with Simon Fanshawe in a series of talks called *Facing Fanshawe* at the Drill Hall. I started writing for gay weekly newspapers including *Capital Gay* and *The Pink Paper*. In those formative years of writing for gay publications, there was no shortage of gay and lesbian films, and I made sure to see all of them. The most outstanding was *My Beautiful Laundrette*, directed by Stephen Frears, starring the then-newcomer Daniel Day-Lewis. This was a revolutionary film, one of the first to depict a non-stereotypical same-sex romance and sexual encounter between two young gay men. I thought it was brilliantly written by Hanif Kureishi. The film inspired me and gave me something to identify with. Other films released at that time included *Desert Hearts*, *Parting Glances*, and *The Passion of Remembrance*, made by Sankofa, an independent Black British film collective featuring the gay director Isaac Julien.

Meanwhile, at the LCP, I had a rude awakening. At the start of the LCP course, I became involved in a student video production about international struggles of the world. It began with a quote from the Black Trinidadian Marxist historian C. L. R. James: 'Great men make history but only history that is possible for them to make. Their freedom of achievement is limited by the necessity of their environment.' So far, so good. Mr James's quote was read out on the soundtrack with photos of Nelson Mandela, Malcolm X, Angela Davis, Winnie Mandela, Gandhi, Paul Robeson, Gerry Adams, and Lech Walesa. The struggles we represented included those in such places as Palestine, South Africa, Nicaragua, and Northern Ireland. Groups such as the miner's wives and Iranian women were also shown. The Brixton uprising was included. However, when I asked for the struggles of the lesbian and gay community to be featured, I was treated with incredulity by my colleagues. When I asked for a photo of the American gay politician and activist Harvey Milk, who had been assassinated in 1978, to be included, the other members of the group refused. As far as they were concerned, the struggles of lesbians and gays were unimportant and, because they hadn't heard of Harvey Milk, they didn't believe that there was any reason for him to be acknowledged alongside Nelson Mandela and the others. I found this experience extremely difficult to comprehend but more significantly, as a gay student, I felt completely isolated. Steve Whitson, my fellow 'sissy', just shrugged his shoulders and showed no feeling of solidarity with me. He told me he had fought all his gay battles in the 1960s and 1970s in America and he wanted to move on from the struggle.

When I approached one of the tutors for advice, I fared no better. My attempt to discuss my sexuality with her, and how to make it relevant in my work, failed. She treated me with contempt and complained that I had approached her simply because she was a woman. She accused me of seeing her as a member of the 'weaker' sex. I was appalled. Nothing could have been further from the truth. I had approached her because she had been assigned our tutor for the project. I admitted to her that I didn't feel comfortable talking to any of the male tutors about my sexuality because none of them struck me as being sympathetic or understanding. She suggested that in future if I needed help or advice, I should phone the London Gay Switchboard. This was a brilliant support organisation. Anonymous volunteers were trained to help anyone who needed advice. The volunteers had to be on the ball because a caller could ask them anything. A caller could be suicidal or ask what gay pubs were near their home. Lesbian Line offered a similar service to women callers.

Despite her delivery, the tutor's advice was sensible. I did end up calling the Switchboard and the nice chap who answered my call was extremely helpful and supportive. In fact, he put me in touch with

Converse Pictures, a lesbian and gay film collective based not far from my home in South London. They helped me enormously to regain my confidence and encouraged me to continue with the degree. Meanwhile, a little bird informed me that the tutor who had been so hostile to me didn't like gay men because her husband had left her for one. Oops.

In declaring my sexuality, I quickly discovered that one of Britain's most progressive, radical, left-wing and Marxist film schools shied away from anything to do with lesbian and gay cinema and politics. When I informed Terry, he explained that, from his perspective, we had no place in the political thinking of Marxists. Terry told me that they saw gay men as wealthy, narcissistic, and decadent. I knew I wasn't wealthy or decadent, but I had to look up the word narcissistic in the dictionary to find out what it meant. Wasn't that either. So I had a battle to fight, and that battle was to help foster an environment of tolerance for gay cinema and the arts.

At that time, there was hardly a film studies course which didn't feature the work of the Russian director Sergei Eisenstein. So, when we were shown his 1925 classic *Battleship Potemkin*, I mentioned in the discussion afterwards that he was gay and one could find homoerotic images in his films. My declaration was met with stony silence. When one of the tutors screened F. W. Murnau's silent melodrama *Sunrise* (1927), another classic often included in film studies, I spoke about Murnau's homosexuality and how it influenced his work, once again to a deafening silence. It soon became apparent to me that I was being irritating to staff and students by making these references, but I didn't stop. Regrettably for me, at no time was there a discussion about it.

I was also shocked to discover that Laura Mulvey, the feminist filmmaker, knew only sparsely about the portrayal of women in British cinema of the 1940s. This came to my attention when I presented a seminar on the subject and showed extracts from *The Wicked Lady* (1945) starring Margaret Lockwood, *Brief Encounter* (1945) starring Celia Johnson, *It Always Rains on Sunday* (1947) starring Googie Withers, and

Black Narcissus (1947) starring Deborah Kerr. Laura was fascinated and asked me if she could borrow the video tape so that she could look at the extracts again. I anticipated a discussion with her once she'd rewatched the extracts, but once again was met with stony silence. She just returned the tape and said 'Thank you.'

In the new year, also on the advice of Switchboard, I visited the Hall-Carpenter Archives which were held at the London Lesbian and Gay Centre. It was located in central London on Cowcross Street, Farringdon. I discovered that the Archives were a treasure trove of gay and lesbian history: newspaper cuttings, journals, books. I wanted to research back issues of *Gay News* for an essay for my degree. They had every copy from 1972 to 1983. What I discovered was Keith Howes's thoroughly researched and informative two-part survey of lesbians and gays in British television. Keith had published this in *Gay News* in 1977 and his groundbreaking work opened my eyes to a history I had only limited knowledge of. This was partly due to the Gay Liberation Movement wanting nothing to do with television. To his credit, Denis Lemon, the editor of *Gay News*, encouraged Keith to give equal attention to film and television. But I discovered that taking our television history seriously was never accepted by gay activists or the gay intelligentsia.

Then, on February 11, 1986 came *Are We Being Served?* a one-day conference at London's County Hall which was organised by the Gays and Broadcasting Project. The Project's research and findings had been published in a report that was presented at this event. The authors of the report challenged broadcasters, especially in television, to examine their own homophobia and that of the institutions they served. Nothing on this scale had been attempted before and the meeting room was packed. Speakers included Mark Finch and Lorraine Trenchard, two of the Project's researchers. The representative from Channel 4 was given a hard time. Launched in 1982, this new television channel had promised to address the needs of viewers from minority groups, but the lesbian and gay community had felt cheated, left out and let down. The campaigning in our community eventually led to programmes such as the Channel 4 series *Out on Tuesday* in 1989, but visibility on the box took longer than we expected.

The following month, in March, I accepted an invitation from John Dower – a former colleague from the Peckham dole office – who was now a film student, to star in his student film, *The Tunnel.* He told me he wanted me to feature because I had 'the most amazing eyes'. Bit of a sweet talker he was. We filmed at two locations: the foot tunnel at Greenwich and at the seaside in Weymouth, but it was there my acting career started and ended. In April, I almost had a brief encounter with my ex-partner David Castell when he took to the stage of the National Film Theatre for an interview with Julie Andrews. I knew David was going to be there. I had read about it in the publicity. I had hoped to see him again and say hello. David was an enthusiastic and knowledgeable interviewer and Julie was a superb interviewee and raconteur. They both looked fabulous. After the interview, Ms Andrews was signing autographs. I had brought with me my original 1965 *Sound of Music* souvenir movie brochure. I was ready to get it signed until all of a sudden that same childhood embarrassment came over me. All the other fans had pristine pictures of Julie, not to mention memorabilia, for her to autograph. And to make matters more excruciating, David was sat next to her at the autographing table. Shamefully, quietly, I slipped out of line because I didn't want David – or Ms. Andrews – to see my dog-eared, tea-stained copy of my souvenir movie brochure. On reflection, I wish I hadn't done this because it would be wonderful to have Ms Andrews's autograph.

In the summer term of 1986, I recorded a video interview with my Nan at her flat in Peckham for a short documentary I was making called *A Few Home Truths.* I was inspired to take on this project after reading a quote in Stuart Hood's *On Television* (1982), a book I found in the LCP library, where he says, 'Most people are unlikely ever to find themselves in front of film or television cameras, in a studio or elsewhere…they will remain anonymous members of the audience for television, of "the public" – two terms which are used in television as if they were the same thing.' My intention was to give a voice to a working-class woman, something you rarely saw on television. Nan was a lively interviewee, with a clear memory of her life growing up in Merthyr Tydfil, the struggles of the 1926 General Strike, and working in a wartime munitions factory. She, as always, spared a few words for Margaret Thatcher. Nan was a great storyteller and her warm, endearing Welsh accent drew listeners in.

She was relaxed, eloquent, disregarded the camera, and enjoyed being asked about her life. It was this experience that gave me an awareness of the importance of first-hand testimony in the recording of social history. A year later, Nan passed away. Shortly after the interview her health began to decline. It was heartbreaking to see this happen. When my sister's daughter Emma was born in May 1987, Nan told us she was determined to attend the christening of her first great-grandchild, in spite of her failing health. Emma was christened on July 2. Nan passed away on August 18. Her wish to attend Emma's christening had been granted. Another wish she had was for us to take her home to Merthyr Tydfil.

On August 30, we travelled all the way to Merthyr and visited 14 Harrison Street, Dowlais, where Nan's brother, our Uncle Jimmy, lived. Her sister, Auntie Anne, lived nearby. Mum's cousin Pat and her husband George joined us from their home in Bristol. It was lovely to see them all again. No. 14 was a tiny house and would have been a miner's cottage in the old days when Nan and her brothers and sisters were born. Mum said it didn't look any different to how it was in wartime when it was crowded with family members, escaping the air raids of London and Manchester (where Nan's brother Jack lived). It still had an outhouse in the yard, a tin bath hung in the kitchen for washing, and electricity was only available downstairs. Uncle Jimmy rented the house from a private landlord. He was a shy man and wasn't the kind to ask his landlord for anything. Thankfully, his rent was a pittance. Jimmy spoke very fast, with a strong Welsh accent, and I couldn't understand him but Mum and her brothers did. After some time situating ourselves with Uncle Jimmy and Auntie Anne, talking about Nan, cousin Jerry arrived.

Anne came running into the house: 'Jerry's coming!' she cried as she and Jimmy disappeared into the yard, slamming the door behind them. Jerry entered and in a loud Welsh voice announced that he had visited London in the 1950s. He said, 'I went all the way to London to visit May and her husband.' Pat quietly explained that Jerry was as mad as a hatter, but he insisted on coming to the cemetery with us to scatter Nan's ashes. Eventually Jimmy and Anne resurfaced and we made our way to Pant Cemetery.

The cemetery was huge and on a hillside. If it hadn't been for Jerry, we would never have found the grave of Nan's parents. It had a headstone and it was a very emotional experience. Although it was a sad occasion, Jerry made us laugh when he 'borrowed' some flowers from someone else's resting place and laid them on the grave. Mum and her brothers, Mike and David, scattered Nan's ashes. Then we said goodbye to Jerry, Jimmy, and Anne and found our way to the beautiful Brecon Beacons where we had lunch. Then we came back to London, all in one day. I had borrowed a camera from Terry to take photos of the visit.

Uncle Jimmy never married. Mum told me that Irish mothers always kept a son at home to take care of them and Jimmy was the son chosen. He couldn't afford a telephone, but Nan had been able to call him at the catholic hall where he socialised. In 1987, the Irish and Welsh communities of Dowlais were still living side by side but keeping their own cultures and religions. He was very close to his niece Pat who kept an eye on him until she informed us that he had passed away in 1997.

Nan's death was expected but very distressing. I had never lost anyone close to me. My childhood and teenage years were spent by her side, listening to her stories. She had a wonderful way of bringing to life her experiences. I am thankful I captured some of this in my

Stephen's grandparents. Clockwise from top left: Henry Bourne, Ada Bourne, Albert 'Bob' Joyce and Mary Joyce with Kathy (Stephen's mother) on her lap. (Author's collection).

Stephen's great-grandmother Hannah Johnson, known as 'Granny' (standing), with one of her neighbours outside 13 Dieppe Street, West Kensington in 1940.
(Author's collection).

From left to right: Kathy Joyce (Stephen's mother), Esther Bruce, Granny Johnson, Michael Joyce and Esther's dog Paddy outside 13 Dieppe Street in 1947.
(Author's collection).

Stephen
(Author's collection).

Stephen with his father, Arthur Bourne (1963).
(Author's collection).

Stephen at St Michael and All Angels Secondary Modern school on Wyndham Road, Camberwell SE5 in 1974. Stephen is in the middle row, third from the left.
(Author's collection).

Sonia Pascal and Stephen in 1982.
(Author's collection, courtesy of Linda Bourne Hull).

BURNING AN ILLUSION

Black Actors in British Cinema

The release last year of *Burning an Illusion* and its enthusiastic reception by audiences marked a milestone in black film history – an opportunity rare in this country to see black people portrayed on the screen with any degree of realism. A comparison with Alexander Korda's *Sanders of the River* (1935), starring Paul Robeson as the faithful African tribal chief, Bosambo, gives food for thought. This season sets out to discover how far film-makers in this country have succeeded in exploring the experience of black people in Britain since the 1930s.

Black people first began to settle in Britain in 1555 and, since that time, they have made positive contributions to the political and cultural framework of this country. However, very few have been given the recognition they deserve. Ira Aldridge (1807-67) was one of the first black actors to achieve success in Britain and he made his most famous appearance in the theatre as Shakespeare's *Othello*. In 1930, Paul Robeson won critical acclaim in Britain for his performance in the same role and went on to play leading roles in several British films. However, black British film history, which can be traced back to the silent era, is a subject which has not been properly researched or recorded since 1948, when Peter Noble published *The Negro in Films*, the pioneer study on this theme. In recent years some American writers, such as Jim Pines in *Blacks in Films* (1975) and Thomas Cripps in *Slow Fade to Black* (1977), have acknowledged that, on several occasions, British film-makers have seriously attempted to explore the complex issues of race relations in this country. However, no British writer has come forward to analyse these films in any depth.

'*What the black actor has managed to give are moments — indelible moments, created, miraculously, beyond the confines of the script: hints of reality, smuggled like contraband into a maudlin tale, and with enough force, if unleashed, to shatter the tale to fragments.*' (*James Baldwin in* The Devil Finds Work – 1976).

With this season we aim to provide a forum for a critical look at black film history in this country and pay a long-overdue tribute to the many fine black artistes who have contributed to British films in the last fifty years.—*Stephen Bourne.*

Stephen Bourne contributes to Staunch, *a magazine which covers a range of subjects from a black perspective.*

Lecture on Paul Robeson **Wed 8 Jun 8.3**

After the screening of *The Proud Valley*, there will be a lecture in NFT3 on Paul Robeson, given by Richard Dyer, a lecturer at Warwick University. (Admission free, no pre-booking).

There will be an exhibition relating to this season in the NFT clubroom.

National Film Theatre
South Bank, Waterloo, SE1

BOX OFFICE Tel 01-928 3232
MEMBERSHIP from 65p weekly or £3.00 monthly (full details from NFT Box Office)
Monthly members may bring up to three guests (see free programme booklet for full details)
TICKETS £2.20 bookable in advance. £1.70 unreserved on sale half an hour before performances

Wed 1 Jun 6.15, 8.30
MIDSHIPMAN EASY

Thu 2 Jun 6.30
SANDERS OF THE RIVER

Sat 4 Jun 4.00
KING SOLOMON'S MINES

Tue 7 Jun 6.00
OLD BONES OF THE RIVER

Wed 8 Jun 6.15
THE PROUD VALLEY

Thu 9 Jun 6.30
THE THIEF OF BAGDAD

Sat 11 Jun 6.15
FIDDLERS THREE/ THE VENTRILOQUIST'S DUMMY

Sun 12 Jun 6.15
POOL OF LONDON

Sat 11 Jun 8.30
MEN OF TWO WORLDS

Sun 12 Jun 8.30
CRY, THE BELOVED COUNTRY

Sun 19 Jun 6.15
SAPPHIRE

Sun 19 Jun 8.30
FLAME IN THE STREETS

Mon 20 Jun 6.30
A TASTE OF HONEY

Mon 20 Jun 8.30
THE L-SHAPED ROOM

Wed 22 Jun 6.30
TO SIR, WITH LOVE

Wed 22 Jun 8.45
LEO THE LAST

Thu 23 Jun 6.15
A WARM DECEMBER

Fri 24 Jun 6.30
THE NATIONAL HEALTH

Fri 24 Jun 8.30
LOVE THY NEIGHBOUR

Sun 26 Jun 4.15
MAN FRIDAY

Sun 26 Jun 6.30
PRESSURE

Tue 28 Jun 6.30
BLACK JOY

Tue 28 Jun 8.35
THE SAILOR'S RETURN

Wed 29 Jun 8.45
BABYLON

Thu 30 Jun 8.45
BURNING AN ILLUSION

Burning an Illusion, a Black British film retrospective curated by Stephen in 1983. National Film Theatre flyer. (Author's collection).

Stephen at the National Film Theatre in 1983.
(Author's collection)

Paul Robeson exhibition flyer (1985).
(Author's collection).

Esther Bruce, Joan Caruana (Mayor of Hammersmith and Fulham) and Stephen at the launch of *Aunt Esther's Story* (1991).
(Author's collection).

Stephen on the set of *Black and White in Colour* in 1991 with (from left to right) crew members Remi Adefarasin (camera), Judi Lee-Headman (sound recordist) and Isaac Julien (director). Photo: Sharron Wallace.

Stephen at the launch of the Southwark Anti-Homophobic Forum (later known as the Southwark LGBT Forum) at Southwark Town Hall in 1995 with (left to right) Chief Inspector Tony London, Chief Superintendent Gerry McBride, Superintendent Matt Baggott and Superintendent David Hynes. Photo: Piers Allardyce.

Stephen at the launch of the second edition of *Black in the British Frame* at Peckham Library in 2001. (Author's collection).

Left to right: activist Peter Tatchell, Stephen and photographer Robert Taylor at the launch of the exhibition *Keep Smiling Through – Black Londoners on the Home Front 1939-1945* at the Cuming Museum in Walworth Road SE17 (2008).
Photo: Andrew Warrington.

Stephen giving a talk about his book *Black Poppies* at Thomson Reuters in Canary Wharf in 2015.

Left to right: Anni Domingo, Stephen, Cleo Sylvestre and Shirley Anderson at Stephen's London South Bank University graduation ceremony at the Royal Festival Hall in 2017.
Photo: Robert Taylor.

Stephen and Ken Sephton at a meeting of The Judy Garland Club in 2005.
Photo: Andrew Warrington.

Stephen's books (2025).
Photo: Alan J. Robertson.

writings and all those years ago in my student film *A Few Home Truths*. I screened the video at a family gathering at my home on August 3, 1986 to the delight of everyone in the room. Nan had never seen herself on the screen before. My aim that evening was much like my aim in my writing, to present something simple and direct. Something personal yet accessible. Later, my cousin Karen told me that her father, Uncle Mike, had cried on the journey home. He thought the video was brilliant and was surprised by some of the things Nan said. He did not realise that she had lived such a hard life. Karen added that she felt strange watching her. She didn't feel as though she was watching her own grandmother. She hadn't realised that she'd had such a hard life but was grateful that I'd given our grandmother, a working-class woman, a chance to relay her methods for survival in the 1930s and 1940s. We were all proud of Nan. When Karen asked her if she enjoyed seeing the video, Nan smiled, laughed, fiddled with her collar and replied: 'It was alright. I enjoyed it. I thought it was good.' She also remarked on the Welsh singing on the soundtrack. 'It choked me up because it brought back so many memories.'

After Nan died, I finally came out as gay to Mum and Dad. The time seemed right to me, especially as I had told my sister and a couple of cousins. There was no earthquake. No tornado. Just a simple acceptance, more love, more protection, which is how it should be. It was a relief. No more secrets.

With the confidence I was gaining, I began to explore ways of expressing my gay self in my college work. In 1987, I produced a short 'scratch' video compilation called *Out from the Shadows*. Scratch video was a British art movement that emerged in the 1980s, a form of outsider art. Generally it didn't have any rules. Freedom of expression was its purpose. It arose in opposition to broadcast television. My video was a simple montage of images of gay male characters from British films of the 1960s. The films included *Victim*, *A Taste of Honey*, *The L-Shaped Room*, and *The Family Way*. I sent a copy to Mark Finch, who was then working for the British Film Institute. His enthusiastic response was encouraging: 'I like it very much: It's rigorous, successful, and even elegant in its own way, even more of an achievement considering your difficult working circumstances'. Mark's supportive words led me to produce *Where There Was Silence*, a more ambitious video documentary for my final-year assessment. This focused on one of the films that I featured in the earlier video: *Victim*. This groundbreaking social drama starred Dirk Bogarde as a respectable, married barrister whose secret gay life is threatened with exposure by a blackmailer.

Before I started work on the video, in 1987–88 I published letters in several magazines and newspapers asking gay men to write to me about *Victim* and the impact it had on their lives when the film was released in 1961. I was overwhelmed by the response. Before the existence of email, the correspondents sent me lengthy handwritten or typewritten letters describing what life had been like for them in the early 1960s. They explained how *Victim* had broken new ground in raising awareness about the draconian law that made it a criminal offence for men to have sex with men. It was impossible to be open about one's sexuality. In those days, unless they were exhibitionists like Quentin Crisp, most gay men led double lives, publicly heterosexual while privately gay but hiding their sexuality in the closet. *Victim* and the publicity surrounding the release of the film undoubtedly contributed to public discourse, which resulted in the partial decriminalisation of homosexuality in 1967. When I began *Where There Was Silence*, I cheekily invited Simon Callow and Ian McKellen to take part. They responded with letters of support for what I was doing, but declined to be part of it. Afterwards, I approached the gay actor Stephen Lind. He readily agreed to read extracts from some of the many letters I had been sent by gay men in which they reminisced about *Victim* and the impact it had on them in the 1960s. He did this beautifully.

While I was conducting my research for this production, I had to cope with the anti-gay sentiment across the country, exhibited most acutely by the police and the media. For example, on January 24, 1987 the Royal Vauxhall Tavern, a popular gay pub and drag venue in South London, was raided by 20 police officers. The AIDS pandemic was at its height and the officers wore rubber gloves. Lily Savage (aka Paul O'Grady) was onstage at the time and famously quipped: 'Looks like we have help with the washing up.' Also in January 1987, Alan Douthwaite became the first police officer to die from an AIDS-related illness. When his body was discovered in his room at a police hostel in Upper Norwood, South London, undertakers refused to collect his body. Afterwards, guidelines were drawn up for funeral directors which said that undertakers should wear plastic gloves and use a body bag when dealing with AIDS victims. After Alan's body was removed, the police instructed the hostel staff to disinfect his room and change its use from a bedroom to a cupboard. At Alan's funeral, the service was conducted by Father Paul Igo who asked for God's forgiveness for 'whatever sins Alan may have committed through human frailty'. Alan's story is just one of many at that time that the gay community had to learn to cope with.

In an edition of BBC television's *Heart of the Matter* on March 8, 1987 the repulsive Conservative MP Geoffrey Dickens openly expressed his disgust with homosexuality and demanded its recriminalisation. His justification was to control the spread of HIV. His assumption was that gay men were responsible for the virus. In 1987, Dickens was allowed to say this unchallenged on national television. Then there was James Anderton, the controversial, outspoken, and homophobic Chief Constable of Greater Manchester, known as 'God's copper'. He also used the media to publicly attack the gay community. However, gays and lesbians were rarely given access to the media to challenge such views. On a personal note, I was deeply affected by this virulent homophobia, but I managed to cope by just simply being myself and not allowing the situation to affect me. I put up a barrier. But worse was to come.

On October 9, 1987 at the Conservative Party Conference in Blackpool, Margaret Thatcher stated that 'Children who need to be taught to respect traditional moral values are being taught they have an inalienable right to be gay.'

Another Tory MP, David Wilshire, proposed Clause 27 (later known as Section 28) with the support of Dame Jill Knight. It was added to the Local Government Bill on December 8, 1987 and not repealed until 2003, when we had a Labour government. The amendment made it illegal for local authorities to promote homosexuality or promote the teaching in any maintained school of the acceptability of homosexuality. In a moment of anger, I confronted Wilshire live on a phone-in radio programme on Greater London Radio (GLR). I had never done such a thing before and I was very nervous, but I overcame this to state my case to Wilshire. I told him that I was a film student who was concerned that my work would be banned, but he didn't understand and just waffled on. I was concerned that my video production was in breach of Section 28, and I feared that it would be banned if I tried to show it in a public venue. Officially the Labour Party opposed Section 28 but when they came into power in 1997, they did not succeed in repealing it until 2003.

For the LGBT+ community this was one of the most serious attacks the Tory government had made on our civil liberties. It proposed the banning of teaching homosexuality in schools, and sought to prevent lesbians and gays from accessing public funds. I felt that my documentary about *Victim* needed to address Wilshire's proposal, and I swiftly changed my original concept to accommodate Section 28. Armed with a video camera, on April 30, 1988 I recorded the Section 28 march in London for inclusion in my documentary. We gathered at the embankment along the Thames and marched to Big Ben. There were some well-known faces on the front line including Ian McKellen, Michael Cashman and Jimi Somerville. Stephen Lind was also there in drag as 'Lotte Cash' (aka Margaret Thatcher). We went round the Houses of Parliament to Lambeth Bridge and then finished at Kennington Park. The mood was one of vitriol directed at Thatcher and her nasty Tory government. I remember a group of lesbians shouting 'Maggie Thatcher is a horse's arse!' over and over again. People from all walks of life attended the march. Businessmen in suits and ties, punks, lesbian feminists, drag queens, and lots of different LGBT+ political groups. Estimates ranged from 10,000 to 30,000. It wasn't celebratory or fun like Pride, but just as noisy. Despite the anger, there was no trouble. There was a strong police presence, however, I don't recall anyone having any bother with them.

For me, it was an exciting and thrilling experience of solidarity. I wasn't a gay activist. I was never drawn into party politics. I had left of centre views, strong opinions, and a desire to express them in the name of building a more equitable society. Section 28 didn't radicalise me, however, it did make me very angry. And I wasn't the only one. Since the 1967 Sexual Offences Act, much progress had been made. We were still fighting, and no longer doing it completely in the shadows. Still, it felt as if Margaret Thatcher and her Tory government were slapping us in the face with Section 28. This happened at a time when some gay men were struggling to live with HIV and facing all kinds of homophobic attitudes. Our morale couldn't have been any lower. We were being forced underground again without power and control. It was an ugly time for the LGBT+ community. Section 28 reminded us that we were still very fragile in the eyes of the law and the only way for our voice to be heard was to take to the streets. I made sure my gay voice was heard at the LCP. I was a founding member of a lesbian and gay society at the LCP which helped bring together isolated students from various departments, including print journalism and photography. We tried to make resources available like popular lesbian and gay journals but the LCP library refused to acquire any of them on account of there being no funds. Curiously, right-wing, homophobic newspapers like *The Sun* were made available.

The thesis I submitted for my graduation in 1988 analysed the films of the 1930s gay Hollywood director James Whale. His most famous films included the First World War drama *Journey's End, Frankenstein,* and its high camp sequel *Bride of Frankenstein* as well as the glorious musical, *Show Boat.* All of them dealt with 'outsiders' and had, in my humble opinion, gay subtexts, so I argued a case for him as a gay *auteur.*

At the graduation assessment in 1988, my tutors questioned me about the form and technical aspects of *Where There Was Silence,* completely ignoring the subject matter. The external examiner was Annette Kuhn, a highly regarded cultural historian and feminist. She, too, was unhelpful. I cannot recall what she said during our one-to-one session – I immediately blanked it – but I do remember that she left me feeling inadequate and a failure. In three years nothing had changed. Disappointed and frustrated, I expected the worst, but I was thrilled when they awarded me a 2:1 with a commendation for my research paper about Black representation in early British film and television. When they gave me the envelope with my result, I immediately took it to the gents' toilet, locked myself in, opened it and burst into tears. I had graduated with a grade I was proud of.

Where There Was Silence wasn't seen widely, but it did generate some interest. In June 1988, just before I graduated, I collaborated with the LCP's Lesbian and Gay Society to organise an event for that year's Pride called *Strength and Pride* at the London College of Printing. The event highlighted my documentary and screenings of several lesbian and gay film and video productions. In the Autumn issue of *Lesbian and Gay Socialist,* Peter Kent-Baguley's positive appraisal of my documentary gave my confidence a boost:

> 'Initially, on my first viewing, I found the recollections of *Victim,* in each case expressed somewhat archly I thought by actor Stephen Lind sitting or standing slightly awkwardly by a table, an interference to the film but, equally, I found the film extracts an intrusion on

> the recollections. However, as the video proceeded the archness and cross-interferences melted and the intimacy and poignancy of the period claustrophobia enveloped me; I felt their feelings and their recollections registered with my history, stored and sorted but not far from sight.'

Gradually, other reviews began to surface including Rupert Smith in *The Pink Paper*. However, when I invited Jack Babuscio, the film critic for *Gay Times*, to see *Where There Was Silence* at our graduation degree show at the British Academy of Film and Television Arts in Piccadilly, he declined. I then sent him a copy of the video and asked him if he would consider reviewing it in the magazine. He declined, stating that he did not review videos or student productions. So I telephoned him at the *Gay Times* office. He took the call and I angrily told him that he was being elitist by ignoring students and that he was wrong to discriminate against the work of lesbians and gays who make videos. Jack accepted the criticisms, apologised, and in the March 1989 issue he published a favourable review. Another battle had been won. Jack wrote: 'It's a work of no small accomplishment...ending with a reference to Section 28... *Where There Was Silence* constitutes a cogent, if somewhat pessimistic, argument on the perils of homophobia, as well as an insightful look at the representation of gays in cinema.'

There were a handful of festival screenings including the 1988 Expo of Student Film and Video, and Frameline's 1989 San Francisco International Lesbian and Gay Film Festival. The video also found a distributor, Albany Video, and seemed likely to take on a life of its own. However, there was one more slap in the face to come. I submitted it for inclusion in the 1988 London Lesbian and Gay Film Festival entitled *A Queer Feeling When I Look at You*. I took it for granted that it would be accepted. Not so. Mark Finch, the co-programmer with Penny Ashbrook, declined. I was devastated.

Mark had been so enthusiastic about the previous 'scratch' video

I had produced, so his refusal to include the new production in the festival didn't make sense to me. He never offered an explanation, which left me feeling more distraught and disillusioned. I realised that I was not going to find any gay solidarity with Mark and that I had to put this disappointment down to 'life'. Sometimes you win, sometimes you lose. Later, on seeing what had been included in the festival, salt was added to the wound. There was a perfect showcase for *Where There Was Silence* in a screening called *Clause for Thought: New British Shorts.* Advertised as 'wildly different British shorts assembled at the advent of Section 28', my modest video would have slotted perfectly into this, alongside Ken Butler's *Before the Act*, Richard Kwietniowski's *Ballad of Reading Gaol*, Stuart Marshall's *Pedagogue*, and Steve Harvey's teasing trailer for *Homo Promo.* 'Filmmakers will be present' said the programme note. I was present, but not as a filmmaker. I had to swallow my pride and attend as a member of the press.

After graduating from the LCP, I didn't have time to mull over re-entering the job market. I had to start applying for jobs straight away. Thankfully, I didn't have to wait long for an opportunity. Of course I had to request references and one of them was provided by Mike Stanhope, LCP's Senior Lecturer in Film Studies. He said, in a reference dated October 6, 1988:

> 'Stephen performed consistently well on the course both in his academic work and in film and video production. In particular his written work, which I supervised, was distinguished by a highly developed ability to research complex material and to present it with lucidity and sophistication. A final-year thesis on the films of James Whale was among the most successful and accomplished pieces of undergraduate work I have read. Stephen's commitment to and knowledge of cinema, especially the popular cinemas of Britain and the USA, is clear, and manifests itself throughout his work in an exemplary combination of passion with rigour and intelligence.'

Oh, if only Mike had told me this during the three years I spent at the LCP! It would have made such a difference to my low self-confidence and feeling of isolation. Still, better late than never.

Chapter 9

Gay Times

I thoroughly enjoyed the perks of being a freelance film critic. Not uncommon were trips to press screenings in a small, cosy viewing theatre on Wardour Street, in Soho, or to a big plush cinema, usually on a Sunday morning, such as the Odeon Leicester Square. I remember going to a viewing theatre to see Whoopi Goldberg's second movie, a crazy, zany comedy called *Jumpin' Jack Flash*. At the screening I recognised the legendary Dilys Powell sitting nearby. She was known as the doyenne of British film critics and was in her 80s then. Ms Powell sat through the film with a bunch of bananas on her lap. I couldn't wait to read her review of Whoopi's fun-packed comedy because I noticed that she slept through most of it. At the time, she was the film critic for *Punch*. One of my favourite movie books is *The Golden Screen*, edited by George Perry and published in 1989. It is a collection of Ms Powell's film reviews from 1939 to 1988. Fifty glorious years of captivating and perceptive film criticism written in a language I could understand and relate to.

Then there was *A Month in the Country* starring Colin Firth and Kenneth Branagh, beautifully shot in rural Yorkshire. It was set just after the First World War and focused on two war veterans trying to come to terms with the horrors of the trenches. I gave it a positive review in a gay newspaper because I appreciated the depiction of Branagh's character as gay, court-martialled, imprisoned, and thrown out of the Army. It is not the main focus of the story, but Branagh created a sympathetic character who in peacetime, despite being gay, is the equal of the film's main character, Birkin, played by Colin Firth. In the film, the two men are emotionally damaged by the war and seek the peace and quiet of the countryside. The day after the review was published I unexpectedly came face to face with Kenneth Branagh in a newspaper shop near my home. How's that for serendipity? I spluttered a 'hello' and he gave me a surprised look. I told him that I had just seen his new film *A Month in the Country* and given him a glowing review in a gay newspaper. I think it was the mention of the word 'gay' that scared him off because his feet didn't touch the ground as he fled from the shop, clutching his copy of *The Guardian* (it must have been *The Guardian* because the shop didn't stock *The Times*). I appreciate that I probably just caught him off guard but have often wondered that if I hadn't mentioned the word 'gay' Mr Branagh might have engaged in conversation with me. I continued reviewing films for the Black newspapers but in 1987, I had a bad experience when the *Caribbean Times* asked me to attend a press screening of Richard Attenborough's anti-apartheid epic *Cry Freedom.* It starred Denzel Washington as the South African activist Steve Biko who was brutalised and murdered by South African security guards in 1977. A top PR company handled the publicity and I called them to request a reservation for the press screening at the Odeon Leicester Square. To my surprise, the request was denied. The press officer informed me that *Caribbean Times* wasn't on their approved press list, and that she hadn't heard of it anyway. I suspected that she had thought I had created the newspaper to get a freebie. I calmly explained to her that *Caribbean Times* was one of the few national weekly Black newspapers in Britain, but she still refused to give me a ticket. Then I threatened to take the matter further. I told her that I would ask the editor of *Caribbean Times* to run a cover story and make a complaint to Mr Attenborough. How would *that* look? There was silence, followed by 'Let me take your number and I'll call you back.' Within the hour the phone rang and a gentleman apologised for the 'misunderstanding', offering me two tickets for the press screening. All they were really interested in was ensuring that the likes of Dilys Powell, Derek Malcolm from *The Guardian*, and Barry Norman from BBC television's *Film 87* were attending and had nice, comfortable seats. They couldn't give a toss about *Caribbean Times*, one of Britain's top Black newspapers. At the screening I noticed that Ms Powell, Mr Malcolm, Mr Norman, and their peers all had the best seats in the cinema, reserved for them of course. I noticed that there were no Black film critics sitting with them.

I had no training to be a film critic, just the experience of doing it. I had been contributing to the Black press for several years but in 1988, the year I graduated, through the arts journalist Pas Paschali, I found an outlet in the queer press. Pas introduced me to *Square Peg*, a deliciously deviant magazine with a queer take on arts, culture, and politics. Apparently it was founded in Derek Jarman's flat – yes, *that* flat – on Charing Cross Road in 1983 and released quarterly until 1992. Self-described as a 'journal for contemporary perverts', Pas took me along to a *Square Peg* collective meeting. They readily accepted my proposal for an article about Black and Asian lesbian and gay representation in mainstream British cinema. I included films like *The L-Shaped Room, Girl Stroke Boy, My Beautiful Laundrette*, and *Mona Lisa*. It all went very well and the article looked great in the journal. However, the next proposal, interviews with several Black and queer filmmakers, led to a painful confrontation. The collective agreed for me to go ahead, which I did, but after submitting the copy they called me in for a meeting. It was like going into the lion's den. The members verbally tore me to shreds, all the while I hadn't even written anything negative about the filmmakers. I didn't gather much of the tirade's substance through their rage. All I could see and hear was a group of mostly white, middle-class queer artists mouthing abuse at me. I liked their magazine and I was thrilled it existed, because it was so different from other gay publications, but I quickly realised that I had nothing in common with any of them. No feeling of solidarity on either side. I ran out of the meeting and burst into tears. Pas ran after me to ask me if I was alright, but I just ignored him and never contacted him or the collective again. Bizarrely, they still published the interviews. *Square Peg* continued to be published quarterly until its dissolution in 1992, and despite my bad experience with them, I continued to read it.

Fortunately, *Gay Times* opened its doors to me. After graduating I sent Peter Burton, the magazine's arts editor, a proposal for a feature which he readily accepted and published in the December 1988 issue. This was *James Whale – Dangerously Indiscreet in Hollywood* and I based it on my college thesis. My debut feature for *Gay Times* looked good in the magazine alongside articles about the artist David Hockney, Hollywood's greatest tap dancer, Ann Miller, the lesbian painter Gluck, and the movie director John Waters. In the same issue my review of a new coffee table book about Josephine Baker was also included. For me, this was a marvellous breakthrough, and I hoped it would bring more opportunities with *Gay Times.*

And it did. Throughout 1989, I reviewed a new book about Judy Garland and the making of her 1954 movie *A Star is Born* and a biography of Cary Grant. I also interviewed the British film actress Sylvia Syms who had co-starred with Dirk Bogarde in *Victim*; the director Colin Gregg and producer Tommaso Jandelli about their film *We Think the World of You* based on J. R. Ackerly's novel; and the jazz singer Adelaide Hall. Then, on January 12, 1990 I had a telephone call from Peter Burton. He informed me that Jack Babuscio had died and he wanted to know if I was interested in taking over as the film critic for *Gay Times.* I was saddened by Jack's death, age 52, from an AIDS-related illness, but I wanted the job. I said yes. I didn't find out until later that Jack had died the day before Peter called me. I was shocked. Peter didn't waste any time contacting me, but I suppose the show had to go on. Jack's final column was published in the February 1990 issue together with an obituary by Peter who described him as 'perhaps the most highly-regarded critic of film viewed from a gay perspective – not least because he had written on the subject with such consistent verve and intelligence over an extended period of time... Without doubt, Jack's intelligent and perceptive writing about film for both *Gay News* and *Gay Times* was an enduring contribution to gay cultural history. He was an ideal contributor – presenting clean copy which rarely needed correction and which always arrived on time.'

I didn't have time to worry about taking over Jack's film column and meeting his high standards, I just had to get on with it. I now had a monthly deadline to meet and we didn't have email in 1990. I used an Amstrad word processor and the copy I printed out had to be photocopied and mailed to Peter (who lived in Brighton) with press stills. It was a tall order, turning this around every month (plus I had a full-time job), but I maintained. My first column, published in March 1990, included reviews of *La Casa de Bernarda Alba* (*The House of Bernarda Alba*), *Steel Magnolias, Glory* (for which Denzel Washington won a Best Supporting Actor Oscar), and a retrospective at the National Film Theatre called *Blue Angels and Violet Nights: Sexuality in Weimar Germany*. For the April issue, I reviewed Steven Spielberg's *Always*, Oliver Stone's *Born on the Fourth of July, Driving Miss Daisy, The Krays*, and the documentary *James Baldwin: The Price of the Ticket*. I had fun putting these together and was thrilled when John Marshall, the editor of *Gay Times*, wrote to me: 'Congratulations on your first two film columns for *Gay Times*. They're wonderfully lively, articulate, informative, and intelligent. More of the same, please, in future.' I was proud to be associated with a popular gay magazine, and welcomed the opportunity to develop as a writer. In addition to the monthly film column, Peter also commissioned me to write features and book reviews.

So far, so good. However, very often, when I requested a press ticket from a film publicist, he or she would say: 'But it's not a gay film.' I would then attempt to explain that gay men go to the cinema to see anything and everything, not just the latest film by a gay director like Rainer Werner Fassbinder or Derek Jarman. Some gay men want escapism too. So yes, I want to review mainstream blockbusters like *Terminator 2* or the reissue of Walt Disney's *Cinderella.* Most of the time my explanation fell on deaf ears. Press screenings would be mysteriously 'full' when I told them what magazine I wrote for. If I did review a film positively I never saw any quotations from my *Gay Times* reviews included on film posters and adverts. I remember when Kevin Costner's Western epic *Dances With Wolves* was released. I sent an advance copy of my review to the publicist and asked him if he would consider quoting me and *Gay Times* on the posters and adverts: 'a graceful, poetic film…a remarkable achievement for first-time director Costner', but it didn't happen. The only occasions it did happen was for three gay films: Ron Peck's *Strip Jack Naked* (*Nighthawks 2*), Derek Jarman's *Edward II*, and Heiner Carow's *Coming Out.*

When I took on the job of film critic for *Gay Times*, I knew I was going to become marginalised. I was never invited to speak on BBC Radio 4 or acknowledged in the mainstream as a film critic. I was not a closeted gay film critic on a broadsheet or homophobic tabloid as I discovered some were.

A year passed and I learned that Derek Jarman was releasing a new film called *The Garden.* I had always felt ambivalent about Derek's films and I decided to use *The Garden* as a reason for writing a critical piece about them. This was something that, as far as I was aware, no gay film critic had done. Someone had to put their head into the lion's cage, and I wanted to be that person, but first I discussed it with Peter. His response was simply to do it. However, I was experiencing feelings of guilt. I questioned whether I should be critiquing a gay film director in print. Derek already had negative criticism and detractors. I drew an analogy that I thought would be helpful. Should a Black film critic critique Spike Lee's work? The answer, of course, is 'yes', because I had to be honest with myself and the readers of my column.

When it was published in the January 1991 issue, an image from *The Garden* was featured on the cover of the magazine. I said:

> 'I have always found Jarman's films problematic. It has always been an uphill struggle to understand and appreciate what is happening in them. I haven't liked them very much. Coming to terms with being gay was hard enough, but coming to terms with Jarman's films is another matter entirely! So, I was pleased (and relieved) when he asked us, the audience, at the press screening of his latest film *The Garden*, to "tell me what you read. Your feelings are the right ones". I understood this to be the invitation I have been waiting for to write honestly about his films, and I thank him for giving me permission to say, at long last, how I, as a gay spectator, truly feel about his films.'

I went on to raise concerns about Derek's presentation of gay sex, his focus on women at the expense of gay characters (i.e. Tilda Swinton as a sort of 'Earth Mother' in some of his films), and his view of Britain under Thatcher's government in *The Last of England* which I found patronising: the vision of a privileged, middle-class aesthete who doesn't have a clue about the inhabitants of what he calls the 'urban landscape'. I said I didn't like *The Garden* either. However, I did admit that I admired both *The Tempest* and *War Requiem.*

In retrospect, I went too far. I wasn't equipped to write a critical piece about Derek's films. I blundered in parts due to my inexperience of the gay scene and the world of queer artists, but when I read it now, I can see where I was coming from and what I was trying to say. At the time, lesbian and gay friends were divided about my appraisal. Some agreed with my comments, others didn't, but I hoped that a conversation had opened up. The most interesting response came from Simon

Watney, an art historian and AIDS activist. In a very long letter which was forwarded to me by *Gay Times*, he attacked me for being a 'puritanical Leftist cultural theorist', but I didn't know what that meant. I just thought I was being honest. Simon said:

> 'Bourne's inability to understand contemporary gay culture is however most obvious in his slick dismissal of the "Think Pink" sequence from *The Garden* as "a silly musical diversion". He seems completely unable to see that by tying together the utopian associations of the Hollywood musical with footage from a Gay Pride march, Jarman constructs one of the most forceful, poetic, and politically charged images in the history of gay cinema. *The Garden*, like all Jarman's films, is complex, quirky, joyful, tragic, and imaginatively true to the dark times in which we live.'

As for Derek, he didn't contact me, and I didn't expect him to. Six years after he died in 1994 I found out what he thought when extracts from his journals were published. In *Smiling in Slow Motion – The Journals of Derek Jarman 1991–1994*, I read the following: 'The concept of positive images was born out of gay liberation in the 1970s; *Gay Times* is of that time and Brighton-based. I don't know how one should describe Brighton, perhaps Façade Amnesia, the town for gay people. There are no queers there, it is often violent, has a huge sex-for-money scene – as there is no other employment. *Gay Times* has been gunning for me – they are theatrical. There was a disgraceful review of my films by their positive image "film critic" Steven [sic] Bourne. Positive images are an illusion, like commercials – they are not the stuff of art.'

Misspelling of my name aside, my review had entered Derek's consciousness and though it wasn't my proudest writing, there were the seedlings of workable critique. I took it in stride. I now understand where Derek was coming from. Looking back, I realise more than ever that we didn't belong to a 'gay community'. The solidarity present existed in pockets. If there had been a common feeling amongst us, if Mark Finch at the British Film Institute had embraced my video and included it in the Lesbian and Gay Film Festival, if the *Square Peg* collective had been friendly towards me, then I might have learned more and been more objective in my critique of Derek's films. But this did not happen, and so I had my limitations as a film critic. I know that. As for Derek, we did meet one more time when he was the subject of a Channel 4 documentary. I attended the press launch and as soon as he recognised me, he walked over and gave me a hug with a cheery 'Hello, Stephen.' We never spoke about *Gay Times*, but I sensed that he truly understood what I was trying to say in the piece, however clumsily. I was simply making waves, just as he did. To Derek's credit, I enjoyed his film version of Christopher Marlowe's *Edward II* and named it as my Best Film of 1991.

I continued writing for *Gay Times* until 1992. Highlights included interviewing several diverse gay film directors including Richard Kwietniowski (*Flames of Passion*), Norman Rene (*Longtime Companion*), Ron Peck (*Strip Jack Naked*), and Isaac Julien *(Young Soul Rebels)* and Terence Davies about Dirk Bogarde. Also in 1991 I named Margi Clarke Best Actress for *Blonde Fist*, written and directed by her brother Frank Clarke. I had thoroughly enjoyed the two films he had written: *Letter to Brezhnev* and *The Fruit Machine* (which I loved). As far as I was concerned, here was a gay film-maker who was able to put honest portrayals of the working-class on the big screen.

One day I had a phone call. 'Hello, love', said a voice with a Liverpool accent. 'It's Margi here. *Gay Times* gave me your number. I hope you don't mind. I want to thank you for naming me your Best Actress. I'm made up. Frank wants to say something too.' Margi put her brother on the phone: 'Hello, kid. Thank you for supporting my film. It means a lot.' What a lovely surprise it was. I was over the moon. I felt like a queen, as they say in Liverpool. I didn't waste any time sending them the cover of *City Limits* with Margi's photo on the cover and a black and white photo portrait of Frank. They signed them and they now have pride of place in my autographed photos album alongside Butterfly McQueen, Evelyn Laye, Barbara Windsor, Jean Alexander (aka Hilda Ogden), June Brown (aka Dot Cotton), Betty Driver, Lena Horne, Cleo Laine, Eartha Kitt, Sir John Mills, Hayley Mills, Sylvia Syms, Lorraine Kelly, June Whitfield, Peggy Ashcroft, Kenny Lynch, Petula Clark, Lily Savage (aka Paul O'Grady), and Larry Grayson.

A split with *Gay Times* occurred in 1992. Peter Burton had asked me to review *The Ballad of the Sad Café*, starring Vanessa Redgrave. I wasn't impressed by her performance in the slightest. Come to find out, Vanessa was Peter's favourite actress. This was the beginning of a run of creative disagreements I was to have with Peter. After this review, he asked me to review *The Naked Lunch*, based on the novel by William Burroughs. I hated the film and did myself no favours by telling this to Peter. The end came when I planned to review the Merchant/Ivory film version of E. M. Forster's novel *Howard's End.* Peter insisted that I read the novel before I reviewed the film but I refused because I didn't have time, even though I liked the film very much. That was that. My final column was published in June 1992. I was cast adrift from *Gay Times.* I wouldn't have minded if I could have continued contributing to the magazine as a feature writer and book reviewer, but Peter wouldn't speak to me. At first, I was deeply hurt by the rejection and I didn't speak about it to anyone. Then I became philosophical and told myself that all good things have to come to an end. I decided to move on.

So after leaving *Gay Times*, I started reviewing films for *Jazz Express* on a freelance basis. I wasn't expected to restrict myself to films of jazz interest; I could write about anything.I wrote a regular film column for several years until it ceased publication. I then approached *Sight and Sound*, a British Film Institute publication. I hoped to join their roster of film critics. In 1997, a new editor called Nick James had taken over and he seemed approachable so I wrote to him. When he called me he said that I would have to write a 'dummy' review of a contemporary film of my choice. I was taken aback. 'But I have more than ten years' experience of writing film reviews, some for Black journals, others for gay publications including two and a half years at *Gay Times*. Can't I send you examples of those?' He laughed and said no, that was not the way to approach a film magazine editor. I would have to write a dummy review for him before he would consider me. I felt like telling him to feck off but instead I agreed to do as I was told. However, after ending the call, I didn't take it any further. In fact, I have never reviewed a film since. I had reached a point of being tired of having to prove myself. It wasn't arrogance. I just felt that it was time to move on and try my hand at other things, and opportunities did come my way.

Chapter 10

The Divas

I have always been drawn to singers of pop songs because I value their storytelling. When Ella Fitzgerald sings something by Cole Porter or Rodgers and Hart, it is to be savoured. In addition to Ella in the 1970s, I was drawn to Dionne Warwick, Roberta Flack, Gladys Knight, Syreeta, Donna Summer, and Ethel Waters, my favourite of all, who I'd been listening to since I was ten years old. Ethel touches my soul. She was an actress on the mic who put drama, beyond whatever her lyrics proclaimed, into her songs. To me, she was genius. For evidence of this, listen to her singing 'Stormy Weather'. She inhabits a character on this song originally written by Ted Koehler and Harold Arlen, and acts out all of its drama for her audience, notably at New York's Cotton Club. This is what draws me to Ethel. So it's no wonder the gospel singer Mahalia Jackson said that without Ethel there wouldn't have been a Billie Holiday, Lena Horne, Sarah Vaughan, Ella Fitzgerald, and Mahalia herself. They all acknowledged Ethel as their main influence because she came before them.

In 1958, Frank Sinatra acknowledged that while growing up he had paid close attention to African-American jazz musicians such as Louis Armstrong and Duke Ellington and singers such as Ethel: 'When I was a youngster struggling to find myself, I heard a lot of Ethel Waters, whose feeling for the blues and great warmth touched me deep down. I shall never forget her.' Sinatra did not forget Ethel or the debt he owed her. In 1976, on the occasion of her 80th birthday, he sent her a letter of congratulations and signed it affectionately, 'Francis Albert'.

I was introduced to Ethel when one of her old films was shown on television in 1968. The BBC showed her 1943 MGM film musical *Cabin in the Sky* in which she co-starred with Lena Horne. I later discovered that both Ethel and Lena had published autobiographies which were easy to access through interlibrary loans. Ethel's *His Eye Is on the Sparrow* (1951) and Lena's *Lena* (1966) were revelations to me because I had no knowledge of the personal and professional struggles of the two stars. Then, in 1973, Donald Bogle's groundbreaking study of Black actors in Hollywood movies was published, *Toms, Coons, Mulattoes, Mammies and Bucks*, which is an insightful reassessment of Black Hollywood. Almost single-handedly, Bogle made it possible for the wider public to appreciate the talents of Hattie McDaniel, Butterfly McQueen, Ethel, Lena, and many others. I still have the paperback of Bogle's book, which I purchased as a teenager. It has been well read, evidenced by the frayed edges, and to this day, is one of my favourite books. I owe a debt of gratitude to Mr Bogle for opening a door, and showing me new ways of looking at Black cinema.

After reading Bogle's book, I read every book I could find on Black Hollywood. A lot of American books were published on the subject in the 1970s, and I managed to find all of them in London at specialist bookshops dotted around, like the Cinema Bookshop off Tottenham Court Road. Ed Mapp's *Blacks in American Films – Today and Yesterday* (1971) was a pillar of this new surge in Black Hollywood publications. In the 1990s, Ed and I struck up a correspondence. On his annual visits to London, we'd meet up for lunch and a catch-up. On the other hand, sadly, Mr Bogle never replied to my letters and, when they were invented, emails. Many times I tried to make contact with him, though all in vain. Throughout my life I have reached out to people I admire because I believe that we have something in common, something to share. I believe this can only be a good, positive thing. The reality is that this good thing rarely materializes, but when it has happened, such as my friendship with Ed Mapp, it has proved to be fruitful and enlightening.

While my Ethel fandom deepened with her autobiography there were yet other stars who competed for my praise and attention. In 1973, Diana Ross's first film, *Lady Sings the Blues*, was released in Britain. I had known about Diana the pop star since early childhood when I listened to her singing such Motown hits as 'Baby Love' with the Supremes. She had to reintroduce herself to me as an actress. In her breakthrough film as the jazz singer Billie Holiday, Diana was elevated to movie stardom on an international scale, the first Black woman to achieve this since Dorothy Dandridge had starred in *Carmen Jones* in 1954. I enjoyed reading about Diana's movie debut and collected all the press clippings I could find in newspapers and magazines. I bought the soundtrack album and more importantly, the paperback reissue of Billie Holiday's autobiography. It had a photo of Diana as Billie on the cover, to tie in with and help promote the release of the movie. Diana's portrayal of Billie reinforced what I knew about the painful challenges Black women faced in show business.

Based on her absence from jazz history books and magazines, you would've thought that Ethel had no clout in this country. Billie and Ella soaked up all the attention, because the powers that be – the jazz historians – had been selective and, in my view, narrow-minded. In the 1970s, I did happen upon a marvellous record shop called 58 Dean Street Records, located in Soho, and it was there I discovered imports of American albums by Ethel. The shop was small, cramped, and crammed with records. Customers couldn't avoid bumping into each other while searching for their favourite singers, none of whom were my beloved Ethel apparently whose notoriety didn't change with her passing in 1977.

For years, Ella, Lena, and Eartha Kitt, as well as our own Shirley Bassey and Cleo Laine, were popular with British audiences, and they made many concert and television appearances here. In the 1970s, Ella, Lena, and Eartha were still visiting Britain and working here. I searched for and collected everything I could find about them in newspapers and magazines. I also saw them on television, usually in variety shows like Eartha in *The Good Old Days*, and Lena in *Song by Song*.

As a birthday treat in 1976, my sister took me to see Diana Ross in concert at the Victoria Palace. I couldn't afford to see Lena on stage until 1980, when she made a memorable appearance at the London Palladium. It was a trial run for her acclaimed one-woman show *The Lady and Her Music*, which opened on Broadway the following year and then came to London's Adelphi Theatre in 1984. It received rave reviews and had sell-out performances, of which I attended three.

After one of the shows I attended, on August 8, 1984 I queued at the stage door with a small group of fans from various walks of life in the hope of seeing Lena up close and asking for her autograph. Despite putting on one of the best shows I'd ever seen, she patiently and graciously spoke to everyone individually and happily signed autographs. My appreciation for her was reaffirmed by the respect she showed her fans. I treasured the few moments I had with her. Thinking back to the first time I had seen her on television in *Cabin in the Sky* at the age of 10, I found myself blurting out 'Miss Horne, I have been a fan of yours for 16 years.' She looked at me, smiled, and drawled, 'But you're just a baby!' I was 26 but looked 16!

Three years later, on May 27, 1987 I met and interviewed Lena's daughter Gail Lumet Buckley when she visited London to promote her book *The Hornes – An American Family*. We met at the hotel where she was staying and it was an enjoyable experience. Afterwards Gail told me she was impressed with my knowledge of her mother's career, especially her films, and relieved that I hadn't asked anything about Lena's private life, 'as interviewers always do'. I had shown respect, the same way Lena had to me all those years ago, and this must have meant something to Gail. Though we never saw each other again, we corresponded for a number of years and she kindly and generously made it possible for me to receive a signed photograph of Lena in MGM's *Till the Clouds Roll By* (1946).

On December 21, 1988 I came face to face with the formidable Eartha Kitt when she was appearing in the London version of Stephen Sondheim's musical *Follies*. I arranged to interview her about her film career for the magazine *Films and Filming* but my friend Sonia, who had already interviewed her, warned me about what to expect. 'She's very eccentric', Sonia said. 'She has had a wooden cage built in her dressing room and she keeps white doves in it. She will expect you to take her a potted rubber plant.' I had to wait ages for her agent to arrange an interview, but something terrible happened to me a few days before it was scheduled to take place. I was assaulted by a tenant in my block of flats. I had witnessed an altercation between him and one of my neighbours which resulted in her being hospitalised. Following his arrest, he was taken to court and bailed. I appeared as a witness and gave evidence against him. Consequently, he planned for his revenge by finding me and punching me in the face. I was knocked unconscious. A neighbour found me lying on the ground in the lift lobby area and called the police and an ambulance. Needless to say, he was arrested again and remained in custody while he waited for the trial, where he was found guilty of the two assaults and sentenced. However, not even a bruised face could keep me from my appointment with Ms Kitt. So when I arrived at the Shaftesbury Theatre to interview her, I was purple as you could imagine with a bruised face.

Eartha took one look at me and showed concern. After taking the potted rubber plant from me, she thanked me and then asked me what had happened to my face. I explained and added that I didn't want to miss the chance to meet her and talk to her about her film career. She was very open and gave me lots of insights about her admittedly few film appearances. At the end of our meeting she insisted that I come and see her in her forthcoming one-woman show which would follow *Follies*. She told me to contact her agent. Later on, when I called her agent, Eartha had indeed reserved two tickets for me, but afterwards I decided not to go backstage and see her because I knew there would be dozens of fans queueing at the stage door.

Growing up in London, I was aware that we had two expatriate divas living here, and I befriended both of them: Elisabeth Welch and the jazz innovator Adelaide Hall. In the 1920s Elisabeth and Adelaide had been together in the casts of two Black Broadway shows: *Runnin' Wild* and *Blackbirds of 1928*. The latter brought them to Paris and the famous Moulin Rouge in 1929. They made London their home in the 1930s. I saw Adelaide in concert for the first time in 1984 when she took part in a jazz festival. In 1985, *The Voice* asked me to interview her. After a period in the wilderness, the release of Francis Ford Coppola's film *The Cotton Club* unexpectedly reinvigorated Adelaide's career. The publicists for Coppola's film had discovered that Adelaide had been a star of the original Cotton Club in New York, and she was invited to the film's British premiere. After this, her phone never stopped ringing.

When I was given her phone number, I called to arrange our interview. She asked me to meet her 'at the entrance to Harrods' in Knightsbridge, but I'd never been there. I wasn't aware it had 16 entrances. On my arrival, I panicked and ran around the building, hoping to see her. To my relief, I recognised her emerging from a taxi. When I introduced myself she smiled, took my arm, and led me to the cafeteria where I conducted the interview. She was a sweet, charming lady and I loved being in her orbit, especially when people recognised her and asked her for an autograph.

I stayed friends with Adelaide and saw her in concert many times. The liveliest was in 1988 at the intimate King's Head Theatre when she invited her friends Beryl Bryden and Barbara Windsor to join her onstage and sing 'Won't You Come Home, Bill Bailey?' Beryl, a larger-than-life jazz singer, happened to have her washboard with her, which she played with gusto. The three ladies raised the roof. It was an unforgettable experience. The following year I worked as a consultant on *Sophisticated Lady*, a Channel 4 television documentary about her life and career, but my efforts to find a publisher for a biography fell on deaf ears. One reputable publisher called me in for an interview and asked questions like 'Did her husband beat her up?' and 'Did she take drugs?' When I pulled a face and said no, I was shown the door. It was a horrible experience. However, in 2001, some years after she had passed away, I did manage to find support for a small publication for the centenary of her birth.

This coincided with my nomination of Adelaide for an English Heritage Blue Plaque. I had high hopes for this, but it was declined. Disappointment followed. Geoffrey Noble, the Blue Plaques Secretary, explained why in a letter dated April 25, 2002: 'I am very sorry to have to confirm that after taking the advice of our Blue Plaques Panel, English Heritage has decided not to erect a plaque to Adelaide Hall. Our Panel noted Miss Hall's long career as a performer and recording artiste: "Creole Love Call", for instance, remains a highlight of Duke Ellington's discography. The Panel concluded, however, that Miss Hall was insufficiently well-known today to justify a plaque.' Noble advised me to nominate her again after a period of ten years.

In 2003, in response to a query I had sent them, English Heritage confirmed that only one of their plaques had been erected for a Black woman: Mary Seacole. They also informed me that a nomination for the activist Claudia Jones, who was a founder member of the Notting Hill Carnival, had been rejected.

I waited patiently for ten years to pass and then nominated Adelaide for the second time. Once again, English Heritage rejected her, so I gave up. Then, in 2020, they contacted me and informed me that Adelaide was one of a number of names that the London Assembly had asked English Heritage to look at. Four years later, on July 9, 2024 I had the joy of being one of the guest speakers at the unveiling of Adelaide's Blue Plaque outside her former home in Collingham Road in Kensington.

I had also been successful with my nomination for Elisabeth Welch, who had passed away in 2003 at the age of 99. Her English Heritage Blue Plaque was unveiled by the playwright and critic Bonnie Greer in 2012 outside Elisabeth's former home in Ovington Court, Kensington. Bonnie remarked on Elisabeth, saying, 'It was a very rare art form that she practiced, the supper clubs, cabaret, and that's about being an actor, as well as being a great singer. For her, it was about freedom, and gives people like me, and many of us, permission to pursue our lives. She gives that to everybody.' Bonnie's perceptive words could be applied to many other Black divas, including Ethel Waters.

After several British publishers declined my proposal for a biography of Elisabeth Welch, an offer came from Anthony Slide, a film historian, to submit it to Scarecrow Press in America. They promptly commissioned it. *Elisabeth Welch – Soft Lights and Sweet Music* was published in 2005, which led to two further biographies for the same publisher: *Ethel Waters – Stormy Weather* (2007) and *Butterfly McQueen Remembered* (2008).

Chapter 11

Black and White in Colour

Some Black television celebrities have claimed that when they were growing up there were no Black people to be seen on British television. In his autobiography *Rising to the Surface* (2022), Lenny Henry describes the version of the world shown to him on TV growing up in the 60s. Instead of black and white, 'They should have called it white-and-white television. If a Black person did come on, viewers thought there was something wrong with the set...The only Black people you saw on television in the 1960s were the Black and White Minstrels.' However, while this may have been Lenny's perception, this was not the case. This misperception may stem from people overlooking representation on television versus cinema. Television's history was ignored for decades. At least until the 80s. And it was the British Film Institute in a joint venture with the BBC who attempted to change this. In 1989, the two organisations co-funded a groundbreaking research project which pieced together the history of Black people in British television from its beginnings in the 1930s. I was part of the research team.

Just before I graduated in the summer of 1988, I was encouraged by a lecturer at the LCP to send my research paper about Black representation in early British film and television to the BFI's Education Department. Shortly afterwards I was invited to give an internal seminar about the paper for some BFI staff. I gave the seminar at the National Film Theatre on October 6, 1988. Kobena Mercer, who was employed at the BFI as a Research Projects Officer, was one of the attendees. Little did I know that this was going to be an important turning point in my life. Two months later, on December 20, I was invited to the BFI to meet Kobena. Richard Paterson was also at the meeting, then-head of the BFI's TV and Projects Unit. It was at this meeting that they offered me a job as a Research Officer for three months starting on January 16, 1989. From the outset, they appreciated my knowledge and ability to do in-depth research. It probably didn't hurt that we came from similar worlds, Kobena, Richard, and I. Kobena was gay and Richard was in an interracial marriage. Although I felt a bit intimidated by Kobena (he was a high flying academic studying for his PhD), having just finished my non-university undergraduate degree (London College of Printing did not gain university status until 2003/2004 when it became part of the London Institute), and Richard, who was going to be my boss, they were very friendly and interested in working with me. I felt ready for the challenge.

They explained that my role was to assist in researching the history of Black people in British television, not film. Television, at least in the UK, has always been treated as the poor relative of film. I don't think this has ever changed, although some academic institutions have begun to offer courses in television studies. I walked out of our first meeting with a big smile on my face. It turned out that the seminar at the NFT had been an audition. Nothing had been mentioned at that time about a research project. I had left the LCP with a bank overdraft and a few months later I was offered a wonderful job with a decent salary. It was only for three months, but who could tell where it would lead.

On my first day at the BFI I was introduced to Therese Daniels, who I'd be working alongside, and the friendly staff of the TV and Projects Unit. They included Veronica Taylor, who organised the television seasons for the NFT and a member of the support staff, Yvonne Salmon.

There was no contact with the senior staff of the BFI. They worked on a different floor at the top of the building. However, shortly after my arrival, I came face to face with Sir Richard Attenborough, then-Chair of the BFI. He followed me into the lift on the ground floor. When I recognised him, I froze. He sensed this and in a warm, friendly voice he asked 'Hello, what do you do?' I mumbled a reply: 'I'm researching the history of Black people on British television.' He smiled and offered some positive words, before I exited at my floor.

On that first day at the BFI my thoughts went back to 1974 and the letter they had sent me following my request for work experience. The rejection letter was bad enough, but exacerbated by the fact that they couldn't possibly consider me without a university degree. With perseverance, hard work, and perhaps a bit of good fortune, in 1988, I found myself with a degree which had led to my dream job. As soon as I started, I made a conscious decision to enjoy every minute. I doubted I'd ever be given such an opportunity again. Little did I expect, once my three months were up, I'd be given a further opportunity to continue at the BFI for another two and a half years, first as a member of the research team and then as a contributor to the two-part television documentary based on our research. Throughout that time, we rediscovered an extraordinary hidden history. With proper funding and institutional support, I was part of the 'Race and Ethnicity' project (as it was originally called) that unearthed a Black British television history vastly different from what we expected.

I continued as I started, with an appetite to make this project as all-embracing and inclusive as my previous research. Before I arrived, the BFI had decided to limit the scope of the research to begin only in 1950. I asked why, because I knew there had been a Black presence from the opening day of the BBC's high-definition television service: November 2, 1936. This continued throughout the BBC's pre-war service (1936–1939), and as soon as the BBC was able to resume television after the war on June 7, 1946. I gave examples. The dance innovators Buck and Bubbles in a variety show on November 2, 1936 and the Trinidadian Edric Connor in *Music Makers* on June 22, 1946. I won the arguments, and we rightly started at the beginning: 1936.

The role of British television in popular culture – and the necessity of preserving its history – needed urgent recognition. By 1989, progress was underway. During the 80s, BFI's National Film Archive was renamed the National Film and Television Archive (NFTVA), and the NFT at South Bank began to include monthly television retrospectives. Despite the noise television was making, there was still little understanding and appreciation for the Black stories which were becoming more common. American television was a model for representation when diverse castings began to matter less during an inclusivity recession in Britain during the early 70s. The result of this was that there was a period of time where viewers began to look at America for Black history, whose story, while important, wasn't that of Black Britons. It was no coincidence this happened immediately after Enoch Powell made his racist 'Rivers of Blood' speech and the popularity of his fictional 'disciple', Alf Garnett, in BBC television's *Till Death Us Do Part*, was at its peak. So aside from popular music and entertainment programming, viewers could hardly be blamed for thinking that a Black presence on British television began unfavourably in 1972 with the launch of Thames's problematic sitcom *Love Thy Neighbour*.

The Race and Ethnicity project aimed through archival research to look at the involvement of Black people in British television, both on screen and behind the camera. When I joined the project I saw the work as a starting point, for there had been very little previous research on the subject. Certainly no one had looked at the pre-1970s history in any depth, and what little had been published tended to be inaccessible.

The research was divided into two: my colleague, Therese Daniels, documented factual programmes, while I focused on drama and entertainment (music, dance, etc.). Our tasks included compiling a database of television programmes from two listings magazines: *Radio*

Times (1936–1989) and *TV Times* (1955–1989). By scanning every page, Therese and I listed every programme we could find with Black on-screen and off-screen involvement. Using this information, we catalogued programmes from our television archives and conducted interviews with important on-screen and off-screen personnel.

Early examples included the Guyanese actor Robert Adams in two Eugene O'Neill plays *The Emperor Jones* (1938) and *All God's Chillun' Got Wings* (1946). Adams also played the Prince of Morocco in *The Merchant of Venice* (1947), the first time a Black actor had played a Shakespearean role on BBC television. The range and depth of programmes we found – especially from the 1950s and 1960s – was surprising. There were, it turned out, many more programmes featuring Black people in the early, formative years than we anticipated. Themes explored included decolonisation, the settlement of African and Caribbean people in postwar Britain, and mixed marriages. This doesn't mean there was no racism, because there was plenty, in fact, to go around. The BBC's *Black and White Minstrel Show* ran from 1958 to 1978 as an example. To counter this harm, though, there were more positive portrayals with Black actors, including Gordon Heath in *Deep Are the Roots* (1950) and *Othello* (1955); Eartha Kitt in *Mrs Patterson* (1956); Uriel Porter in *Dixon of Dock Green* ('The Black Noah') (1957); Cy Grant in *Home of the Brave* (1957); Bertice Reading in an excerpt from the Royal Court production of Carson McCullers's *The Member of the Wedding* (1957); Lloyd Reckord in Ted Willis's *Armchair Theatre: Hot Summer Night* (1959); Earl Cameron in *Drama '64: A Fear of Strangers* (1964) and Errol John in *Rainbow City* (1967). Prominence was given to many Black singers and entertainers too, from Winifred Atwell to Paul Robeson, but in most pre-1970s television programming, Black people were quite clearly spoken about and referred to rather than directly addressed.

Before the existence of videotape (from the late 1960s), British television programmes were transmitted live and could only be recorded if they were filmed on 35mm stock directly from the television screen.

This process was known as telerecording but, due to the high costs and technical problems, it was a format rarely used. Consequently, only a fraction of our early television output has survived.

Thanks to the funding and support we received, we were able to unearth many fascinating dramas and documentaries which redefined our understanding of British television history. For instance, there were two compelling BBC documentaries: Jack Gold's *West Indians* (1963) with a commentary by the Barbadian poet and writer George Lamming, and Philip Donnellan's poetic *The Colony* (1964), filmed on location in Birmingham's Black community, in neighbourhoods like Handsworth. When we met Donnellan we discovered a maverick who had spent years making documentaries for the BBC which gave a voice to real people who were usually excluded. Donnellan's *The Colony* was an hour-long programme in which members of Birmingham's Black community, nurses, teachers, bus conductors and railway signalmen; museum attendants and more, talked about how they felt to be Black and Brummie. This was further evidence that British television, in its formative years, had something to be proud of.

There was also *Freedom Road* (1964), an impressive documentary with a concert format in which an outstanding cast of Black singers performed songs of protest from the days of slavery to the civil rights movement. Highlights included Cleo Laine's 'Strange Fruit', Pearl Prescod's 'We Shall Overcome', and Madeleine Bell's 'What Did You Do in School Today? a duet with George Webb. Others in the cast included Cy Grant and Nadia Cattouse. *Freedom Road* was praised for its originality and won several international awards including the Golden Plaque at the Berlin Television Festival.

In drama, there was writer John Hopkins who wrote the hard-hitting and thought-provoking episode of *Z Cars* ('A Place of Safety') (1964) as well as *Fable*, his controversial and disturbing *Wednesday Play* (for the namesake series) from 1965, in which he reversed apartheid and located it in Britain. When we interviewed Hopkins for the project, he described

A Place of Safety as 'the best or the most completely realised episode of *Z Cars*' that he wrote. Regarding *Fable*, Hopkins said that Thomas Baptiste, one of the Black members of the cast, told him that it would not be understood, that people would say 'That's what happens if you make Blacks policemen and put them in control.' And Hopkins replied 'Oh no, that couldn't happen. Everyone will understand that it's an ironic comment.' After *Fable* was shown, Hopkins got a letter from a white viewer which said 'Boy, you showed them what would happen if *they* came to power.'

Another highlight was rediscovering the BBC's telerecording of *A Man from the Sun* which had been deposited in the NFTVA. This was a superb drama-documentary first shown in 1956. It was an early attempt to explore the lives of the 'Windrush Generation' in post-war Britain. It was transmitted live from a BBC studio with filmed inserts.

When I organised a private screening of *A Man from the Sun* at the BFI, I was thrilled when John Elliot, the creator, and several cast members, including Cy Grant, Nadia Cattouse, and Pauline Henriques attended. Elliot told us that he scripted and produced the drama because he was genuinely concerned about the attitudes of the British towards Caribbean settlers, aware that some were welcoming, but others were hostile. Elliot felt the need to explore 'the clash between the mythical Britain and actual grotty real Britain, which West Indians would face when they got here.' Pauline said that, as a Black actress, it was a landmark docudrama for her: 'It was about working-class Black people, and we were portrayed as real people, not as stereotypes. It gave a voice to Black people who, unlike myself, had recently arrived in Britain. It was a very good, very lively play...It was a play for the day, right for the time, and I felt it was a very exciting thing for the BBC to do.'

Finding Pauline was one of my achievements. I had listed some of her appearances in early BBC television plays, starting with *All God's Chillun' Got Wings* (1946) and ending with *A Man from the Sun.* Then all traces of her vanished. When I mentioned her name to various Black actors I interviewed, they said they had never heard of her. And then

I had a breakthrough. Pearl Connor told me that Pauline had left the acting profession in the 1960s to do social work. She worked for years for the Brook Advisory Service, supporting unmarried mothers who wanted to keep their babies. It turned out that the Brook Advisory Service was based on Tottenham Court Road, right opposite Stephen Street where the BFI was located. So I went in there and asked them if they knew Pauline Henriques. The staff were baffled until I mentioned that she was Black at which point their confusion lessened. They said she had worked for them, but they knew her as Pauline Benjamin (her married name at the time). They agreed to forward a letter to her and within a week I made contact with and visited Pauline, now in retirement, at her home in Brighton. She told me she was delighted that someone had found out about her acting career, which she had abandoned in 1960, and was a willing and insightful interviewee. We remained friends until she passed away in 1998.

One of the joys of the project was that Therese and I were given unlimited access to all of the television archives, not just the NFTVA and BBC, but all the ITV archives. They were treasure troves and, with the willing support of the archivists, and with hard work and a little bit of luck (because the archives were still in the process of being catalogued), we found some real gems. I shall never forget the day I was digging around in the BBC's archive when I came across a rusty old can of film. Little did I know that I was about to rediscover a forgotten experimental telerecording from 1947. It is probably the BBC's earliest known recording of a live performance by an entertainer. When I put the 35mm film on a steenbeck, I was thrilled to discover my friend Adelaide Hall singing and dancing in a show called *Variety in Sepia.* This was transmitted live from the BBC's studio at Radiolympia in Earl's Court. A mutual friend arranged a dinner at his home for Adelaide and myself where we surprised her with the footage which had been transferred to a videotape. Adelaide hadn't seen it and was completely unaware of its existence. She was delighted.

Another proud moment for me was rediscovering a very important archive holding called *The Big Pride.* In the 1950s, the Guyanese writer Jan Carew and his Jamaican wife, Sylvia Wynter, were part of the generation of talented African and Caribbean poets, novelists and playwrights who lived and worked here. In 1961, they were commissioned to adapt their BBC radio drama *The University of Hunger* for ITV's *Drama '61* series. It was based on events that had actually happened in Guyana in 1958: three men had broken out of prison and tried to escape, not only from their past, but the harsh reality of their lives. However, the recording that was made of this compelling drama, retitled *The Big Pride* for television, remained forgotten until I persuaded the NFTVA to acquire the damaged negative, restore it, and make a new viewing copy. I was aware of its historical importance because very few examples of the early plays of African and Caribbean writers have survived in our television archives. Among those which will never be seen again are three by the Trinidadian Errol John: *Moon on a Rainbow Shawl* (ITV, 1960), which was adapted from his acclaimed stage drama produced at the Royal Court two years earlier, *The Dawn* (BBC, 1963) and *The Wednesday Play* ('The Exiles') (BBC1, 1969). If I hadn't succeeded in persuading the NFTVA to acquire and restore *The Big Pride*, an important work by two major Caribbean writers would have been lost forever.

As soon as the NFTVA had restored *The Big Pride*, I organised a public screening at the NFT in 1997. 36 years after its first transmission, this hour-long television play was shown again. The cinema was packed and included the likes of Herbert Wise, the producer of *The Big Pride*, and several cast members including Nadia Cattouse and Tommy Eytle. Just ten minutes before I was about to introduce the screening, Jan Carew arrived from America and to the delight and surprise of the audience I was able to introduce him to them as the co-writer of the play. Afterwards, in a question-and-answer session, the Trinidadian Pearl Connor complimented me on finding this play. She also informed everyone that it was an example of what good things Black British actors were capable of achieving in 1961 with agents like herself who were willing to fight for them to get decent parts.

Eventually the whole project evolved into a two-part television documentary called *Black and White in Colour.* At first I felt as if I had been thrown into the deep end. However, the work, though demanding, was very exciting and took on a whole new dimension, especially when Isaac Julien was assigned the role of director.

I admired Isaac's work: *The Passion of Remembrance* (1986), made with the Sankofa Film and Video Collective, and the beautiful *Looking for Langston* (1989). Isaac was an openly gay artist and filmmaker who identified with the queer arts movement. He had recently completed *Young Soul Rebels,* his first feature for the BFI, and despite not directly having TV credentials, this put him in a strong position to be assigned the role of director for *Black and White in Colour.* At a pre-production meeting Isaac admitted he wasn't a great fan of television and had little knowledge of the contribution made by Black personnel. He quickly changed his mind when Therese and I began to show him some of the programmes we had found in the archives such as *A Man from the Sun* and *Fable.* He was particularly taken by *Z Cars* ('A Place of Safety') because he was unaware that BBC television could be so inventive and cutting edge in the 1960s. He was delighted that Elisabeth Welch, who he only knew from singing 'Stormy Weather' in Derek Jarman's film *The Tempest,* had had a long and eventful television career that had begun in the 1930s. Isaac grew fond of two actor friends I recommended for the documentary: Thomas 'Tommy' Baptiste and Cleo Sylvestre. He later cast Tommy and Cleo in his short film *The Attendant* (1993). When I asked Isaac if I could be an extra in *The Attendant* he agreed and offered me the role of one of the semi-naked, leather-thonged angels who materialise in the museum attendant's homoerotic fantasies. I'm not a prude, but I declined, much to the amusement of Isaac.

I liked Isaac but we were worlds apart. Or so we thought. I assumed that he came from an affluent, privileged middle-class background and he assumed the same about me until, one day, when we were alone in the office, we began a conversation and we realised we both came from similar working class backgrounds in two inner-city communities: Isaac from North London and myself from South London. However, we didn't really connect as gay men because we existed in two completely different subsets of this world. This was brought home to me when Isaac asked if I had been to Kinky Gerlinky, an influential nightclub in the West End that attracted, amongst others, queer people including Boy George. I made Isaac laugh when I told him I'd much rather spend the evening in front of the telly watching *Coronation Street* with a cup of tea and a custard cream.

Originally Therese and I had reservations about Isaac taking on the role of director for *Black and White in Colour.* We had suggested other Black directors who had more experience in television, such as Colin Prescod. As it turned out, Isaac brought a sharp sense of his own personal vision to the project. He also invited the director John Akomfrah to join us as a consultant and Professor Stuart Hall to narrate the programmes.

The recording of the interviews was intense and exhausting. 54 interviews were crammed into a two-week schedule in the summer of 1991. Isaac insisted on surrounding himself with as many Black crew members as possible. So he recruited Remi Adefarasin on camera (a few years later Remi was Oscar nominated for his cinematography on *Elizabeth* starring Cate Blanchett), Judi Lee-Headman on sound, Tammy Harewood on makeup, Karlene Page as a runner, amongst others.

The majority of the interviews were conducted by Therese, Isaac, and myself. The list of interviewees was impressive: Michael Abbensetts; Norman Beaton; Pearl Connor; Farrukh Dhondy (my former teacher); John Elliot; Brenda Emmanus; Paul Gilroy; Cy Grant; Pauline Henriques; Lenny Henry; Linton Kwesi Johnson; Kenny Lynch; Carmen Munroe; Horace Ove; Jim Pines; Colin Prescod; Lloyd Reckord; Rudolph Walker, and Elisabeth Welch. My favourite filming day was July 24, 1991 when I interviewed four women I had become very close to: Cleo Sylvestre, Pearl Connor, Pauline Henriques, and Elisabeth Welch. Not everyone made it into the documentaries, but the unedited recordings of the 54 interviews were deposited into the NFTVA's archives.

During post-production, when Isaac was editing the documentaries, his film *Young Soul Rebels* was released. Isaac invited me to the premiere along with many of his friends, family, and associates. I interviewed him for *Gay Times* and they put an image from the film on that month's cover. One day in the edit suite, Isaac was upset by a disparaging review by the outspoken but sometimes vicious critic Alexander Walker in the *Evening Standard*. Not long after Isaac read the review in the *Standard*, I bumped into Mr Walker at a press screening, and I told him he was very unkind to Isaac and unfair to his film. Mr Walker looked surprised, but I vanished before he could respond.

Before the *Black and White in Colour* documentaries were screened on television, I showcased the first programme in a season at the NFT in April 1992. I was wholly responsible for curating the first Black British television retrospective for *TV on BFI South Bank*. I contextualised the documentary by including dramas, documentaries, music programmes, not all of them seen in the documentary, and these covered the period 1936 to 1966. The 'sneak preview' of the first programme was followed by a panel discussion, chaired by Isaac, which included Pearl Connor, Carmen Munroe, and Thomas Baptiste.

To their credit, in June 1992, the BBC decided to showcase the two-part *Black and White in Colour* documentaries in a week-long season of some of the programmes we had featured. A positive outcome of the project was a collection of 28 interviews edited by Jim Pines and published in a BFI book called *Black and White in Colour – Black People in British Television Since 1936*.

In 1993, *Black and White in Colour* was nominated for the BFI's award for Best Archival Achievement. Therese and I had undertaken the bulk of the archival research, and yet neither of us were named on the nomination (that honour went to Isaac and Colin MacCabe). Neither were we informed about this nomination or invited to the award ceremony. I received a letter of apology from Colin MacCabe. I also received one from Wilf Stevenson, the BFI's Director: 'Although there is a high ticket demand for the evening, if such a request had been made on your behalf we would have endeavoured to provide you with an invitation'. Such is life, but I moved on and made up my mind to write a book based on the research I had undertaken.

Chapter 12

Remembering Aunt Esther

As Aunt Esther lay dying in hospital from a heart attack with me by her side, the doctor asked me who I was. I explained I was her nephew. The doctor looked at me, a young white man, and at Esther, an elderly Black woman, and asked, suspiciously, 'How?' Aunt Esther, in a great deal of pain, managed to squeeze my hand and say quietly, 'She doesn't believe we're related because you're a different colour.'

Although Esther was born and raised in a predominantly white community, she never had a problem with her identity as a Black or mixed heritage woman because her father was a proud and independent Guyanese gentleman. He instilled in his daughter what it meant to be Black and proud, and told her to remember she was as good as anyone else. Joseph always made a defiant stand against racism and retaliated against anyone who discriminated against him and his daughter. Joseph had come to London before the First World War and never returned to Guyana. As a working-class man on a low income, it simply wasn't possible. Esther never visited Guyana, although she corresponded with family members – including her grandmother – until the 1940s.

After Joseph was killed in a tragic accident during the London Blitz in 1941, Esther was adopted by my great-grandmother as a young adult. By the time I was born, she was well part of our family. Growing up, I spent many happy times listening to Aunt Esther telling me about her life. But by the late 1980s, I decided it would be a good idea to start recording these conversations on audio cassettes. During many conversations over the next few years I uncovered a wealth of information about her life as a working-class Black British woman spanning eight decades. In one of these interviews she recalled an encounter in the 1930s with another Black citizen of Fulham: the Jamaican activist Marcus Garvey. Such was the neighbourhood during wartime, full of community spirit. Esther was a friendly, outgoing woman who integrated easily into the culturally diverse London of post-war Britain. She was always helping someone in need, especially members of her community. She once told me that, in the 1960s, she made friends with a young nurse who had come here from Jamaica. One day the nurse burst into tears. Esther asked what had upset her and she replied, 'It's the matron at the hospital. She keeps giving me all the horrible jobs.' Esther then went to the hospital and found the matron. 'What happened next?' I asked. 'I wiped the floor with her', she replied. The nurse didn't report any more incidents.

Esther told me that she was horrified by the attacks on Black citizens during the Notting Hill race riots of 1958, not far from where she lived in Fulham. She, like so many in my family, was angered by Enoch Powell's inflammatory 'Rivers of Blood' speech in 1968 and the subsequent rise in support for the racist National Front. From Aunt Esther I learned about the importance of first-hand testimony in the recording and documenting of history. Little did I know that this information would form the basis of my first book, *Aunt Esther's Story.*

The book came into existence because, in 1991, I attended the launch of *West Indian Women at War – British Racism in World War II* at the Imperial War Museum. I spoke to the book's co-author, Colin Douglas, about Aunt Esther. It was a case of being in the right place at the right time, because Colin worked in Hammersmith and Fulham council's press office. He informed me about the work of Sav Kyriacou and the

Ethnic Communities Oral History Project (ECOHP), which was based in the borough. Thanks to Colin, I made contact with Sav, and I gave him the transcripts of some of the taped interviews. When the ECOHP commissioned the book, Sav explained to me that it would have to include Esther telling her own story in her own words, with some context from myself. With Sav's enthusiastic support, *Aunt Esther's Story* was published very quickly and launched at the Centre 181 Gallery in Hammersmith on October 14, 1991. At the launch, in addition to several family members including Mum and Dad, and Esther's cousin Lee and his daughter Brenda, there was Hammersmith and Fulham's Mayor, Joan Caruana.

Aunt Esther's Story was considered groundbreaking, because very few autobiographies and biographies had been written by or about Black women in British history. *The History of Mary Prince, a West Indian Slave*, the first autobiographical woman slave narrative, written by the Bermudian Mary Prince, had been published as early as 1831, but it was not reprinted until 1987. *Wonderful Adventures of Mary Seacole in Many Lands* by Mary Seacole, first published in 1857, had been reprinted with great success in 1984, and helped to raise the profile of the celebrated Jamaican doctress. An earlier ECOHP title, *The Motherland Calls – African Caribbean Experiences*, published in 1989, included interviews with several women who settled here after the Second World War.

In 1995, Sav wrote a chapter about the work of the ECOHP for *Literacy, Language and Community Publishing – Essays in Adult Education.* Regarding *Aunt Esther's Story* he said, 'I felt the story read beautifully and was funny and charming. I took it to my committee and they jumped at the chance to publish it as it was local, oral history and she had a diverse community background. I was surprised at how well it read and wondered how much Stephen was putting his own stamp on it. I asked him for copies of the tapes and was relieved when I listened to them as they were almost word for word. I noticed that more than anything it was the punctuation that made it read so easily. Stephen is a writer and I think this helped him in the transcription process.' In 1992, the ECOHP, Aunt Esther and I found ourselves shortlisted for the Arts Council's Raymond Williams Prize for Community Publishing. The feminist magazine *Spare Rib* put Aunt Esther on their cover. The reviews were fantastic. Kadija George in *Black Arts* said: 'The book is informative and important...the format makes it easy to read. It is ideal for schools to use as a tool for generating interest not only in another aspect of Black working-class life but working-class life in general.' *Aunt Esther's Story* and the recognition it brought was the genesis of my career as an author with a distinctive style that people appreciated. I sent a copy, along with a story I'd published about my upbringing in Peckham and Camberwell, to my friend David Robinson. He was the film critic for *The Times* and Charlie Chaplin's official biographer. He was most enthusiastic: 'I think they are absolutely terrific. You have achieved a style that is absolutely pure and direct; and succeeded in the almost impossible – eradicating any "literary" taint. I think you should do a lot of writing while you have this beautiful, incomparable style. Believe me – and always heed the words of an older man.'

Esther and I attended several events to promote the book. At one of them, a curious young Black woman approached us and asked her: 'Where do you come from?' Aunt Esther replied, 'Fulham'. The young woman looked confused: 'But what island did you come from before that?' Esther replied: 'England'. I intervened and explained to Esther that the young woman thought she was from the Caribbean. To the majority of young Black people, Black elders came here from Africa or the Caribbean. The concept of a Black elder being British-born was still not understood unless you came from the culturally diverse communities of London's East End, Cardiff, or Liverpool.

The success of the book gave my aunt a sense of pride at the end of her life. It was my hope that a documentary could be made about her. So I interviewed Aunt Esther on broadcast quality videotapes and submitted a proposal for a documentary to a number of television departments, as well as the British Film Institute's New Directors scheme. Unlike the positive reviews we had for the book, the rejection letters for the documentary were depressing. Laurence Rees, Editor from BBC's *Timewatch* wrote (March 29, 1993):

> 'I read your proposal with very great interest. However, I am afraid I don't think that *Aunt Esther's Story* is right for *Timewatch* at the minute. I think it unlikely that such a personal story would fit within the current mix of programmes which I am planning. I am sorry to be the bearer of such disappointing news but wish you the very best of good fortune in finding a home for the idea elsewhere.'

The rejections went on and on. However, in 2007, I *was* interviewed about Aunt Esther and her father Joseph for the BBC's *The Edwardian Family Album.* It looked as if she was going to be seen in a television documentary after all. To my dismay, the director called me just after he had completed editing the programme with some bad news. He said that the 'powers that be' at the BBC didn't want to have a white man talking about a Black aunt and ordered the sequence to be cut. He was as gutted as I was, but he kindly showed me his 'director's cut' so that I could see how it would have looked.

In 1992, Aunt Esther suffered a stroke. Her recovery was long and difficult, during which I became her main carer and supported her all the way. Her beloved pets, a dog, Meg, and a cat, Bruno, were looked after by a neighbour. While she remained in hospital, I was shocked at the number of elderly people in her ward who had no one to visit them and advocate for their needs. Once Esther was able to speak again, she took quite a few hospital staff to task if she thought they were in the wrong or neglecting the elderly patients in her ward.

On returning home, she was reunited with her beloved Meg and Bruno. Her return was an emotional moment for all of us because for a time it looked as if Esther wouldn't survive. I was so proud of her.

Though she was wheelchair-bound and needed support from various social services, she was home. The additional support came with some teething problems as Esther valued her independence. She was assigned a young man to be her carer, but she quietly told me she couldn't bring herself to ask him to take her smalls to the laundrette. It embarrassed her. He was a nice lad and Esther got on well with him, so it didn't take much for me to persuade her to let him take all of her washing to the laundrette. Another time she told me that the meals on wheels service only brought her English food and she was bored with it. Esther enjoyed Caribbean food so I persuaded her to request it. When I next visited I asked her what had happened. She replied: 'Yeah, they brought me Caribbean food alright. The same boring meat and veg with a bit of rice on the side!'

Following her poor health Esther grew isolated and lonely. I visited her when I could and often spoke to her on the phone, as did my mum and her cousin Lee. She had two friendly neighbours on her street, Irene and Pauline, who kept an eye on her. So I spoke to social services about finding her a senior citizens club which would give her something to look forward to. On one visit she told me that she had been taken to a club nearby, and save for one nice Black lady, it was all white people who paid her no mind. Eventually, an accommodating and multicultural local club was found for her. She loved it and soon made friends who she proudly introduced to me. The club did her a power of good and made her feel less isolated. They organised a number of day trips in their mini bus, and I told Esther she had to send me a postcard from the places she visited, even though they were only day trips. She enjoyed doing that and I enjoyed collecting the postcards. I joined them once on a visit to the Imperial War Museum because they needed some extra hands and I could move Aunt Esther around in her wheelchair. We had such a good time that day.

Although she'd make a fairly good recovery, in 1994 Esther suffered from heart failure and had to be admitted to hospital again. The African women who cleaned the wards and pushed the tea trolleys made a big fuss of Esther and braided her hair. Aunt Esther enjoyed that. Aunt Esther passed away in her sleep on Sunday morning, July 17, 1994. She was 81. Before she passed away, Esther told me to 'Let John Major bury me.' She hated the Tories and what they had done to the country. So when I organised her funeral, I made sure the state paid for it.

At her funeral, Mum, Dad, and I sang Susan Warner's 'Jesus Bids Us Shine' with the congregation, and we all wept. The vicar explained to everyone that this was one of the hymns Aunt Esther enjoyed singing with Granny Johnson. A few weeks later, I accompanied my mother to Fulham Cemetery, and we scattered Aunt Esther's ashes under a willow tree near her parents' unmarked grave. Granny Johnson rests nearby.

Jesus bids us shine with a pure clear light,
Like a little candle burning in the night.
In the world is darkness; so we must shine –
You in your small corner, and I in mine.

Jesus bids us shine first of all for Him;
Well He sees and knows it if our light grows dim.
He looks down from heav'n to see us shine –
You in your small corner, and I in mine.

In 1996, a second, revised edition of *Aunt Esther's Story* was published by the ECOHP, and in 2004 I contributed an entry about her to the *Oxford Dictionary of National Biography* (ODNB). The editors recognised that the ODNB had a habit of overlooking Black historical figures. Paul Robeson was one of the few Black people from history in the ODNB before 2004 when the editors began to commission more entries about Black Britons. So Aunt Esther took her place among the 57,000 entries that include Elizabeth I, Oscar Wilde, and Winston Churchill, and I knew that she would be looking down and chuckling about this.

My sister and I were raised to look upon Esther as our adopted aunt, and if people asked questions about my family's relationship with her, I would reply truthfully: 'Not all white people come from all-white families.' However, in 2010 a member of the Black and Asian Studies Association (BASA) accused me of trading on Aunt Esther to give me some kind of credibility in my Black British history work. I was deeply hurt. Another BASA member jumped to my defence. This was Alex Pascall who was a trailblazing broadcaster, famous for his groundbreaking BBC radio series *Black Londoners*. He was also an oral historian. Alex had come here from Grenada in 1959. He said, 'This calls for serious discussion as many may not be aware of the way "aunty" and "uncle" are used as forms of respect for elders as well as family and friendship links. In later years, we also developed the "brother" and "sister" link. This is culturally deep among Caribbeans and Africans and rules out the question or notion of colour; I would leave room for the ones who are uncomfortable. I have had insight into Stephen's book and the way he referenced Aunt Esther, nothing is wrong with that. Maybe we should use the sentiments of Stephen's book to debate or discuss the issue of adoption and family relationship… May I in conclusion return to an old saying of my father: "There are three sides to every story: yours, mine, and the facts", please give me something factual that will add flavour to the pot. In the meantime, I goin' to see what aunty or uncle cooking today.'

Chapter 13

The 90s

I enjoyed the 1990s. On the work front, it was a decade of surprises. By the time my contracts with the BFI and *Gay Times* had ended, I became a founding member of the Black and Asian Studies Association (BASA). The inaugural meeting of BASA took place at the Institute of Commonwealth Studies on December 4, 1990. Attendees included Hakim Adi, Peter Fryer, Jeffrey Green, David Killingray, Roger Lambo, Howard Rye, and Marika Sherwood. The Association was established to foster research and to provide information about the history of Black and Asian people in Britain. We all had our own specialist interests in Black and Asian British history. For example, Peter had written the acclaimed and influential *Staying Power* (1984), Howard was an authority on jazz, Marika had written *Many Struggles – West Indian Workers and Service Personnel in Britain 1939–45*, and before the decade was over, Jeffrey had written the fascinating *Black Edwardians*. BASA launched a newsletter in September 1991, edited by Marika until 2007. BASA would also put on conferences where we could share our research. Towards the end of the decade, members also worked with organisations, such as the Imperial War Museum, to assist them in highlighting the Black and Asian presence in their collections. All of this was done with no funding. All of our work was voluntary.

I put together *Out of the Archives*, the National Film Theatre's first lesbian and gay television season in July 1992. Screenings included Joe Orton's extraordinary *Entertaining Mr Sloane* (1968), starring Sheila Hancock and Edward Woodward; the lesbian drama *Girl* (1974), starring Alison Steadman; and *Only Connect* (1979), written by Gay Sweatshop's Drew Griffiths and Noel Greig. The season was so popular it became an annual event every July for ten years throughout which I was proudly the curator.

The future looked promising, but nothing could've prepared me for an opportunity that came my way in 1993. It was my friend Terry who suggested that I speak to his friend Jim Hiley who was a radio producer. Jim was employed by an independent company called Ladbroke Radio and they made programmes for BBC Radio 2. When I met Jim, I was sceptical. Thoughts of Terry Wogan and his dreadful 'Floral Dance' came to mind. 'I don't listen to Radio 2,' I told him, 'and I doubt I can come up with ideas for them'. To his credit, Jim persisted. He sensed that I could think of a suitable programme idea. 'Well, one series the station should do is a celebration of Black British, African, and Caribbean musicians and singers from the 1930s to the 1960s', I proposed. Jim asked me to name some of the artists I'd include. From the top of my head I replied, 'The cabaret legend Leslie 'Hutch' Hutchinson from Grenada, the British-born innovative jazz composer Reginald Foresythe, British-born contralto Evelyn Dove, band leader Ken 'Snakehips' Johnson from Guyana, who was killed in the London Blitz, Nigerian composer Fela Sowande, Trinidadian folk singer Edric Connor', and more. The only condition was no Americans. No Paul Robeson, Duke Ellington, Louis Armstrong or Ella Fitzgerald. This series has to be *British* focused. Jim thought it was a strong idea and asked me to put together a proposal with names, short biographies, music selections, and possible guests. Not only did BBC Radio 2 like it, they asked Jim to extend the series from the original six programmes to nine. It was hard work, but I enjoyed it, especially when I interviewed such famous guests as Adelaide Hall (about Evelyn Dove), Elisabeth Welch (about 'Hutch'), Petula Clark (about Edric Connor), Harry Secombe (about Winifred Atwell) and Spike Milligan (about Ray Ellington).

While researching the recordings of the artists in the BBC Music Library, I encountered a member of staff who chastised me for taking the idea for the series to the BBC. He was surprised that Radio 2 had commissioned it, and completely dismissed the idea as something worthwhile. He also specifically questioned why I was making a special case for Black British artists. As far as he was concerned, with the exception of 'Hutch', the names I had selected for the programmes were forgotten and insignificant. I was deeply offended by his attitude and on subsequent visits, I kept my distance from him.

We struggled to find a suitable title for the series. I suggested *Rhapsody in Black* which nobody liked. In the end, when nothing outstanding came to mind, we reluctantly agreed on *Salutations* which was suggested by a member of staff at Ladbroke Radio. We had no choice because the series had to be submitted to the BBC. It was broadcast from September 1993. With Jim's professionalism and radio know-how and my expertise, the series was not only classy but beautifully presented by Moira Stuart. The BBC were impressed with *Salutations*, even more so when Jim and I received the Commission for Racial Equality's Race in the Media Award for Best Radio Documentary. It was presented to us at the Hyatt Carlton Hotel by the actor Rudolph Walker. It also opened a door for me to make more programmes for Radio 2 throughout the 1990s. Every idea I suggested was accepted and in 1994, for the second year running, we received the Race in the Media Award for Best Radio Documentary. This time it was for *Black in the West End*, a celebration of Black musical theatre in London.

In complete contrast to *Black in the West End*, I also proposed *The Betty Driver Story*, a celebration of the former singer who had been playing the barmaid Betty 'Hotpot' Turpin since 1969, a popular character in *Coronation Street*. She had given up singing in the 1960s to become a character actress, but I had rediscovered some of her early recordings and realised that she had an amazing story to tell. BBC Radio 2 commissioned it and in 1994 I found myself with a producer in Manchester interviewing Betty and her sister Freda. They were lovely, down-to-earth souls unafraid of recounting how their pushy stage-mother had forced shy Betty into the limelight. I remained in touch with Betty until she passed away in 2011. I had been a fan of The Street – as much as any child can be a fan of mature television – since I was a little lad. I could relate to the working-class characters, especially the larger-than-life women like Elsie Tanner and Ena Sharples who dominated life in a back street in Greater Manchester. My earliest memory was seeing Ena's pal Martha Longhurst die from a heart attack in the Rovers Return public house, her glasses in one hand and a glass of milk stout in the other. For me, to visit Manchester and the set of *Corrie* was a dream come true. For Betty's tribute I also interviewed some of the cast including William Roache (Ken Barlow) and Julie Goodyear (Bet Lynch).

For *The Betty Driver Story* I suggested that Cilla Black be the presenter. Cilla had often spoken about her love for *Corrie.* She remembered seeing the first episode when the series was launched in 1960, but the powers that be at Ladbroke Radio laughed in my face. They said that not only was she a big television star for the 'other side' (aka ITV), she would never agree to presenting a radio programme for the BBC. How wrong they were. Not only did I get to meet and befriend the great Betty Driver, but Cilla too! However, on the day that Cilla came to Ladbroke Radio to record the programme, we had to contend with her strange husband Bobby. While Cilla was friendly and incredibly funny, Bobby was quite rude to everyone. This embarrassed Cilla but it was obvious that she loved the bones of him and wouldn't make a move without him.

In 1991, to mark the 30th anniversary of the release of the film *Victim* starring Dirk Bogarde, I proposed a small monograph about the film, to include its history and impact on gay men, to the Gay Men's Press. They turned it down, but determined to explore the film's impact in another context, in 1992, I featured it in a talk entitled *Brief Encounters* during the sixth London Lesbian and Gay Film Festival. In addition to *Victim*, I drew attention to other early British films with a queer presence. It was at this talk that I befriended a member of the audience, Mark Gatiss. He was an up-and-coming actor, writer, and brilliant impersonator of Sir John Gielgud. He was soon to become nationally famous as a member of The League of Gentlemen, the sketch comedy team. Mark and I discussed his interest in James Whale, the out-Hollywood film director of *Frankenstein* fame. I loaned Mark a copy of my 1988 thesis about Whale. Mark had been contracted to write a biography of him for Cassell, the publishing house that had created a Lesbian and Gay Studies list. The commissioning editors were Steve Cook and Roz Hopkins. Another friend, Keith Howes, had been commissioned by them to write *Broadcasting It – An Encyclopaedia of Homosexuality on Film, Radio, and TV in the UK 1923–1993*. Encouraged by their support for Mark and Keith, I sent Steve and Roz a book proposal but they understandably asked me to play the waiting game while they established the press as a commercially viable venture. Thankfully, their first batch of titles were very popular and my book, *Brief Encounters – Lesbians and Gays in British Cinema 1930–1971*, was commissioned.

When *Brief Encounters* was published in 1996, the reviews were generally favourable. Andy Simmons in *Gay Times* described the book as 'The first specifically British delve into the representation of queers in the nation's cinema…a fab companion to a film guide.' He added that 'We must crown Bourne as the Miss Marple of British cinema.' But there were criticisms, too. Jonathan Sanders in *Gay and Lesbian Humanist* critiqued me for working from a 'positive images' standpoint that seemed to him 'a bit outdated in the queer politics era'. Sanders rejected *Victim* as a film that promoted 'a gloomy acknowledgement of an unavoidable disability.' I didn't agree with Sanders but I appreciated that some critics – especially those who related to queer politics – rejected the older films.

I felt that we needed to reassess them, including *Victim*, and not dismiss them as historical relics that didn't have any value. Only then could we come to a better understanding of what they represented and the impact they had made, especially on gay audiences. The only mention in a broadsheet was at least favourable. This came from Philip French in *The Observer*: 'It is written with a love of and understanding of mainstream British cinema rare among movie historians.' Perhaps Mr French was referring to the absence in my writing of academic theory and jargon. Who knows?

I also received congratulatory letters from Dirk Bogarde, Ian McKellen, which I appreciated, and the director and screenwriter Bryan Forbes who said: 'Thank you so much for sending me that dedicated copy of your excellent book which I devoured over my cornflakes this morning. I do congratulate you – you have produced a thoughtful and timely reminder that some of us did blaze a lonely trail, even if we often had to cover our tracks to circumvent the British Board of Censors.'

I received only one request for an interview. It was from Keith Howes, who wrote about me in the April 1997 edition of a gay Australian magazine called *Outrage*. The article bore the bold yet promising title: 'A Star is Bourne.' 'Stephen Bourne has a swathe of inky black hair, a slight frame and large Bette Davis eyes. He may speak softly and look like a waif, but when he says shut up and listen, you listen! No messing about with our Stephen. Meet the totally dedicated, focused professional... There are stories of grown men and women scattering when he is in the vicinity, and fax machines positively melting when the Bourne dander is up. Which, considering the ignorance and prejudice surrounding his two main areas of interest (popular gay culture and popular black culture), could be quite a regular occurrence. Any truth in the rumours, duckie?'

To which I replied, 'I am told I have a reputation for being "difficult", but this is simply not true. I am very passionate about my work, and feel very unhappy with the apathy shown by the lesbian and gay media.

When I face this indifference, I have a tendency to become agitated and show my frustration. I have always been determined to fight against this apathy, but more often than not I am knocked back. So this is sometimes interpreted as my being "difficult." But what the hell, if I don't push my work and speak up for what I believe in, then no one else will.'

It is interesting to read this now. The frustration I refer to was borne out of the apathy and indifference shown towards my annual *Out of the Archives* television seasons and also *Brief Encounters* by the lesbian and gay media of the 1990s. This did not happen with my work on Black culture. In 1996, when I programmed *Black on White TV*, the second Black British television retrospective at BFI Southbank, the Black British media embraced it and promoted it. Which is why I had the fortune of attracting large audiences to my tributes to the actors Norman Beaton and Carmen Munroe. I also felt that my work on gay culture was being marginalised because I did not come from an academic background. I did not teach in a university. Keith wrote, 'A highbrow buff he ain't, but a great stirrer he is.' In the write-up he later quoted me saying, 'It has always worried me that so-called lesbian and gay cultural historians in Britain have avoided exploring gay British cinema outside the *Carry On* films and Derek Jarman.' Keith explained that my interest in gay and lesbian images grew alongside my own coming out, 'which was, like most coming outs, a very long process. Only when he was studying for his arts degree did he begin to explore hitherto forbidden early British cinema.'

In October 1997, I presented my first Black History Month event. This took place at the Sojourner Truth Centre, a community venue in Sumner Road, Peckham. I spoke about Aunt Esther and the book we had co-authored. I also showed some extracts from the video recording I had made in 1993. Little did I know that this would be the first of many Black History Month events I would be involved in. At first I was apprehensive about giving talks in public. For me, lectures by academics were always dry and unexciting. I didn't want to replicate that experience. However, I soon learned that to capture people's attention, it was also important to be natural and draw them gently into my world. I achieved this by being myself, being natural. Since that time, people who have attended my talks have commented that I spoke to them as if they were in my living room, by creating an intimate experience. I discovered that it was possible, even in large lecture theatres. I also learned to keep my talks relatively concise, about 45 mins, as some academics tended to go on too long and send everyone to sleep. Following a talk, question-and-answer sessions are also important to me because I want to give people the opportunity to interact. And I have found that there are always questions to be asked.

In the 1990s, I began making occasional appearances on television. The first was BBC1's *Biteback* in 1995 where I criticised television's poor representation of gays and lesbians, especially in magazine-type programmes. These features tended to be lightweight and trivial, often failing to deal with some of the serious issues in the lives of our community. I also took part in Channel 4's *Black Divas* (1996) and BBC1's *Black Britain* (1997). I believe I was the only interviewee to feature in two Paul Robeson documentaries, one British, one American: *Paul Robeson – Speak of Me As I Am* (1998) for BBC1 and *Paul Robeson – Here I Stand*, an *American Masters* production which was first shown in the USA in 1999.

In *Here I Stand* I spoke about Robeson's film work in Britain in the 1930s. The interview, filmed in my London flat, got off to an embarrassing start. The documentary was directed by an African-American filmmaker called St Clair Bourne, and in the days before the internet, he had no idea what I looked like. He assumed I was going to be Black. When we met he exclaimed, in front of the crew (because we shared the same surname), 'I expect your ancestors owned my ancestors.' The look of horror on my face said it all and I uttered something along the lines of 'Excuse me? You know nothing about my family history, so please do not make assumptions.' Despite the awkward start, the interview went extremely well. St Clair proved to be an excellent interviewer. 27 years later in 2024, I accidently discovered the complete unedited interview on PBS's website in *American Masters Digital Archive.* I had been included along with all the other interviewees for *Here I Stand* like Hakim Adi and Harry Belafonte. After recovering from the shock of seeing my younger self, I watched the interview and I have to say I was impressed with the way I came across: confident, articulate, passionate, and knowledgeable. I was pleased that there existed some evidence of how I projected myself at that time.

I have often looked at 1998 as the watershed moment in my career as an historian of Black culture and history. On a personal and societal level, so much happened to draw attention to the Black world. My personal involvement included taking part in BASA's Paul Robeson centenary conference; programming *Songs of Freedom*, a Paul Robeson film and television retrospective for BFI Southbank; and writing another book for Cassell: *Black in the British Frame – Black People in British Film and Television 1896–1996.*

Black in the British Frame was one of several important Black British history books that surfaced during 1998. It seemed that publishers were finally recognising the relevance of the subject. 22 years later something similar happened following the Black Lives Matter demonstrations which followed the brutal murder of George Floyd. Other titles included Hakim Adi's *West Africans in Britain 1900–1960*; Jeffrey Green's *Black Edwardians*; Delia Jarrett-Macauley's *The Life of Una Marson*; and Sam King's autobiography *Climbing Up the Rough Side of the Mountain.*

In 1998, the British Film Institute still had its African Caribbean Unit, to which I made regular contributions to its *Black Film Bulletin.* At the same time, the BBC also still had its African Caribbean Unit, which allowed due praise to be placed on the 50th anniversary of Windrush. Mike Phillips and Trevor Phillips's *Windrush* book coincided with an excellent four-part television documentary series, also called *Windrush*, broadcast on BBC2 in May/June 1998. The series was shown in the BBC's ambitious Windrush season which included other television and radio programmes such as the all-star Windrush Gala Concert shown on BBC2 on July 25. For my part, BBC Radio 2 asked me to research and script a five-part series which I called *Their Long Voyage Home.* It was broadcast throughout July 1998. When I discussed the idea, I suggested that we focus on women because so much of the Windrush narratives focused on men. I also asked for a Black woman to present the series, and suggested the actress Carmen Munroe and the newsreader Moira Stuart, but Trevor McDonald had already been offered the job. For *Their Long Voyage Home* I suggested three women be interviewed: Helen Denniston, whose Jamaican father Oswald had been a passenger on the Windrush in 1948; Pearl Connor-Mogotsi, a Trinidadian who had also arrived here in 1948 and been an important figure in Black arts and politics for decades; and Brenda Clough, born in Guyana, who had come here as a teenager at the end of the 1950s with her family. Brenda was related to Aunt Esther. Interviews with the women were interspersed with songs and poetry readings by Black artists covering several decades.

In 1998, the main highlight for me was the publication of *Black in the British Frame.* In the book I state that one of the keys to a Black future in Britain is the rediscovery of the Black achievers and realities of the past. I strongly believed that we needed to build a positive foundation in Black British history so that young Black people would feel empowered. I wanted the book to be accessible to a wide readership and my style reflected this. I wasn't interested in writing books for the academic market. *Black in the British Frame* was well received and attracted some positive reviews, especially in some of our Black newspapers and journals. Two years after publication, in her book *Who Do You Think You Are – Imagining the New Britain,* Yasmin Alibhai-Brown described *Black in the British Frame* as 'a detailed, painstaking account of Black people on the screen in Britain'.

Regrettably, there was no acknowledgement in the mainstream print media, but I was helped enormously by Noreen Harewood, an enthusiastic young Black woman who worked in Cassell's press and marketing department. She admitted to me that her colleagues – who were mostly white and middle class women – didn't have a clue how to market *Black in the British Frame.* So, on the quiet, she printed hundreds of small A5 flyers which I distributed to bookshops across London, mainly those on Charing Cross Road, including Foyles. I also left them on buses and tubes. Within a year of its publication, Cassell informed me that the book had sold out its first print run. They even commissioned a second, revised edition which was published in 2001. When *The Voice* newspaper nominated *Black in the British Frame* in its Literature category for its Annual Community Awards, I took Noreen as my guest to the awards ceremony at the Hilton Hotel on Park Lane. I was also nominated in the Race Relations category. I didn't win anything, but I was thrilled to be nominated and photographed on stage with the broadcaster Brenda Emmanus, Daniel De-Gale (the first Black individual in Britain to receive a stem cell transplant from an unrelated donor), and Stephen Lawrence's father, Neville.

Best of all was Lola Young's review about *Black in the British Frame* in the *BASA Newsletter* (September 1998): 'Bourne makes it clear from the outset that he has not set out to add to the emerging body of critical/theoretical material on the subject: his is a linear narrative, a largely descriptive account of some key moments... But Bourne's modest preface and carefully framed title, if anything, underplay the full extent of the wealth of material contained in this most useful work of reference... The focus on British media is one of the strong points of this book since studies are so underdeveloped, especially when compared to the output on North American media. People tend to forget we have a history in this country which has, in part at least, been captured in various genres and modes on television and film... Where there are gaps in "official" documentation, Bourne fills these in with what is clearly an extensive and possibly unique resource: his interviews with people directly involved with the film and television industries...Bourne's engaging honesty and enthusiasm, together with the creation of what is effectively a source book for the field of study more than compensate for any shortcomings...Important also is that the general reader will find the author's style informative and accessible: the text serves as an indispensable work of reference for anyone with an interest in this as yet under-researched, but crucial area of study.'

At the end of the 1990s, I had every reason to feel optimistic about the future, especially with my Black British history work. I expected this to develop with the coming of the new millennium, however, nothing could have been further from the truth. Meanwhile, my life took an unexpected turn when I became a 'critical friend' to the Metropolitan Police.

Chapter 14

Why I Befriended the Police

My relationship to the Metropolitan Police, since my unfortunate run-in with two officers opposite my home on Peckham Road in 1980, has changed drastically. Since the mid-1990s, I have been active in the London Borough of Southwark as a voluntary independent adviser (or 'critical friend') to the police. This relationship began when I realised how easy it was to stand on the sidelines and criticise the police without doing anything constructive to change how they go about their work. My role with them began in 1994. In Southwark, through my work with the tenant's association on my estate, I was introduced to Inspector Richard Heselden. He arranged a meeting with one of his senior officers, Superintendent Gerry McBride, who was in charge of Walworth Division. Gerry was the most senior police officer I had met and his warmth and friendliness shattered my preconception that senior police officers were all autocratic and dictatorial. This helped me to learn to trust police officers of all ranks, but not to be afraid to challenge them if necessary. I must have made an impression because this meeting led to Gerry inviting me to join a local multi-agency police and community forum known as the Southwark Police and Community Consultative Group (SPCCG). It was Lord Scarman who recommended partnership work between the police and the communities they served in his famous report on the Brixton uprising of April 1981. Despite my reservations, I found that the SPCCG was really quite useful as a platform for debating important crime issues in our community. Looking back at the SPCCG's annual report for 1994–95, the most prevalent crime issues at the time included racial harassment, street robbery, with a concerning amount of youth involvement. The youth's involvement in crime was a symptom of a larger issue, of which there were many more symptoms like the lack of youth facilities, a rise in school expulsions, and youth unemployment. There was willingness on the part of the senior police officers in the group to work with us and make a difference. On April 27, 1994, having quickly established a strong working relationship with Gerry and his colleagues from Southwark Police, I found myself at the opening of the new Walworth Police Station in Manor Place, off Walworth Road. Gerry had invited me and it was at this event that he introduced me to Lord Scarman and the Commissioner Paul Condon.

The SPCCG was a friendly group with occasional conflicts, which made meetings lively and interesting. I enjoyed taking part but was oblivious to how different my life's trajectory would be for it. On Saturday, June 18, 1994 violence erupted after the Pride Festival in Lambeth's Brockwell Park. Some LGBT+ revellers were attacked by homophobic thugs as they left the park. As someone who had been the victim of homophobic abuse at secondary school, I felt strongly that there was not enough awareness of homophobic hate crimes. A meeting of the SPCCG on June 28, 1994 was attended by a local gay man who was not a member of the group, but who bravely stood up and complained to the police and Southwark Council about the recent violence after the Pride celebrations. He also drew attention to police apathy towards victims of homophobia in our own borough. This gave me the confidence to speak out too, and I immediately endorsed what the man had said. It was a serious coming out statement, because very few members of the group were aware that I was gay. I was informed by members I spoke to afterwards that homophobic crime had not come to the attention of the SPCCG before. Neither was there evidence that the group had had openly gay members before I joined, so it took a great deal of courage on my part to inform the group that I was gay in this particular forum, especially in front of several senior police officers. When I told my Dad what I had done, he was horrified because of his more traditional understanding of the law. He was very protective of Linda and me, even as adults. He believed that the police could arrest me just for telling them I was gay. I assured him that this would not happen.

The reaction at the SPCCG meeting was interesting. A senior police officer said, defensively, 'There are no homophonic (sic) incidents in Southwark because no one reports them to us.' It had not occurred to him that the reason for this was a lack of trust on the part of LGBT+ victims. We suffered in silence rather than calling 999 or visiting a police station to make a report. I challenged the officer's misleading perception and asked for a multi-agency group to be set up to look at homophobic hate crime and its under-reporting in Southwark. Within a week, I was contacted by Donnachadh McCarthy, a local Liberal Democrat councillor, who had been informed about what had been discussed. Consequently, a public meeting was organised for May 18, 1995 at Southwark Town Hall on Peckham Road. This was a memorable event. Over 100 people attended, mostly from the LGBT+ community. During the meeting council representatives and senior police officers from Southwark were questioned and challenged about homophobic crime in the borough. A few months later, on September 27, 1995, one day after the SPCCG celebrated its 10th birthday, the historic first meeting of Southwark's Anti-Homophobic Forum (SAHF, later renamed the LGBT Forum), chaired by Councillor McCarthy, was held at the Town Hall. It was one of the first locally-based multi-agency panels in Britain to specifically address homophobic hate crime.

In 1995, one of my favourite television programmes was *The Bill.* Although I loved the show, I was concerned upon reflection that, since it debuted in 1984, the series hadn't featured a gay police officer. I wrote to its producer, Michael Chapman, and asked him if there was a possibility of introducing a gay officer. His reply was shocking: 'I can't think that having homosexuals hanging around the place is going to commend the programme usefully to the public.' At the same time the press officer for *The Bill* said that she did not realise there was a Lesbian and Gay Police Association (it had over 200 members) and that the production team wasn't prejudiced. She said, 'We're willing to bring it in as a social issue but we don't deal with the home lives of the police officers.' I campaigned for this alone and I got my right of reply by writing a feature about this for *The Stage* newspaper ('One PC missing from *The Bill*', April 20, 1995). Three years later, Michael Chapman retired after producing 1144 episodes. I'm not suggesting that I had anything to do with this but in 2001, Hywel Simons joined the regular cast of *The Bill* as an openly gay copper, Sergeant Craig Gilmore.

From my work with the police sprung the opportunity to attend meetings at New Scotland Yard. These were meetings of the London Lesbian and Gay Policing Initiative (LLGPI) which had been formed in 1990. It was at these meetings that I met a number of activists from across London who had been working with the police. These included Griffith Vaughan Williams who had been active in one of the first campaigning groups, the Campaign for Homosexual Equality (CHE), since the 1960s. For me, Griff proved to be a source of never-ending information about the history of gay men in Britain. In 1999, the LLGPI was disbanded to make way for the Met's LGBT+ Advisory Group.

I was also invited to two police training colleges – Hendon in northwest London and Bramshill in Hampshire – to take part in equal opportunities courses that had started to address homophobia. On May 1, 1996 I received a thank you letter from The Police Staff College in Bramshill, which read, 'Your honest and open appraisal of the position regarding relationships with the police was well received by course members. You raised a number of different issues which they will be thinking about for a long time, and you encouraged them to look at matters from a different point of view.'

Before I undertook this work, I was completely inexperienced and had no training for it. I just attended the courses and spoke about the relationship between the police and the community as I experienced it. Quite simply, I realised that victims of homophobic crime needed to build up trust in the police in order to give them the necessary confidence to report such incidents so that the true extent of the problem would become apparent. My approach was to use my previous relationships with local officers in Southwark to raise this issue with them in a mutually supportive way. In doing so, a meaningful dialogue was established and progress was made. I was not confrontational because I learned early on that the police will not listen or engage if they are shouted at. Not that I had a problem with some of the more assertive approaches taken by other LGBT+ activists in other forums. Everyone has their own way of achieving results. I just found that my own personal way of cultivating trust and confidence worked in Southwark.

Towards the end of 1996, for my police and community work, I received a Civic Award from the London Borough of Southwark, and I was nominated for the Mike Rhodes Award which was given annually to 'someone who has contributed most to promoting an understanding of lesbian and gay life'. I didn't win. The award went to the playwright Jonathan Harvey for his screenplay of the popular film *Beautiful Thing*. My loss aside, I was thrilled that The Mike Rhodes Trust had nominated a gay man who had worked voluntarily on the frontline of his community.

An important event in the history of the SAHF took place on November 26, 1997. It was on this day that we launched our *Speak Out* anti-homophobic crime campaign at Southwark Town Hall. It was the first borough-wide campaign in Britain to encourage victims of homophobic crime to report incidents and to give a strong message to those attacking and targeting LGBT+ people that such behaviour was totally unacceptable. The lesbian activist Angela Mason from Stonewall was our main guest speaker. Afterwards, I wrote to Angela at Stonewall and asked if it would be possible for me to become involved with the work of the organisation. I wanted to participate in the excellent campaigning work that they undertook. I believed they could draw upon my local work and knowledge, but when she called me I was taken aback by her offer to 'stuff envelopes'. That was not what I had in mind. I politely declined. Following the success of the *Speak Out* campaign in 1997–98, the work of the SAHF was taken to another level when, on April 30, 1999 the Admiral Duncan pub on Old Compton Street, Soho, at the heart of London's gay district, was the scene of a bomb blast. The Neo-Nazi David Copeland was responsible. He was trying to stir up race hate and homophobia by organising a series of bombings. At the Admiral Duncan, Copeland detonated a nail bomb that killed three people and injured over seventy. Copeland's first attack, in Electric Avenue, in the heart of Brixton's Black community, had occurred on April 17. Following a second attack on April 24 in Brick Lane, the centre of the Bengali community in the East End of London, the SAHF and other LGBT+ advisers across London, warned the police that we would be next. In Southwark, a Chief Inspector who worked as the borough's community liaison officer did not take us seriously.

In the wake of the first two bombings, a public meeting was organised at Southwark Town Hall for the local Black and minority ethnic communities, but the Chief Inspector excluded the LGBT+ community. SAHF members, including the new Chair Linda Bellos and myself, argued that we should be included because we feared our community would also be targeted by the bomber, but the Chief Inspector disagreed. So Linda and I forced our way into the meeting. A few days later is when the Admiral Duncan was targeted by Copeland,

and the Metropolitan Police (and our Chief Inspector) finally understood that the LGBT+ community were as vulnerable to hate crimes as other minorities. It was an important landmark in the SAHF's history. As for the Chief Inspector, he retired and Southwark Police launched its Community Safety Unit (CSU) which focused on hate crimes in the borough.

Until then, our main link to the local police was a single Chief Inspector who was a dedicated Community Liaison Officer. In the CSU, an entire team of officers addressed hate crimes in Southwark, including racially-aggravated crimes, domestic violence, and homophobic offences. One of my SAHF responsibilities was to visit the CSU office in Walworth Police Station and offer advice on some of the recent reports of homophobic crime in the borough.

1999 was a landmark year for police and community relations. In addition to the lessons learned from the Copeland bombings, the Macpherson Report, investigating the murder of the Black teenager Stephen Lawrence, was published in April. It conferred a sense of validation to people who already knew that the Met Police was institutionally racist. It also created a great deal of media attention for the same reason. There was important work still to be done. One of its recommendations was to have a personal impact. Macpherson wanted every London borough commander to set up an independent advisory group (IAG). This idea had its origins in the 1996 Stephen Lawrence Inquiry which recommended that 'there must be a change so that there is genuine partnership between the police and all sections of the community. This cannot be achieved by the police alone. The onus is upon them to start the process. Co-operation must be genuine and vigorous. The active involvement of people from diverse ethnic groups is essential. Otherwise there will be no acceptance of change, and policing by consent may be the victim.'

In Southwark, the police service was divided into three separate divisions: Southwark, Walworth, and Peckham. Each division was run by a different Superintendent and I knew all of them from the SPCCG. However, in 1999, the divisions were scrapped and Southwark became one police borough with a single commander in charge. The first to be appointed was Trevor Pearman. As a result of the bridge-building work I had already accomplished with Southwark Police, I was invited by Chief Superintendent Pearman to become a member of his IAG. On December 15, 1999 at Southwark Police Station, I attended the inaugural meeting of the group with a small group of key players from the Southwark community. They included Keib Thomas (Southwark Action for Voluntary Organisations), John Gorsuch (Nunhead Residents Association), Mr Rajput (South East Muslim Association), Shirley Oldhamstead (Downtown Residents Association) and Gerry Forde (Southwark Victim Support Scheme). During the first year of the IAG, others joined the original lineup, and they all came from diverse backgrounds. They included Reg Gyasi (ASCO Tenants Association), Debbie Welch (Cultural Unity), Althea Smith (Southwark Group of Tenants Organisation), Jennifer Blake (CEO of Safe 'N' Sound Youth Project), Avril Jones (Custody Visitor,) and Dayon Haynes (Custody Visitor). At the time of writing, Althea, Jennifer, Avril, Dayon, and myself are still members of the group. Soon after joining the IAG, I discovered that the police and some of the other community members only saw me as a gay adviser, which is not what I wanted. I was happy to consult on any issues relating to the LGBT+ community, but I made everyone aware that I wanted to consult on a much broader range of incidents that impacted the Southwark community. I felt that it was important for the police to see me as a gay member of the Southwark community, but not solely as a member of the borough's gay community.

As a member of the Southwark IAG, I have consulted on a number of high-profile critical incidents, most notably the murder of the 10-year-old Nigerian-British schoolboy Damilola Taylor on the North Peckham Estate on November 27, 2000. The IAG wasn't even a year old when we found ourselves consulting with the police on what has been the IAG's most distressing case. I first heard about it when a local Superintendent, Charlie Griggs, called me at home to inform me that a child had been attacked on Blakes Road while on his way home from Peckham Library. He had been stabbed and was found bleeding in a stairwell on the North Peckham Estate.

During the early stage of the murder investigation, the police needed Peckham's community on their side. However, local people, especially those who lived on the estate and belonged to the Black community, did not trust them and would not speak to them. It was for this reason that bridges needed to be built, and the activist Linda Bellos with two IAG members, Althea Smith and Debbie Welch, became invaluable to the police as independent advisers, especially when reaching out to the local Black community. The rest of us on the IAG also played an important role, and the police consulted with us throughout the long and difficult investigation.

Some of us were asked by the police to volunteer to staff telephones at Peckham Police Station where they had set up a special incident room. This was an attempt to encourage members of the public to use a helpline and share information that may assist the police with the investigation. This is the only occasion I have known Southwark police to do this. They were, without doubt, keen to catch those involved in Damilola's murder.

Early on, I remember Superintendent Griggs calling me again and asking for advice about a public meeting that was being planned at the Harris Academy on Peckham Road. He expressed his concern that a Black community leader insisted that it be organised for Black people only. I explained that, while I understood the politics involved in such a request, it wouldn't be right to separate people at such a sensitive and difficult time. The police needed the wider community on board. When the meeting went ahead, everyone was welcome.

This case affected me deeply. In addition to the death of a young child in my community, Damilola was attacked on Blakes Road. When I was a young lad, and we lived in nearby Cronin Road, we visited great aunt Lil who lived on Blakes Road in a flat over her grocers shop. I also found out that Damilola had been a pupil at my former primary school, Oliver Goldsmith, on Peckham Road. His murder made news across the globe. A relative in Australia wrote to my mum and expressed her sadness that a young child could be the victim of such a senseless crime. I witnessed the concern the local community openly expressed in Peckham and Camberwell from the shock of Damilola's murder. His smiling face peered at us from hundreds of posters that were posted in windows in shops and people's homes, especially along Peckham Road and Peckham High Street. The posters asked people to come forward with information. I have never seen anything on this large a scale before or since. As for the IAG and the police, it brought us together in ways that we could not have imagined on that day in December 1999 when the group had its first meeting. The police learned a lot from us. This exchange cemented the relationship between the IAG and the police.

Since that time, I have advised on a number of major critical incidents in Southwark, mainly by taking part in Gold Groups. These are strategic meetings, chaired by the borough commander, designed to improve responses to critical incidents that impact the community. In 2009, I sat in as an adviser on a series of Gold Group meetings, chaired by the borough commander, Wayne Chance, which focused on the tragic fire at Lakanal House on the Sceaux Gardens estate, where I had grown up. Six people died and at least 20 were injured. As a former resident of the estate, I was familiar with Lakanal House. I also knew the layout of the flats that were destroyed in the fire because I lived in a similar high rise. I witnessed the fire as it happened from my own home at the top of a high-rise, which was not that far away. I had a good relationship and friendship with Superintendent Victor Olisa who attended our IAG meetings. It was Victor who asked me to attend the Gold Group meetings. Others in attendance included our MP, Harriet Harman, the Area Commander, David Zinzan, and senior representatives from

Southwark Council and the London Fire Brigade. Based on what I knew about the layout of the flats in Lakanal House, I asked difficult and informed questions. '*Why were the victims of the fire told to stay put instead of being advised to access the fire escape balconies before they succumbed to the smoke inhalation?* My questions were not answered. I was told that I would have to wait until the coroner's inquest. So I waited. Patiently. However, by the time the inquest took place in 2013, Ms Harman did not respond to my emails asking if I could consult with her about the questions I had asked at the Gold Group. Then in 2017, a fire broke out in another high-rise, Grenfell Tower, in North Kensington, West London. 72 people died with more than an additional 70 injured. It seemed to me that lessons had not been learned from the Lakanal House tragedy. I still live on the top floor of a high-rise, but I have given up asking Southwark Council and the London Fire Brigade to talk to me about my fire safety concerns. They're not interested in talking to social housing tenants. I have often felt frustrated that despite having a lot of success in helping to reform the police, Southwark Council and the London Fire Brigade tend to shy away from interacting with key actors in their community.

For my work as a critical friend to the police, I received a Metropolitan Police Volunteer award from the former Police Commissioner, Sir John Stevens, at a ceremony in City Hall in 2003. This acknowledgement of my contribution to improving police and community relations meant a great deal to me. I remain committed to this work because I find it rewarding, and the police need to have their communities on their side to carry out their work effectively. As an IAG member for over 25 years, I have seen many examples of police and community partnership working at its best, particularly during the Damilola Taylor murder investigation. Though the police get it wrong some of the time, and they have an institutional history marked by racism, sexism, and homophobia, in my encounters with actual officers, I'm reminded of how hardworking and dedicated they are. They exist in a system that has historically treated people with impunity and prejudice, but they are trying to correct it. This is why I continue to be a trusted partner to the police.

I believe that with the right tools and community support, the police can get it right more often. It is not an easy task. Working in partnership with the police is unpaid, time consuming, sometimes difficult, always taxing, but ultimately enriching and rewarding work. I have been told by some of my family and friends that I am mad to give up my precious spare time to do this, but I will continue to serve my community and be a critical friend to the police as long as I am asked to, and as long as I can make a difference.

Alongside my work as an independent adviser, I have uncovered many fascinating stories of police history, mostly focused on Southwark. I have enjoyed sharing these stories with police officers, some of whom are interested in the history of their organisation. For example, for LGBT History Month in 2025 I gave a talk about Sergeant Harry Daley (1901–1971) who was openly gay at a time when it was a criminal offence. I also uncovered the story of Superintendent Robert Branford (1820–69), a mixed heritage police officer who rose through the ranks in Southwark. When this story came to the attention of our Borough Commander, Chief Superintendent Seb Adjei-Addoh, he invited me to give a talk about Branford to senior police officers. This took place in the briefing room at Peckham Police Station on October 3, 2023. It was followed by a room-naming ceremony in Branford's honour. Positive feedback from some of the officers who attended this event showed that my commitment to educating them about their own past has been a great success.

Chapter 15

Silence on the Publishing Front

As the 1990s drew to a close, I felt positive and optimistic about my future in the new millennium. I was encouraged by the successes of the 1990s and looked forward to more of the same. The popularity of *Brief Encounters* and *Black in the British Frame* led me to believe I would have a productive career as a writer of groundbreaking books. Then something unexpected happened. Shortly into the new millennium, I was invited by the Media Studies department of De Montfort University in Leicester to give a seminar to their staff about *Black in the British Frame* which led to a generous offer of a three-year bursary to undertake research for a Doctor of Philosophy degree (PhD). I accepted the offer and chose to research the representation of gay men in British television drama as the subject of my thesis. I thoroughly enjoyed researching and writing this. By the time I graduated, my PhD had become a Master of Philosophy (MPhil) degree. I found it impossible to cope with the demands of the PhD. There was too much emphasis on theory and I found the majority of my readings extremely difficult to comprehend. It took me three years to complete. While I appreciated the opportunity to experience what it is like to be a university student, I decided that the world of academia was not for me. It seemed to be mutual, because even with my literary output, with the exception of London

South Bank University, I am hardly ever invited to give lectures about my work in universities. The world of academia has always been an alien presence in my life, even when I was in it. It is a world that few escape from and few can access. I would suggest that this mindset is not so much race- or class-based, but very much about the control of power. The academic gatekeepers, namely the professors, regard themselves as impeccably progressive, supporting every liberal cause, and yet they exist in a protected ivory tower. Exclusive, not inclusive. There will be those who disagree with me, but they haven't lived my life.

For instance, in my own research, it has proved impossible to access the writings of academics. They are mostly published in journals for which you need to pay a subscription, and only if you work in academia is it possible to access these journals for free. On rare occasions I have personally contacted academics whose writing I am interested in and asked if they could take pity on me and send me the article, only to be ignored or declined. Without a university job, I haven't been able to apply for various academic research grants such as those awarded by the British Academy or the Arts and Humanities Research Council (AHRC).

My disenchantment with academia didn't put a damper on the entire millennium, as I'd soon enter a collaboration with the broadcasting historian Keith Howes and the television producer Stephen Jeffery-Poulter. We worked on a proposal for a television documentary about the history of gay men in British television. There had already been *Black and White in Colour* (1992) about Black people in British television, and this was followed by *A Night in With the Girls* (BBC2, 1997), which celebrated the contribution made by women to the development of television. It was only a matter of time before a similar archive- and interview-based documentary was made about gay men, or so I thought. Regrettably our proposal was rejected by everyone we took it to, including the BBC and Channel 4.

Then I was approached by David Olusoga, a television researcher.

He had read *Black in the British Frame* and was keen to collaborate with me on a proposal for a television documentary which would be based on the book. At the time, David was working for an independent company called Brook Lapping. We worked hard on the proposal, focusing on the British film aspects of *Black in the British Frame.* So far, so good. Brook Lapping submitted the proposal to a commissioning editor at Channel 4 and she appeared to like it. Development money was made available for David and I to collaborate on a more in-depth proposal, but it was all in vain. Although we were paid for writing the proposal, the Commissioning Editor turned down the documentary. I cannot recall why, only that David and I were deeply disappointed and went our separate ways. Some years later David was responsible for writing a series of outstanding history books including *The World's War* (2015) and *Black and British – A Forgotten History* (2016) as well as making some excellent television documentaries.

I should have seen these rejections as warnings of things to come, for in a short space of time, with the exception of *The Voice*, the Black newspapers and journals of the 1990s that I had written for gradually disappeared. So did the African Caribbean Units of the BBC and the BFI, which also meant the loss of the BFI's *Black Film Bulletin.* I had hoped that my book *Black in the British Frame* would have provided these organisations with a foundation to build upon but it became clear to me that this was not going to be the case. However, the film director Menelik Shabazz did launch a new magazine called *Black Filmmaker* and asked me to be a voluntary contributor on a freelance basis. Menelik did not have the budget to pay contributors, but it was a classy magazine and one that I was happy to support. I liked Menelik. He was a gentleman and appreciated my work on Black British cinema, especially *Black in the British Frame.*

At this time, *Black Filmmaker* was one of the very few journals to commission me to write for them. I tried in vain to write for the main-stream newspapers, but it was impossible. It was like talking to a brick wall. Deeply frustrated, there I was, with two decades of writing experience, three books published, expertise in Black British history and gay culture, with no outlets for my work. In time, I did make a breakthrough when the editor of a new journal called *BBC History Magazine* commissioned my proposal for a feature about the lives of Black Britons on the home front during the Second World War. 'We Also Served' was published in their September 2000 issue to coincide with the 60th anniversary of the beginning of the Blitz. Among those I highlighted were the community leader Dr Harold Moody, Joseph Cozier, an evacuee I had interviewed, the entertainer Adelaide Hall, and the bandleader Ken 'Snakehips' Johnson, who had been killed during an air raid. There was also a panel by Oku Ekpenyon relaying the story of her Nigerian-born father's experiences as an air raid warden. For me, this was work in progress and the publication of this article planted an idea in my head to research and write a full-length book about the subject, but in the interim I had to earn a living.

When my bursary at De Montfort University ended in 2002, I started applying for part-time jobs. It was the only way forward if I was to continue being a writer. I wasn't actively working on a book at that time but I was seriously considering approaching publishers with a proposal for a book about Black British citizens on the home front during the Second World War. I was eventually employed as a part-time library assistant in Southwark, and though I had to survive on a small income, it enabled me to pursue publishers. The first library I worked at was Nunhead on Gordon Road but after a short time, I was sent to Brandon, which was hidden amongst the tower blocks on the vast post-war Brandon estate near Walworth Road.

I settled into library work quickly. I enjoyed the different tasks we were given such as shelving books and answering telephone queries, but most of all I liked to interact with the public. Some of them could be challenging. There was one incident at Nunhead that involved a middle-class visitor notorious for late returns on her books. She always argued with members of staff if we requested the fines. One time, she returned one of J.K. Rowling's Harry Potter paperbacks, but it was soaking wet. She didn't offer an explanation so I asked her what had happened to it. She said her son had dropped it in the bath. No apology was offered, and when I explained to her that I couldn't accept the book in that condition and would have to request that she pay for a replacement, she hit the roof. Thankfully my manager intervened and supported what I had said but the woman still refused to pay for the book. Another time, at Brandon, a mother arrived with a small boy who couldn't have been more than four years old. After she had settled him at a computer in the children's section, she made for the exit. 'Excuse me', I said. 'You're not going to leave him unattended, are you?' She looked at me and explained, 'Oh, he'll be alright. I'm just going to the shops. His grandad is in the pub and he can see him across the square.' I took a deep breath. 'I'm sorry, but you cannot leave him', I said. 'He is too young.' The customer began to argue but I interrupted her and explained 'I am a library assistant, not an unpaid child minder. What happens if I'm shelving a Catherine Cookson at the other end of the library and a stranger walks off with him? I'm not prepared to take the responsibility.' With that she muttered something rude under her breath and shouted to the little boy, 'Come on, you're going to the shops with me.' The visitors were mostly friendly and interesting to talk to. My best days, though, were spent reading to children from local primary schools who visited the libraries.

Meanwhile, as I persevered on my writing journey, I quickly learned that the 'big' publishers would not talk to me unless I had an agent. No agent, no publisher. Simple policy. I remember a conversation with the switchboard operator at Harper Collins. When I informed her I was an author and wanted to speak to a commissioning editor, she flatly refused to put me through to anyone. 'Our editors will only speak to agents', she said. So I tried to find an agent. I wrote to quite a few but it proved a hopeless task. In spite of my successes with *Aunt Esther's*

Story (two separate editions in 1991 and 1996), and the two Cassell books, *Brief Encounters* and *Black in the British Frame*, no agent would take me on. Only one responded with a phone call. She was apologetic but explained that there was 'no market for books about Black British history'. Eventually I grew tired of trawling through the *Writers' and Artists' Yearbook* and contacting agents, only to be rejected every time. So I stopped. In addition to the idea for the Black community on the home front book, my proposals for books about Black British theatre and gay men in British television drama (based on my MPhil thesis) had to be shelved. These books should have been published. I felt the time was right and I couldn't understand why agents and publishers were so resistant. I suspected that they were all white and middle-class and this made my books problematic for them. I simply wasn't on their wavelength. I did seek honest feedback from friends on how to improve my book proposals, but this too was in vain. I found that the library job kept me grounded and sane. It provided me with a structure to my week. A routine. I was a forward-thinking person, and optimistic that something wonderful would happen despite the run of bad luck.

In October of 2002, I was invited by the Imperial War Museum (IWM) to adapt the *BBC History Magazine* article for an illustrated presentation during their Black History Month programme. With pressure from Marika Sherwood, my BASA colleague, the museum agreed that they should be acknowledging the Black presence in various conflicts. It was Helena Stride and Grant Rogers in the museum's Education Department that made it possible. In addition to my talk about the home front, Ben Bousquet and Colin Douglas – who was instrumental in *Aunt Esther's Story* getting published – were also engaged by the museum as speakers in the programme. Helena and Grant established these as annual events every October in the museum's calendar. With my contacts in Southwark Council, and the help of some friends in neighbouring Lambeth, we were able to draw a large number of Black attendees year on year. One of my proud moments was giving a vibrant talk to a full audience about Black women in Britain during the Second World War which coincided with the IWM's *Women and War* exhibition on October 15, 2003. It was the biggest audience I had ever had for a talk, at least 250.

My research eventually brought me to a local venue, the Cuming Museum on Walworth Road. They liked a proposal I had put together for an exhibition called *Keep Smiling Through – Black Londoners on the Home Front 1939 to 1945*. The museum successfully applied for funding from the Heritage Lottery Fund and the exhibition was launched on April 10, 2008. I had curated the exhibition with the enthusiastic support of the museum staff. Using historical material and personal memorabilia such as books, photographs, music sheets, and diaries, it showcased a range of Black Londoners who took part in the war effort. They included the community leader Dr Harold Moody, broadcaster Una Marson, fire watcher Esther Bruce (Aunt Esther), singer and entertainer Adelaide Hall; so many familiar names, and more. We also reserved a space for local Black elders, mostly from West Africa and the Caribbean, to put together a display of art work that represented how their countries had supported the British during the war. It was a success and remained open for six months. At the same time, the IWM invited me to join an advisory group for their exhibition *From War to Windrush* which highlighted the contribution of Black men and women from the Caribbean and Britain during the First and Second World Wars. The other consultants included Arthur Torrington from the Windrush Foundation, Colin Douglas, Rev Dr Rosemarie Mallett and Dr Hakim Adi. The opening on June 12, 2008 was attended by some of the remarkable men and women who had served in the Second World War including Sam King, Lilian Bader, Laurent Phillpotts and Nadia Cattouse. Among the exhibits on display were pages from the Empire Windrush passenger list; the telegram from King George V and Queen Mary expressing their sympathy for the death of Walter Tull, the former Tottenham Hotspur footballer and British Army Officer who was killed in action in 1918; photos and audio testimony from Connie Mark who joined the Auxiliary Territorial Service (ATS) in Jamaica in 1943; and the MBE belonging to Sam King who returned to Britain on the Empire Windrush after serving in the RAF.

These exhibitions gave me valuable experience in working with others on a subject that was close to my heart, however, no amount of experience, it seemed, could lend me the credibility required to publish books about Black Britons on the home front. I tried my hand at the publishing journey again, still agentless. One independent publisher, who shall remain nameless, who specialised in publishing books about the Second World War, informed me that they couldn't possibly consider a book about the home front that 'detracted from the popular image of Winston Churchill, King George VI, Queen Elizabeth and Vera Lynn'. I found it very upsetting to go to work in the library and see our Black Interest sections dominated by imported African-American books, especially in the children's section. I felt very strongly that young people were being denied access to stories about Black Britons while many books were made available to them about African-Americans such as Dr Martin Luther King Jr and Rosa Parks.

How did I cope with the rejections for the home front book? Well, I didn't take to drink or drugs. As an atheist, it wasn't an option to turn to God or a religion. I knew that I was in the right place and doing the right thing. I didn't need anyone to tell me that. I persevered because I am the product of a close-knit working-class family and they helped give me the strength I needed to pursue my work, against the odds. I was also driven by the warmth and acceptance of members of the Black community who have always embraced my work by attending my talks, giving me positive feedback, and buying my books. This has always been the case. Their support has never wavered. I have never had to answer the question 'Why is a white man telling us about our history?' I have simply been left alone to do what I do best and I believe this has a lot to do with being a diligent researcher and presenting facts in an accessible way.

I had a breakthrough in 2005 when Southwark Council agreed to fund the publication of my book about local Black history. *Speak of Me As I Am – The Black Presence in Southwark since 1600* was a modest book but it gave me an opportunity to write about my discovery of John Primero, a Black Tudor from Camberwell, as well as other Black historical figures with connections to my borough: Dr Harold Moody, Una Marson, Sam King, Marianne Jean-Baptiste, and Rio Ferdinand among them. It did well, but only in Southwark. It proved difficult to publicise the book outside my London borough.

During Black History Month that year, I was invited to a local event to sell copies of *Speak of Me As I Am.* Tables were provided for sellers to display their books. As people began to arrive, I recognised a well-known Black Member of Parliament. The MP came to my table, picked up a copy of my new book, and began walking away. I called after the MP, 'Excuse me. That'll be £5 please.' I was then subjected to a disconcerting glare. Then the MP threw the book onto the table and walked off. I was shocked. For a fleeting moment I thought that the MP was going to engage in a conversation about my work. I would have appreciated that. Instead, I was confronted by an arrogant MP with no manners. I have no idea why the MP behaved so rudely. For me, it was a lost opportunity. It would have meant so much to me to discuss my work with the MP and find out their views on Black British history and how we could work together to encourage the teaching of it in our schools.

Meanwhile, back at the IWM, I continued to give talks and also participated in *Whose Remembrance?* a documentary about the participation of Black and Asian servicemen and women in the two world wars. It was the IWM's first Arts and Humanities Research Council-supported research project. The IWM temporarily closed while it underwent a large-scale renovation. It reopened in 2014 in time for the start of the centenary of the First World War. However, by the time it reopened my contacts at the IWM had departed, and there were no more opportunities to give talks there. In 2014, when I inquired if I could present another Black History Month talk that year, I was politely informed that I would have to pay for the use of one of their rooms and there would be no fee because they no longer had a budget for such events. An insider explained to me that the IWM was no longer community-focused. It was now a corporate organisation. I do not know if this was true. All I know is that my relationship with the IWM had come to an end.

In my private life, I had to face two heartbreaking losses. Dad sadly was diagnosed with asbestosis. This was the effect of his work in the 1960s and 1970s as a pipe fitter. He was exposed to asbestos when he removed the lagging on pipes in industrial buildings. It was a cruel blow to all of us, but Dad suffered the most. He passed away on April 1, 2007 at the age of 75. Not long afterwards, Mum was diagnosed with an aggressive form of breast cancer which she battled bravely, but it took her from us on March 28, 2010 at the age of 78. The passing of both parents so close together was unbearable. The loss of my lovely, protective parents shook me to the core. My sister felt the same. When Dad's health began to deteriorate, Linda relocated him and Mum from their home in Bideford, North Devon (where they had settled in 1997) to her family home in West Cork in the Republic of Ireland. When we were younger, Linda had told me that if she had children she didn't want to raise them in London. True to her word, she found a home with her husband Richard and children Emma, Michael, and Molly in a rugged but beautiful and peaceful part of rural Ireland.

Linda cared for Mum and Dad, but it was only for a short time. When they were gone I felt as if I had lost the foundation of my existence. They loved us unconditionally all our lives. It was a difficult time and for a while I existed in a state of utter depression. I wasn't aware I was depressed. That realisation came later. But at the time I found it hard to manage even simple daily tasks. I just felt tired all the time. I did reach out to a handful of friends and family members for support but I didn't trouble Linda because she had her own grieving to cope with, though we remained in regular contact, and I visited when I could. There were no funerals. Linda and I agreed to have our parents cremated. We had private ceremonies for them in Linda's beautiful garden where we buried their ashes. First Dad, then Mum. Together. Only myself, Linda, her husband, and three children attended. It was what our parents wished for. No fuss.

My depression lasted about one year after Mum passed away. Then something unexpected happened to help snap me out of it. I had shared how I felt with Diane Johnson, the Personal Assistant to Wayne Chance, Southwark's Borough Commander. She then spoke to Superintendent Steve Deehan about it and he reached out to me and asked if he could visit me at my home. When he came, he told me how sorry he was about the loss of my parents and said that he and his colleagues, including the Borough Commander, were there to help me if I needed it. He assured me that they saw me as part of the police family. It is hard to explain, but immediately following Steve's visit and kind words, the grief began to pass. It has never completely gone away and I don't think it ever will, but when I look back I believe it was this unexpected visit that helped me to put things in perspective and move on. Then another unexpected thing happened which helped me through the bad patch. I had built up a friendship with another police officer, Sergeant Dave Gwyther. He offered me a seaside break in his family's holiday home in Broadstairs on the Kent coast. Free of charge. He said that it was the least he could do in return for all the hard voluntary work I undertook for the police. Dave explained that he and his wife took their children to the seaside fisherman's cottage during school holidays but they were happy for me to stay there by myself during term times. I was ecstatic. I loved the seaside but rarely took time to venture outside London. I made quite a few visits to Broadstairs where I found myself able to relax. Meanwhile, I was seriously considering leaving the library service to concentrate on writing full-time because I, at last, had a breakthrough with the home front book. A publisher had shown an interest. There was, indeed, a light at the end of the tunnel.

Chapter 16

The Turning Point

To recap, it took me almost ten years to find a publisher for my book *Mother Country – Britain's Black Community on the Home Front 1939–45*. A decade of nos, of redirections, and dead-ends. 'Your book is too niche.' 'Black people do not buy books.' I heard it all. I didn't give up hope. One of the reasons for this was my concern that primary schools were ignoring historical Black Britons and our own civil rights movement. Some schools made an exception for the Crimean nurse, Mary Seacole, but when I was invited to a secondary school for girls in Brixton to give a talk for Black History Month, the walls of the classroom I entered said it all. They were covered with posters of African-American women from history: Sojourner Truth, Mary McLeod Bethune, Rosa Parks, Alice Walker, Angela Davis, Michelle Obama, and others. No Mary Seacole or any other Black British women. The young women in the classroom were captivated by the stories of the Black British women I presented and the photographs I showed them. They could relate to them. Finally, after years of knocking on publisher's doors, I made a breakthrough with The History Press. The genie was about to be released from his bottle.

I cannot recall how I found them. It may have been while I was browsing books in the library where I worked and checking out the names of their publishers. I found out that The History Press specialised in publishing titles devoted to local and specialist history. It claimed to be Britain's largest independent publisher in this field, which meant I didn't need an agent when I approached them. I sent them the proposal. To my relief, they agreed to publish *Mother Country* just a few months before I had lost my mother. I had finally turned a corner. Meanwhile, I was advised to join The Society of Authors, which I did, and they have since been a wonderful source of support and practical help, especially with publishing contracts. I completely gave up trying to find a literary agent.

For *Mother Country* I applied for and received a grant from the Arts Council of England which let me do in-depth research for the book. From the British Library I was able to cover the cost of copies of back issues of the wartime newsletters of the League of Coloured Peoples. I also purchased a complete set of bound volumes of the BBC journal *London Calling* (1939–58) which gave me insights into BBC broadcasts across the former British Empire, including the Caribbean and West Africa, in wartime.

In the book I wanted to include a chapter about the home front experiences of Black elders from West Africa and the Caribbean but I couldn't access any funding to travel to these places. I realised that I didn't need to go far and that London had Black elders from all the places I wanted to go. I found Loleta Jemmott from Barbados and Olu Richards from Sierra Leone at the Southwark Pensioners Centre. Cerene Palmer from Jamaica was a member of the local Safer Neighbourhood Ward Panel that I chaired. And Randol Dacosta from Barbados had been my next door neighbour for years. They were all children during the Second World War and willingly agreed to be interviewed. Their revelations enriched the book greatly. I was surprised at how their home front experiences in Sierra Leone and the Caribbean mirrored the lives of the British. They had food rationing, air raid wardens, blackouts and air raid alerts, even though they were not bombed. They were loyal to Britain, too, and, as British subjects, no matter how poor they were, they would donate money to help what they referred to as the 'Mother Country'. The citizens of these countries also had sons and daughters who volunteered as service personnel. They left their homelands to join the British army, navy, and Royal Air Force. Connie Mark, who was from Jamaica, put it simply in her interview, 'We were brought up that England was our Mother Country and obviously when your mother has problems, you've got to come and help her.' I truly enjoyed this additional research for the book and learned so much about these places. The history was there on my doorstep.

I also included a chapter about something close to my heart. In my experience, no one had ever questioned what would have happened to Britain's Black citizens if Hitler had invaded these shores. There had been Norman Longmate's *If Britain Had Fallen*, published in 1972, about the effects of a Nazi invasion on this country. However, the author didn't mention the fate of Britain's Black population. So I wrote to him. He replied: 'Yours is the first letter to ask what would have happened to the Black residents in the event of a successful German invasion.' But he confessed that he hadn't considered it, and was unable to answer my question. I ended the book by stating that prominent Black people like Learie Constantine and Dr Harold Moody would probably have ended up in the hands of the Gestapo. The rest, including my Aunt Esther, would have been rounded up and interned in concentration camps which was the fate suffered by Black Germans and Europeans in the Holocaust.

When *Mother Country* was published on September 23, 2010 to coincide with the 70th anniversary of the London Blitz, the playwright and broadcaster Bonnie Greer provided the following endorsement for the back cover, 'Stephen Bourne brings great natural scholarship and passion to a largely hidden story. He is highly accessible, accurate, and surprising. You always walk away from his work knowing something that you didn't know, that you didn't even suspect. *Mother Country* is quite simply a home-grown triumph.'

I discovered that the 'pain barrier' I had faced for years disappeared. The constant rejections of the book and other titles had been hard to deal with but as soon as I saw *Mother Country* in print, I found that I had shattered the glass ceiling and made an important breakthrough. The sense of relief was overwhelming, however, it wasn't lost on me that there was still work to do. This book was a new venture for The History Press and they were uncertain about how successful it would be. I do recall The History Press being cautious about publishing *Mother Country* because of what they perceived to be its minority interest. There was a belief in the publishing world that Black British non-fiction books did not sell. Consequently, they believed that there was no market for them. *Mother Country* wasn't an exception to the rule, but proof that the rule was nonsense, and thus marked the beginning of a long and productive relationship with The History Press.

The History Press were impressed with the hard work I had undertaken to generate interest in the book. The sales were excellent, and they readily commissioned the second proposal I sent to them, a companion to *Mother Country*, called *The Motherland Calls – Britain's Black Servicemen and Women 1939–45*. The new book focused on the African, Caribbean, and Black British citizens who volunteered to support the war effort by joining the armed forces. As British citizens, they wanted to play their part in fighting Nazi Germany and its allies. I recognised that very little attention had been given to these trailblazers. In the numerous books I had read about the Second World War, hardly any acknowledged the support from across the British Empire. Among those I included were Britain's Lilian Bader (WAAF), Guyana's Cy Grant (RAF), Trinidad's Ulric Cross (RAF), Nigeria's Peter Thomas (RAF), Sierra Leone's Johnny Smythe (RAF) and Jamaica's Billy Strachan (RAF), Connie Mark (ATS), and Sam King (RAF).

I had known Sam King for a while. He had lived in my London borough since arriving on the Empire Windrush in 1948. In 1983, he became the first Black Mayor of Southwark. I had written about him in *Speak of Me As I Am.* Our paths had crossed at various community events, mostly during Black History Month. When I questioned him about leaving Jamaica in 1944 to join the RAF, he replied: 'I don't think the British Empire was perfect, but it was better than Nazi Germany.' He also made the following statement about racism in Britain which resonated with me, 'For every third of the average English people who are unreasonable to us there is another third who will go out of their way to help you. The other third couldn't care less one way or the other as long as their football team plays on Saturday and they can get beer in the pubs.' When I nominated Sam for a Southwark Heritage Blue Plaque in 2010, he received the honour following a huge number of votes from the public.

There were two moments during the writing stage of *The Motherland Calls* that left me feeling very emotional. In 1941, Cassian Waight, a 30-year-old civil servant from Belize City, British Honduras, volunteered for the RAF. By 1944, Cass had become a wireless operator/air gunner on a Lancaster bomber with 101 Squadron. In 1944, Cass and his crew were prominently featured in an edition of *London Calling.* While searching through the wartime copies, I noticed a photograph of the crew, including Cass, on the cover of the March 19–25 issue. Further investigation revealed that they were known as the 'League of Nations' crew because they had members from across the British Empire including the Caribbean, South Africa, and Canada. I also found out that before the edition of *London Calling* was published, the 'League of Nations' crew had flown their last mission. In February 1944, Cass was among the three crew members who had died due to a fire on the Lancaster that they couldn't escape in time. This tragic story unravelled very quickly. From discovering Cass on the cover of *London Calling* I managed, in just one afternoon, to identify him and discover what had happened to him.

The other story that moved me to tears was that of the southern Nigerian Isaac Fadoyebo. He was one of almost 100,000 African soldiers shipped to Asia by the British in 1943–44 to join the fight against the invading Japanese. It was one of the war's most brutal campaigns. In 1944, Isaac's unit were getting closer to the Japanese in the Burmese jungle, unprepared for the horror that was to come. The Japanese opened fire on them. Not only was Isaac injured, but he was aware that in Japanese-occupied territory the Japanese did not take prisoners unless they were white British. When the Japanese found the wounded Isaac, they left him to die. Stranded behind enemy lines, Isaac was lucky to be near a village of Bengalis of Indian origin who, unlike many of the Burmese, supported the British. The villagers saved his life by giving him shelter. He said: 'They were sent by God to take care of me.' Isaac remained hidden by the villagers for nine months. In December 1944, the Japanese retreated and the British Army marched into the village and liberated Isaac. Amazed to still be alive, Isaac returned home to Nigeria. In his village he was given a hero's welcome from family and friends who believed he had been killed. It was the following quote from Isaac that brought tears to my eyes: 'If people have taken you as dead, and you suddenly appear, the tendency is for them to throw sand on you because by throwing sand on you, if you are a ghost, you disappear.' The villagers threw sand on Isaac but he did not disappear.

When *The Motherland Calls* was published in 2012, it was cold-shouldered by the mainstream print media and there were even fewer reviews than there had been for *Mother Country*. However, the *Britain at War* magazine (July 2013) named it their Book of the Month. The book found its readers, probably by word-of-mouth and the hard work on my part to raise its profile (I gave a number of talks at community level to achieve this and distributed flyers provided by my publisher). I did have one small breakthrough with the *Times Educational Supplement* who, on January 23, 2013 published a short article called 'Honour Black Britons' that I had written about the failure of British schools to acknowledge Black British history.

The History Press were enthusiastic about my next proposal: *Black Poppies – Britain's Black Community and the Great War*. With the centenary of the First World War on the horizon, I thought that it would be a good idea to publish something that coincided with this important date in the calendar. I explained in my proposal that I did not intend to focus solely on the servicemen, but that I'd include chapters about the wider Black community in Britain at that time – 1914 to 1918 – with a closing chapter about the terrible race riots of 1919 in which the community came under attack. *Black Poppies* was commissioned and I spent most of 2013 writing it. At first I worried about not being a military historian, but I soon overcame this when I told myself that you didn't have to be one to write a book about the First World War. To help my understanding of the war, I visited several local public libraries and looked for books which had a distilled version of the conflict. I also decided to stick to my way of writing history by focusing on first-hand testimony when I could find it.

I found that information about Black servicemen in the conflict was sparse and conflicting. Once again, with no institutional support or access to funding, my additional research had limitations. At one point, I didn't feel as if I had enough information to fill a book and I panicked. I put myself under a great deal of pressure, which induced terrible migraines. At one point the pain in my head was so bad that I went to A&E at nearby King's College Hospital. I was advised to have a brain scan, which I did, but thankfully there was nothing sinister in my head, just the pressure of writing *Black Poppies*. This book continued to be a nightmare to write, but I persevered and eventually completed it. When I submitted the book, I convinced myself it was going to be a disaster. I believed the title alone was going to get me into trouble and generate hostility from First World War experts. I couldn't have been more wrong, because *Black Poppies* became my most successful book following its publication on August 4, 2014. In fact, my editor at The History Press informed me that due to pre-orders, the first print-run of five hundred copies had sold out before the official publication date. He asked me what I had been doing to promote the book and I explained that earlier in the year I had been hyper-active on social networking services, mainly Facebook and Twitter, and all through 2013 I had been posting information about the book. Due to high demand, The History Press immediately reprinted the book and continued to do so throughout the centenary period.

Black Poppies touched a nerve in the Black community. This happened because no one had ever explored the contribution of Black servicemen in any depth. Black readers were ready for it because it filled a gap. I was told on more than one occasion that it was the title of the book and the striking cover photo of a Black sailor and soldier that attracted readers to it. In the book I included examples of racism, but I believe it was the positive stories that empowered Black readers. I wrote about the comradeship with white soldiers that some Black soldiers experienced under fire on the battlefields. The examples I gave included the brave and heroic Walter Tull and Norman Manley who successfully integrated into the Royal Field Artillery and served as a gun layer on the Western Front. It was these stories Black readers connected to. Many readers told me that they'd only been told negative stories. The 'racism' narrative dominates and for some it can be soul destroying to only ingest this kind of history. I learned that it was important to acknowledge that in British history not all white people were racist and not all Black people saw themselves as victims.

Black Poppies was the breakthrough book I had been waiting for. It was a success and opened doors for me. I was invited to my first Literary Festival (in Havant) and won my first literature prize (from Southwark Arts). I also gave numerous talks throughout the centenary period at a wide variety of venues. There were many highlights, including the magnificent library in Birmingham which had recently opened, and then there was the retired midwives group at King's College Hospital. They were a wonderful, receptive audience. With one exception, an Irishwoman, they were all African and Caribbean. They loved the *Black*

Poppies talk. One of them, a Jamaican, wanted to adopt Herbert Morris, the Jamaican lad who had been shot at dawn in 1917 for desertion, a heartbreaking story. When I was asked where I had been born, I replied St Giles' Hospital in nearby Camberwell. One of the retired midwives shouted across the room, 'Mabel! Mabel! Wake up! He's one of yours.' Mabel, in her nineties and fast asleep, had delivered babies at St Giles' Hospital in the 1950s.

In Liverpool's Childwall Academy, a young lad sat through my *Black Poppies* talk with his arms folded and no expression on his face. Afterwards he said, 'When you started talking I thought your book was going to be boring and you were going to be boring, but now I think your book is amazing and you are amazing.' I took a deep breath of relief and thanked him. A talk at the National Maritime Museum in Greenwich was attended by Adrian Bader, the grandson of Marcus Bailey, the sailor I had featured on the cover of *Black Poppies*. That was another special encounter.

In January 2015, I received an invitation from a theatre director to give a talk about *Black Poppies* at the Globe Theatre. He was staging a production of Shakespeare's *Othello* and setting it in the trenches of the First World War. It was going to be presented to school children. That meant a lot to me. Later that year I was invited to give the same talk about *Black Poppies* at my former primary school, Oliver Goldsmith, on Peckham Road. The pupils were excited to discover that I had been a student at the school and asked endearing if not hilarious questions like whether I'd fought in the First World War. I hadn't been back there since I had left in 1969. It proved a memorable occasion.

The popularity of *Black Poppies* continued to soar. At the request of PC Scotty Frost, I gave a talk for the Southwark Police Cadets, most of whom came from African and Caribbean families. Scotty was one of those rare officers who thought outside the box to create a positive environment for his cadets, and they loved him for it. He then asked me to help him put together a summer project for his cadets, inspired by the First World War centenary. I made a list of First World War memorials around the borough that Scotty and I brought the cadets to. After photographing the memorials, we put together an exhibition which we presented at several venues in the borough, including public libraries, Southwark Cathedral, and Southwark Council's head office at Tooley Street.

Interest in *Black Poppies* continued to grow. A history teacher at a North London academy found me on social media. When we spoke he explained that he had to teach his students about the First World War as part of the history curriculum, but the majority of them came from African and Caribbean backgrounds. He wanted to convey to them a relevant portrayal of the war from a perspective they could empathise with. I accepted his invitation to visit the Academy and talk about *Black Poppies*. His students gave me a warm welcome. They responded positively to the images of Black servicemen and the stories I told about them.

I was encouraged by the success of *Black Poppies*, and I thoroughly enjoyed giving the talks. However, life makes sure to keep you humble. For Black History Month in 2016, I was invited to talk about *Black Poppies* to an audience at the Houses of Parliament. This was going to be part of their series of First World War talks. Invitations were sent to every member of the House of Lords and every Member of Parliament, including my own MP, Harriet Harman. The public was also invited and I was thrilled to see many Black attendees, including parents with their children. About 80 people came, none of them from the House of Lords, only one an MP, a Conservative. I was deeply disappointed with the lack of interest shown by our Parliamentarians. After the talk, the Tory MP asked me if he could take the floor. I agreed and what came next was surprising. After introducing himself he apologised to me and the audience for the absence of his fellow Parliamentarians. A few weeks later he invited me to the Houses of Parliament for a cup of tea and a chat. He promised to promote the book and suggested that I visit the Department for Education (DfE) and try to persuade them to raise the book's profile amongst teachers.

When I visited the DfE, I truly believed I was going to make a breakthrough. The meeting took place with several civil servants at their headquarters on Great Smith Street in Westminster. Unfortunately, nothing came of it. I informed them that all I wanted was for history teachers in British primary schools and academies to know that *Black Poppies* existed. It didn't matter to me if they ignored the book. I just wanted them to know it existed so they could make a choice whether to use it in their classrooms or not. They said they were unable to promote a book. It would set a precedent. Instead, they suggested that I approach newspapers to ask them for coverage, an approach I'd tried many times without success. They didn't offer me any help. I felt frozen out.

In 2018, I accepted an invitation from the Army's Black Asian Minority Ethnic (BAME) network to talk about *Black Poppies* at a conference at Tidworth Camp, a British Army military installation in Wiltshire. Over 500 servicemen and women attended and their positive response was overwhelming. It made me realise more than ever that this book was having a powerful effect, yet I couldn't help but to wonder how influential *Black Poppies* could have been if the mainstream print media had been more supportive.

It saddened me that the book was ignored by the BBC during the centenary commemorations. In 2014, I reached out to Adrian Van Klaveren, when he was the Controller of the Great War Centenary at the BBC. He assured me he would spread the word about the book to programme makers across the BBC. You know how that goes. Reviews were favourable, but only one was published in a broadsheet. When I read it, the relief I felt brought me to tears. It was written by Bernardine Evaristo who described *Black Poppies* in *The Independent* (September 11, 2014) as a slim but important book with fascinating insights:

> 'Bourne is brilliant at framing the bigger picture through individual stories. He zooms in on several soldiers from varying backgrounds and classes...Until historians and cultural map-makers stop ignoring the historical presence of people of colour, books such as this one provide a powerful, revelatory counterbalance to the whitewashing of British history.'

This was the first and, to date, only review of any of my books in a broadsheet. *Black Poppies'* popularity continued and in 2019, five years after its original publication, a revised, second edition was published by The History Press.

Though I'd been searching so long for mainstream validation, the most impactful moment from my *Black Poppies* journey would be this. In August 2016, a letter was forwarded to me by The History Press. It had been sent to them by a Black prison inmate who had read the book and wanted to reach out to me. He requested photocopies of some of the photos in the book, which I immediately sent him. He planned to put together a small exhibition in the prison for Black History Month. I was deeply moved when I read what he had to say. Here is an extract: 'I am at present an unfortunate prisoner in Her Majesties prison HMP Thameside. The reason that I am writing to you is because I have just finished your book *Black Poppies* which has given me a rare insight into the lives of early Black people of great courage and pride, living, working and standing strong. This has brought great pride into my life, bringing about a sense of pride, ownership and something I can't quite put my finger on. Looking at the pictures was like seeing familiar faces observed growing up around me over the years. I was very impressed with the construction and well thought out content in this book. God bless you.'

Chapter 17

A Career Outside the Spotlight

Recognition is important to all of us. We need reassurance that we are on the right path, doing the right thing. I need reassurance that my books are being read and acknowledged. I also want recognition for the amazing people I have written about in my books. They are Black people who have contributed something important to this country and made a difference. In time, I discovered that the recognition for both myself and the people I write about comes, not from the mainstream print media, but elsewhere.

The existence of Black History Month (BHM) every October has been important to me. It has provided many opportunities to share my research and books with the Black community, filling in the existing gaps in history lessons in our schools and in our history books. I have no shortage of examples showcasing the positive response to my work. It's been an extreme privilege. I recall a memory from after a BHM talk I gave in 2008 about the contribution of Caribbean people to the Second World War when an elderly Black woman approached me and silently pushed a £20 note into my hand. I was surprised and was about to give it back when her daughter came forward and explained, 'Mummy wants you to have it. She came here from Jamaica in the 1950s to work as a nurse, and she says you are the first person who has acknowledged what her island did for England during the war. This is her way of saying thank you.' Around the same time, I gave a similar talk for a group of Black elders at the Southwark Pensioners Centre, not far from my home. Afterwards one of the women asked me how much I was being paid. I replied, 'Nothing. I'm doing this for nothing.' She shook her head. 'Come', she said to the other Black elders, 'Let us show our appreciation.' With that she took off her hat and passed it around the group. She collected about £7 and gave it to me.

After the publication of *Black Poppies*, I received a great deal of positive feedback, but one incident I'll never forget occurred when I jumped onto a bus outside Liverpool Street station and the young Black driver cried out 'Black Poppies!' I was taken aback and asked him how he knew I had written the book. He told me that he loved the book, had learned a great deal from it, and wished he had had a book like that when he was at school. I asked again, how did he know I had written it. He replied: 'I was curious to know what you looked like so I googled you.' At that point the people queuing behind me became impatient.

It was Cynthia Hamilton who brought me to the attention of Valerie Brandes at Jacaranda Books. She heard me on a Radio 4 programme and then searched online for my details to pass on to Valerie. Cynthia thought I'd be a great fit for Jacaranda because of my focus on Black British personalities, rather than American, for a change. She told me that Jacaranda was one of the few Black-owned independent book publishers in Britain. Founded in 2011 by Valerie, its aim is to promote inclusivity and diversity in publishing. When I met Valerie and her team, which included Cynthia, we discussed possible ideas for a book.

I informed them about my collection of Evelyn Dove photographs and memorabilia. Evelyn had embraced the worlds of jazz, musical theatre and, most importantly, cabaret, in a career that spanned five decades from the 1920s through to the 1960s. A Black British diva with movie star looks, she captivated audiences and admirers across Europe. At the height of her fame, she replaced Josephine Baker as the star attraction in a revue at the Casino de Paris. She refused to be constrained by her race or middle-class West African and English backgrounds. Evelyn was a woman ahead of her time. She flew past barriers and faced up to her own personal struggles with determination and defiance.

By the time Evelyn passed away in 1987, her contributions had been forgotten, except by her friend Isabelle Lucas. When I met Isabelle in 1989, she told me all about Evelyn and showed me the photographs and memorabilia she had saved. In 1993, Isabelle was a great help when I included Evelyn in my BBC Radio 2 series *Salutations*. When Isabelle suffered a heart attack, she asked me to take responsibility for Evelyn's collection. She feared that when she passed away it would end up in a rubbish skip. When I showed some of the photographs to Valerie and her team, they were fascinated by Evelyn's story, as well as her beauty and glamour. She was a lost Black British star and Jacaranda immediately contracted me to write a book about her. *Evelyn Dove – Britain's Black Cabaret Queen* was published in 2016 and launched at the Royal Academy of Music where she had been a student during the First World War. Sadly, Radio 4's *Woman's Hour* declined to interview me about the book, despite Evelyn's working with the BBC. In 1925, she was one of the first Black women to sing on BBC radio and in 1946, she was the first to have her own BBC television series.

I proposed another book to Jacaranda to coincide with the 70th anniversary of the arrival of the Empire Windrush and founding of the National Health Service in 1948. I wanted to compile a coffee table book about the lives of Black women in Britain spanning the ten years from the start of the Second World War in 1939 to 1948. It is a period in which a diverse range of Black women from various social classes and professions made an important contribution to this country, whether it be the armed services, the BBC, or nursing and entertainment. The women include Lilian Bader, Una Marson, Josephine Baker, Nurse Ademola, Cleo Laine, Winifred Atwell, and many others. Some of them I had known personally, such as Pauline Henriques, Pearl Connor-Mogotsi, Nadia Cattouse, Elisabeth Welch, and Adelaide Hall. I also wanted to acknowledge Mona Baptiste, who was one of the few women on the Windrush. A rarely seen photo of her with other Windrush arrivals was featured on the front cover. *War to Windrush – Black Women in Britain 1939–48* was launched at BFI Southbank on June 4, 2018. It was a great success and many people attended. After I had given a talk about the book, attendees queued for a signed copy. Afterwards, I was approached by a frail elderly Black woman who seemed to be disoriented. I asked her if I could help. She said she had received a letter about her status in this country.

This was the time of the Windrush Scandal. A political action by Prime Minister Theresa May's Tory government that generated public outrage. It concerned people mostly from the Caribbean, who were wrongly detained, denied legal rights, threatened with deportation and, in at least 83 cases, wrongly deported from the United Kingdom by the Home Office. I tried my best to advise her. I was aware that the Black Cultural Archives (BCA) were giving free advice to people who had arrived in Britain before 1973 and were concerned about their status as British subjects. I suggested that she contact the BCA as soon as possible. She knew they were located in Windrush Square, Brixton. She thanked me and departed.

It was David Somerset, a film programmer at BFI Southbank, who made it possible for me to present the *War to Windrush* event. However, the wider programme planning team proved trickier to deal with. I had curated the 10th *Out of the Archives* retrospective in 2001, but I had to wait 18 years to curate another. This was *Forgotten Black TV Drama* which opened in February 2019. In collaboration with Lez Cooke, an Honorary Research Fellow at the University of London, we presented a selection of British television dramas from 1961 to 1985, many of them not seen since they were first broadcast. We showcased the work of some of the most outstanding African and Caribbean writers of their generation, such as Jan Carew, Sylvia Wynter, Barry Reckord, Michael Abbensetts, Jamal Ali, Buchi Emecheta, Caryl Phillips, Mustapha Matura, and Trix Worrell. The screenings unfortunately failed to attract large Black audiences, which had been my intention. A friend explained to me that BFI Southbank was still viewed by many in the Black community as a predominantly white, middle-class organisation.

Soon afterwards, I proposed a similar retrospective, *Forgotten Gay TV Drama*, to coincide with the publication of my book *Playing Gay in the Golden Age of British Television*, but the programme planning team turned it down. I was informed by a member of staff – off the record – that a retrospective which focused specifically on gay men would not be acceptable. BFI Southbank preferred to focus their attention on the LGBTQIA+ community at large. BFI Flare, the London LGBTQIA+ Film Festival, had already replaced the London Lesbian and Gay Film Festival. I was heartbroken that a gay-specific event was no longer possible.

While I was finally enjoying recognition and success with my Black British history books, I had to play the waiting game for a gay history book to be commissioned. I hadn't written one since *Brief Encounters* in 1996. I had tried in vain to find a publisher for a book based on my MPhil thesis about gay men in television drama. I couldn't even get commissioned to write for our monthly gay magazines: *Gay Times* or *Attitude.* Then something unexpected happened. A publisher came to *me.* For LGBT History Month in February 2012, *BBC History Magazine* published a two-page article I had written for them about various gay men's lives in the Second World War. I included, amongst others, the RAF hero Ian Gleed who had been decorated by King George VI for his bravery in the Battle of Britain; Dudley Cave, who had been a prisoner of war and in later life became an activist who campaigned for the lifting of the ban on homosexuals in the armed services; the flamboyant Quentin Crisp, and entertainer Noel Coward. I was contacted by a commissioning editor called Tomasz Hoskins who was employed by the publisher I. B. Tauris. When I googled I. B. Tauris, I was a bit wary. They looked too academic for me. Too much like Routledge. That would mean writing in a completely different style and not receiving an advance. Nothing could have been further from the truth. When I met Tomasz he told me that he liked my writing style, because it was free of academic jargon and theory, and wondered if I would be interested in expanding the article into a book and, yes, that I would be paid an advance. It hadn't occurred to me that the article could be extended into a book. I had already come to terms with the fact that no publisher was interested in publishing my gay history books. Then out of the blue, I was contacted by a publisher and given an opportunity to write one. I suggested to Tomasz that I also include the First World War while we were still in the centenary period, which he agreed was a good idea. He then asked me if I would include lesbians. I said I could, but only if he extended the contract by a couple of years (so that I could do the necessary research) and pay me more money. He declined and we agreed to focus the book on gay men only. Tomasz then scheduled the publication date for July 27, 2017 to coincide with the 50th anniversary of the partial decriminalisation of male same-sex acts. Tomasz also asked if we could change the title from my choice, which was *Carve Their Names With Pride*, to his choice, *Fighting Proud*. I didn't object, but secretly I preferred my own title.

Fighting Proud became a wonderful voyage of discovery. Tomasz agreed that I could refrain from rewriting at length the stories of some of the iconic gay men from the two world wars who were already famous, such as Wilfred Owen, Lawrence of Arabia, Ivor Novello, and Alan Turing. These men had been well served by biographers. Instead, I included short profiles about them in a section called 'Not Forgotten'. I wanted to concentrate on gay men whose lives were not well known. During the writing process, I discovered fascinating men I had never heard about, men who hadn't been given a place in gay history, such as the writer Hector Bolitho and the RAF's Richard Rumbold. Most of the stories came from fragments I had collected through the years. They were brief references I had found in books about the two world wars. At the heart of the book was Montague 'Monty' Glover, who served in the army in the First World War, and his young partner Ralph Hall, who served in the RAF in the Second World War. Ralph's love letters to Monty had somehow survived the wartime censor and after the two men had passed away, the letters were discovered and saved by the gay writer and ephemera collector James Gardiner. We owe James a debt of gratitude.

Television rarely recognised my work, but there were a few exceptions. In 2011, I agreed to be interviewed by Lenny Henry about Black servicemen in the Second World War for BBC1's *National Treasures Live.* The recording took place at the Imperial War Museum, however Lenny was two hours late, which didn't go down too well with the BBC production staff or the museum. When he eventually arrived, he took one look at me and said 'So, *you're* the Black historian?' He had been informed that he was going to interview a Black historian. He added: 'What university did you go to?' I quickly replied 'I left school with feck all and didn't go to university. I have taught myself'. That left him speechless, and I doubt many people can say they have done that to Mr Henry. A few years later, in 2015, Lenny interviewed me again, this time for the BBC Radio 4 series *Raising the Bar* about Black British film and television. This time he was much more relaxed and friendly and we got on fine.

In 2017, I was thrilled to be recognised with two wonderful honours, both of them completely unexpected. First came a Special Achievement Award from the Screen Nation Film and Television Awards which are also known as the 'Black BAFTAs'. The awards had been created by Charles Thompson in 2003 to raise the profile of Black British and international film and television talent of African heritage.

This was something the British Academy of Film and Television Arts (BAFTA) had rarely done. Charles had always been a champion of my work, especially my 1998 book *Black in the British Frame*. The honour, in recognition of my groundbreaking historical work on Black British film and television, was presented to me by my friend, the actress Anni Domingo. I took as my guests to the ceremony Valerie Brandes from Jacaranda Books and Jazzmine Breary, a member of her team. We all had a great time.

Recognition also came from London South Bank University (LSBU) who honoured me with an Honorary Fellowship. I was presented with this at a graduation ceremony which was held at the Royal Festival Hall on London's South Bank. This was my first experience of a graduation ceremony. I was truly overwhelmed. I had missed out in 1988 when the film school of the London College of Printing declined to notify its graduates about their ceremony because it didn't fit with their Marxist politics. I also missed out on the graduation ceremony for my MPhil degree at De Montfort University because my Dad was terminally ill and I was in distress. So this LSBU event meant a lot to me. In addition to sharing the stage in a cap and gown with LSBU's senior academics, I faced over two hundred students (who were graduating that afternoon) and their guests in the audience. My own guests included Anni Domingo, Cleo Sylvestre, Shirley Anderson, a friend from the 1970s; the photographer Robert Taylor, who took some wonderful images of the event, as well as Avril Jones (Chair of the Southwark IAG), and police constable Scotty Frost, but it saddened me that my parents were no longer around to enjoy the recognition. It was gratifying to have been given the Honorary Fellowship not only for my Black and gay history work, but also for my voluntary role as an independent adviser to the Metropolitan Police. I realised I had come a long way from being an educationally disadvantaged teenager in the 1970s.

There was another surprise awaiting me in 2019 when the Booker Prize winner Bernardine Evaristo named me her Black History Month hero on Facebook and other social media platforms. Bernardine said: 'Stephen Bourne is a hero of our history, who has published countless books, always accessible to all, on the hidden stories of our presence on these shores. Let's honour Stephen for quietly shining a light on our history.'

2017 was also the year I joined the Historical Association, and I immediately began writing articles for two of their journals: *HA News* and *The Historian*. One of my articles was a personal story entitled 'What Got Me into History' and this led to an invitation from BBC Radio 4's *Four Thought* programme to present this as one of their talks. The recording was made in 2020 during lockdown. This was the first time I had ventured out during that strange and disturbing time. When I travelled on the underground to Oxford Circus, the train carriages were practically empty. On walking to BBC Broadcasting House, I was shocked at how few people there were at Oxford Circus and on Oxford Street, which was usually one of the busiest areas of London. It reminded me of a dystopian sci-fi movie. In the open plan offices of Broadcasting House there were rows and rows of empty desks. Social distancing was required for the few people who were in the building, but as far as the recording went, it was business as usual. In fact, it went very well and my contribution to *Four Thought* was broadcast on September 9, 2020.

Writing books hasn't earned me a fortune. That only happens if you're a celebrity with a name and you have the support of an agent and an accountant to manage your affairs. In truth, I have barely earned a living from writing, but I have managed to scrape by. Dad always encouraged my sister and I to be thrifty and that has put me in good stead. If you cannot afford to shop for food at Marks and Spencer, then move onto a cheaper supermarket like Iceland. I remember Dad saying: 'Never loan anyone money and never borrow it and always pay your rent on time so you can keep a roof over your head.' My parents' love for their children and grandchildren was unwavering.

A couple of months before he passed away, Dad and I spent some time on our own. He was very ill and frail, but he managed to stand up and asked me to do likewise. He placed his hands on my shoulders and said, simply, how proud he was of my achievements. I had often wondered how he, as a straight, working-class man coped with having a son who was gay and wrote Black British history books for a living. But I knew the answer all along. He was always a loving, caring father who accepted me for who I am. During my lifetime I have always been upset by stories of fathers who were unable to come to terms with their sons being gay or, at worst, showing violence and disowning them. I want it known that it doesn't have to be this way. My dad is a shining example of what the father of a gay son should be.

Chapter 18

Black Poppies Man

When I worked as a part-time library assistant throughout Southwark, local primary school children would visit us and some would bring their homework projects. As staff, we would help find the information they needed. I shall never forget when one girl, no more than 10, wandered about the children's section of Brandon Library, near Walworth Road, during one of my shifts. She was in a daze, clutching a piece of paper. When I asked her if I could help she informed me that her teacher had given her some homework. She had to find out about evacuees from the Second World War, but she didn't know what an evacuee was. I explained this to her. 'In wartime children who were sent away from their homes in the cities to the safety of the countryside were called evacuees.' I then showed her the photo of the group of Black evacuees on the cover of my then-recently published book *Mother Country – Britain's Black Community on the Home Front, 1939–45*. There was also a photo of another evacuee, a small boy with his suitcase, included in the book's illustrations. Seeing an image of evacuees that looked like her made a huge difference. The look of surprise on the girl's face turned into one of recognition. Not only did she become engaged in the homework project, but she produced a really interesting piece of work which included the photocopies I made for her of the Black evacuees. I hoped that her teacher would be impressed.

At the Historical Association's annual conference in May of 2022, I spoke about the lack of children's history books that included the lives of Black Britons. Until then, there had been only a handful of exceptions including several picture books for young readers. One of my favourites is Michaela Morgan's beautifully-illustrated *Walter Tull's Scrapbook* (2012). Eight years later David Olusoga adapted his adult book *Black and British* for teenagers. In 2022, the television presenter Alison Hammond wrote the quirky and engaging *Black in Time – The Most Awesome Black Britons from Yesterday to Today.* Regrettably Alison omitted one of the most important Black Britons from history: Dr Harold Moody.

My first attempt at writing a children's Black British history book was in 2008 when I enlisted the support of Southwark Council for a short biography on Dr Harold Moody. This was aimed at primary school children in the borough. Dr Moody had travelled from Jamaica to Britain in 1904 to study medicine. After qualifying as a doctor, he made his home in Peckham, serving both the community as a popular GP and becoming a figurehead in the British civil rights movement. In 1931, he founded and led The League of Coloured Peoples, one of the first organisations to address the needs of Black Britons. Dr Moody was a trailblazer who Edward Scobie likened to America's Dr Martin Luther King Jr when he wrote one of the earliest Black British history books, *Black Britannia* (1972).

Funded by the Southwark Alliance, *Dr Harold Moody* was published with a striking cover designed by a pupil of Peckham's St Thomas the Apostle College. Copies were distributed free of charge to every library and primary school in Southwark. Dr Moody has been honoured with an English Heritage Blue Plaque and a park in his name not far from his former home in Nunhead. A bronze portrait sculpted by his brother Ronald in 1946 is also displayed in Peckham Library, and yet still more needs to be done to acknowledge him nationally.

Following the publication of *Black Poppies* in 2014, I received requests from school teachers and parents to write a children's version of *Black Poppies*. What surprised and empowered them most were the stories in the book that showed comradeship between Black and white servicemen on the battlefields of the Great War. This was not the case in America where Black and white servicemen were segregated. We did not segregate and in some instances, Black recruits were welcomed and integrated into British army regiments. This doesn't mean discrimination did not exist. It was almost impossible for Black soldiers to be promoted, though some exceptions were made for men like Walter Tull. This was, after all, the time of the British Empire where Black people across the world were living under colonial rule.

Over time, I noticed that more and more Black fiction books for children were being commissioned and published. Most of these focused on the arrival of the Empire Windrush in 1948 and the Windrush generation, but schools still needed more Black history books. So in 2021, I asked The History Press if I could adapt *Black Poppies* for primary school children. They had never published a children's book before, but they readily agreed and their support and encouragement was tremendous.

Though the new *Black Poppies* was aimed at eight to twelve year olds, I recommended it to anyone in any age group. In addition to a new cover design by Tom Clohosy Cole, who had illustrated Michael Morpurgo's *War Horse*, I included a number of stories which I adapted from the adult version. I then added new information and images. Alongside familiar chapters, readers heard for the first time about a police constable from Newport who joined the Welsh Guards in 1915 and an African-American who made his home in Britain and worked as coal miner until 1915 when he joined the army and served in the war. Published in 2022, the young readers' edition of *Black Poppies* has been a great success.

Shortly after the children's version of *Black Poppies* was published, I was invited by the local police to take part in a day of activities at the Black Prince Trust, a youth centre in neighbouring Lambeth. I was given a half-hour slot to talk about the book to about 30 young Black people from the local area between the ages of six and 16. I arrived with some reservations. Some of the kids were playing basketball while others were being entertained by a police officer who was spinning plates. He explained to me that he had worked in a circus before he joined the police. Other activities were going on and I didn't think the kids would want to stop what they were doing and listen to me. However, when they were brought into the room, I found that they were attentive and enjoyed the talk. Some of them asked interesting questions. About one week later, on my birthday, I was walking along Lambeth Road when two young Black children came towards me on their skateboards. One of them recognised me. 'Dad! Dad!' he shouted. 'Look. It's the Black Poppies man!' The children stopped and looked up at me. I smiled and their Dad approached us. 'What's a Black Poppies man?' he asked. The children's faces were familiar. They had been sitting in the front row of the young people at the recent talk. I explained this to their Dad and presented him with a copy of the flyer for the book. This recognition meant everything to me. It was a sign that I had been doing the right thing for over 40 years. I realised that being identified by children as someone who had made an impact on them was the most important encouragement. It is moments like these, and there have now been quite a few, including the prison inmate, bus driver and now the children, who have all connected to *Black Poppies* and my other Black British history work.

I can only hope that the incredible life stories I have been uncovering from British history have been given the breadth and depth they deserve. I hope that I have brought a sense of purpose and continuity to these people, whether they come from the Black or gay communities. I am eternally curious about people and their stories and people in turn have generously repaid that curiosity to me and my books over the years. The journey has been bumpy at times, but ultimately rewarding.

Nothing in my life has been planned. When my first book was published in 1991, I had no idea if I would write another. Now I find it hard to believe that I have had over 25 books published, against the odds. It is an extraordinary achievement for someone who left school educationally disadvantaged. No one can be as surprised as I am. Yet, the work continues.

When I am asked what advice I would give to young people, I reply 'Follow your hearts and be inquisitive. Ask questions. Do not accept everything you are told. Find out for yourself and, if it seems right to you, stay with it. Be diligent, professional and friendly and always wear a smile on your face.'

Acknowledgements

Thanks go to David Hankin for digitally remastering some of the photographs; Keith Howes for his constructive comments on early drafts of the book; my sister Linda Hull for checking my spelling and grammar; Chief Inspector Aaron Barnes for his constructive comments about Chapter 14 'Why I Befriended the Police'; Nick Goodall for his support; and Valerie Brandes and her Jacaranda team: Magdalene Abraha, Yusef Bushara, Kamillah Brandes and Zain Kazerooni for their enthusiastic response to the proposal and for commissioning *Thursday's Child.*

About the Author

Stephen Bourne has been a published author of history books since 1991. His best-known are *Black in the British Frame – The Black Experience in British Film and Television*, *Black Poppies – Britain's Black Community and the Great War* which he has adapted for children, *Evelyn Dove – Britain's Black Cabaret Queen*, *War to Windrush – Black Women in Britain 1939–48* and *Trailblazers of Black British Theatre*. He is also the author of *Fighting Proud* which focuses on the lives of gay men in the two world wars and *Playing Gay in the Golden Age of British Television*.

Stephen graduated from the London College of Printing in 1988 with a Bachelor of Arts degree in Film and Video and De Montfort University in 2006 with a Master of Philosophy degree. In 2017 Stephen was honoured with a Screen Nation ('Black BAFTA') award for his documentation of Black British film and television. Also in 2017 Stephen was recognised by London South Bank University with an Honorary Fellowship for his contribution to diversity and voluntary work as a community adviser to the Metropolitan Police.

For further information about Stephen's books go to www.stephenbourne.co.uk

photo credit: Alan J. Robertson